MARCHING
WITH DR. KING

MARCHING WITH DR. KING

Ralph Helstein and the United Packinghouse Workers of America

Cyril Robinson

 PRAEGER

AN IMPRINT OF ABC-CLIO, LLC
Santa Barbara, California • Denver, Colorado • Oxford, England

Library of Congress Cataloging-in-Publication Data

Robinson, Cyril D.
   Marching with Dr. King : Ralph Helstein and the United Packinghouse Workers of America / Cyril Robinson.
      p. cm.
   Includes bibliographical references and index.
   ISBN 978–0–313–38418–9 (hard copy : alk. paper) — ISBN 978–0–313–38419–6 (ebook)
   1. Helstein, Ralph. 2. Labor leaders—United States—Biography. 3. United Packinghouse Workers of America—History. 4. Packing-house workers—Labor unions—United States—History. I. Title.
   HD6509.H45R63   2011
   331.88'164909092—dc22   2011010792
   [B]

ISBN: 978–0–313–38418–9
EISBN: 978–0–313–38419–6

15 14 13 12 11   1 2 3 4 5

This book is also available on the World Wide Web as an eBook.
Visit www.abc-clio.com for details.

Praeger
An Imprint of ABC-CLIO, LLC

ABC-CLIO, LLC
130 Cremona Drive, P.O. Box 1911
Santa Barbara, California 93116-1911

This book is printed on acid-free paper ∞

Manufactured in the United States of America

This book is dedicated to Les Orear, worker, union organizer, journalist, photographer, and founder and president of the Illinois Labor History Society.

Contents

A photo essay follows page 145.

Preface

Why a biography of Ralph Helstein, a person very few readers have ever heard of, and why have I chosen to write it?

As I thought more about and learned more about Helstein, it became clear to me that I held a certain kinship to Helstein—his religion, his profession, his convictions, his culture, and his dedication to social justice paralleled mine.

Helstein, then the union's general counsel, was elected president of the United Packinghouse Workers Union of America (UPWA) in 1946 as the compromise candidate of the left and right. Although electing an attorney as president seemed strange because the UPWA had insisted that the union must be led by a packinghouse worker, Helstein had shown his leadership ability and was not a partisan of any political wing. As it turned out, the choice was fortuitous because Helstein was able to steer the union through a disastrous 1948 strike; begin an antidiscrimination program that strengthened the union; and bring to the workers all kinds of benefits in wage hikes, working conditions, and health and vacation benefits.

That he held strong and consistent views on freedom of speech allowed the union to avoid the political rifts current in other unions during the McCarthy red-baiting period. Helstein also foresaw the problems brought on by changes in the industry because of automation, elimination of jobs, and movement of packing operations from the Midwest to the Southwest. When these plants began to shut down, most workers received severance pay and job protection found nowhere else in industry.

Helstein led his union during particularly turbulent times. The post–World War II environment was a time of left–right splits throughout the country, and the UPWA was no exception. This was a time when the CIO was going through anti-red purges. The Congress of Industrial Organizations (CIO) accused the UPWA of being Communist dominated—and with some reason because a high percentage of its officers either were in the recent past or were now Communist Party members. Yet to my knowledge, no one ever accused Helstein himself of being a Communist Party member or of being a Communist—not that it would have phased him.

Although Helstein was not religious in the traditional sense, his brand of Judaism, as a social activist and a believer in prophetic Judaism and social justice, played an important role in his thinking and planning. His presidency of the UPWA follows a long line of Jewish labor leaders such as Samuel Gompers, David Dubinsky, and Sidney Hillman, all of whom had a view of their trade union leadership broader and were more socially active than most of the leaders of their time.

Finally, in 1968, before his retirement, he engineered a long-sought merger with the Amalgamated Meatcutters. No doubt he foresaw the problems such a move would make both for the UPWA and for him personally. His progressive policies and opinions were unwelcome in his post with the Amalgamated, where he was relegated to a non-policy administrative function. He soon retired, and physical problems that had dogged him for many years made his last years unfulfilling. He died in 1985 of a heart attack. At his funeral, family, friends, associates, and nationally known figures spoke glowingly of his life and of the irreplaceable loss of such a moral and intellectual giant.

In writing a biography, a writer takes on a heavy responsibility—what to disclose and what not to disclose, a tendency to either respect too much or detest too much his subject, concern about wounding with disclosures his relatives or friends who saw a totally different man from the one the writer feels an obligation to his readers to reveal. In this work, I never faced those decisions. Like any human being, Helstein arguably made some mistakes and made some bitter decisions affecting his friends that he thought necessary to save the union. He had some personal views such as believing that union officials should have very modest salaries, meaning that all other officials in the union received substantially lower salaries than officials in other unions. This caused some resentment, but to my knowledge, no one ever complained to him about it.

In sum, readers will find no exposés here. What they will find is a man and the union he led like no other on this earth. His story and this union's story deserves to be told. That's what I have tried to do.

I felt a closeness to Helstein because as lawyer, I could understand his belief that the law should be used as a tool to correct some of the abuses and inequalities found in our society. As he did, I believed in labor unions as a means for workers to collectively combine to fight for a better life for themselves and their families. As a secular Jew, I was interested in finding just what importance Judaism had for Helstein in carrying out those social objectives.

Two historians, Rick Halpern and Roger Horowitz, were in the process of completing their dissertations and turning them into books at the time I started my study. In the course of their project, they had interviewed most of the actors in the UPWA drama.[1] Another writer, interested in Jewish union leaders, had interviewed Helstein about how his Jewish background influenced his policies.[2]

I want to thank a number of people whose participation made this book possible. First and foremost is Les Orear. Orear was an organizer for the union, then editor of the *Packinghouse Worker*, the UPWA's official publication, and thereafter founder of the Illinois Labor History Society (ILHS), an organization dedicated to preserving the history of unionism and educating the public and present union members about that history. It was the ILHS that provided a grant that permitted me to conduct interviews for this project, and it was Orear that over the years provided corrections and filled in gaps in my knowledge as the work progressed. In the text, the reader will find in the prose of Orear the grit of this union's soul. In addition, Les' daughter, Lynn, was extremely helpful in searching through ILHS files for documents and photos.

I wish also to thank Nina and her sister Toni; Helstein's daughters; and Helstein's wife, Rachel for the information on Ralph's childhood and his philosophy. A separate thanks is due Nina, who, over dinners in restaurants, gave me numerous interviews that I recorded among the sounds of dishes being rearranged and meal orders taken. She also generously read and corrected drafts of the book.

Brad Lyttle, a friend in Chicago, provided a home for me in my many trips to Chicago. Dissertations and subsequent books and articles by Rick Halpern and Roger Horowitz were indispensable in providing an understanding of the development of union policies, and the interviews of union officials, including several of Helstein were especially helpful and often cited. I would also like to thank Professor Robbie Lieberman of the history department of Southern Illinois University, who made valuable editorial suggestions and could always be counted on to be available with ideas that moved the manuscript toward publication. Dan Sharon, retired reference librarian at Spertus Institute, Asher library, Chicago, read and corrected faults in the manuscript and over the years provided continual research counsel.

The library at the University of Wisconsin at Madison, where much of Helstein's and the UPWA's records reside, helpfully supplied copies of the Halpern–Horowitz tape recordings and knowledgeably provided access and guidance in my trips to Madison to find, examine, and copy records. I especially want to thank Harry Miller, reference archivist, Wisconsin Historical Society, for his extensive help in searching and finding what I needed.

Morris Library personnel at Southern Illinois University at Carbondale made my research easier by access to interlibrary loans and to material, books, and newspapers from their archives. Almost all the computer assistance came from my friend, Don Ugent, who was has a wealth of expertise in this area.

This book never would have seen the light of day without the support of Michael Millman of Praeger Press.

Introduction

Ralph Helstein[1] was first general counsel and then from 1946 to November 1972, when he retired, president of the United Packinghouse Workers of America (UPWA).[2] How this Jewish lawyer, raised as an Orthodox Jew, became and maintained his leadership of a predominantly black worker organization, whose predominant business was slaughtering and marketing pig products, is a fascinating story.

I met Helstein only one time, in 1952, as a recently hired lawyer with Cotton, Fruchtman[3] and Watt, the law firm that represented the union. Such a personal diversion in a biography would be inappropriate except that it shows an important side of Helstein, a characteristic he used in his management of the UPWA.

Soon after I started at the law firm, I was notified that Helstein wanted to see me. I met him at the union's office in downtown Chicago, located in the Transportation Building at the corner of Dearborn and Harrison Streets.[4]

Helstein was a balding man of small stature, friendly and welcoming, with a firm, direct delivery.[5] If I was to work with and represent workers, he explained, I had to understand their work experience. There was only one way to do this, and that was by sharing that experience. While I looked on, he called the head officer of a small (about 250 employees) packinghouse, William Davies Packing Co., situated in the Chicago Stockyards area. He told me that he wanted me to work for the company so I might gain some experience in packing. He asked that I be moved around from job to job to vary my experience.

That he, the head of the union with which the company was then negotiating a contract, could ask his adversary to allow a young lawyer to enter its employ as a worker, at the time, struck me as astounding. It showed both the amount of trust Helstein garnered even from his adversaries and his concern that these workers be represented by someone who understood and empathized with their problems, not only intellectually but experientially as well. In addition, as we will see, he sought to make up in me for the lack he always felt in himself—never having shared that work experience with the workers he led.

Jews as Labor Leaders

Helstein was a Jew and ended up as leader of a labor union. Was this trajectory as a Jewish leader of a trade union unique? Or is there a history of Jewish leaders of labor unions? And if so, what leads Jews to join and become active in labor unions? And to what extent, if any, did Helstein's Jewishness affect his leadership of the union?

Like many Jews, Helstein was a secular Jew, but his Jewishness definitely influenced, if it did not determine, how he lived his life. Many times he characterized his faith as "prophetic Judaism." Helstein had definite views as to social activism, what some people would call radical. Prophetic Judaism was not unique to Helstein but was part of Jewish culture, character, and history.

Joe Rapoport,[6] a radical Jewish unionist and supporter of many radical causes, gives a traditional base for his own views. We Jews are reminded of it every year at Passover with the words "evodim boyinu be-mitsrayim, we were slaves in the land of Egypt." We have a history as antislavery fighters in the Exodus from Egypt to the Promised Land. In this, we acted on the general principle of supporting minority workers in their fight for economic rights—for a living wage, for the right to a job, for protective legislation and union recognition.[7]

Gerald Sorin, who interviewed 170 Jewish radicals, concluded that his interviews strongly suggest that the Jewish socialists were a prophetic minority,[8] responding to biblical norms of social justice interpreted in modern context. They were men and women who had been deeply immersed in the moral commandments of the Torah and Talmud, in messianic belief systems, traditions of *tsedaka* (not mere charity but righteousness and justice toward others), mutual aid, and communal responsibility.[9] Sorin concludes:

> Jewish socialists contributed significantly to keeping the concepts of human interdependence and government responsibility for social welfare in the political dialogue. And they shared responsibility for several decades of reform legislation. These men and women, in addition, created a wide-ranging web of fraternal organizations which transmitted the values of the Left to succeeding generations.

And they were a prophetic minority, too—not because they accurately predicted the future but because they worked at educating and mobilizing the best in people and at sustaining loyalty to the highest ideals of social justice. They worked, like Isaiah and Amos and Micah and Hosea, with whom they were so familiar, at hastening the coming of a just, peaceful, and beautiful world.[10]

This radicalism was more than a political persuasion. According to Rapoport, political life was part of a working-class way of life that in turn led to and was intertwined with Jewish political life.

We had schools, lecture series, theatrical groups, literary groups, folk choruses, and mandolin orchestras. There were special summer camps where we could take a vacation and spend time together. There were weekend excursions for camping and hiking. There was the visiting with friends in the evenings. All of these things were a binder for trade union and political struggles. It caught my imagination and encouraged my participation in the movement.[11]

Workers in the first decade of the twentieth century were militant, but Jewish workers were the most militant of any immigrant group. Jewish trade unions grew the fastest. More Jews were Socialists, and on the East Coast, where most Jews congregated, they were able to elect a congressman and many mayors and state legislators.[12] Although most non-Jewish immigrants to the United States were of peasant origin, Jewish immigrants were largely town dwellers, skilled artisans, or laborers.[13]

Statistically, Jews were the largest ethnic faction of the American Communist Party. Jews were "concentrated in the clothing industries [so] that Jewish Communists could and did play an important role in the labor movement without modifying their ethnic identification." Many of the major leaders of the party were Jews.[14] One difference between Jews and most other ethnic groups was that as second-generation Jews moved into professions—teachers, social workers, lawyers, librarians—they retained their liberal or radical ideas.[15] In 1935, a large Jewish contingent of Communists took over leadership of the American Federation of Teachers in New York City, Chicago, and Philadelphia.[16]

Jewish social workers were active in founding a whole series of social service agencies and accompanying trade unions: the State, County, and Municipal Workers of America; the United Federal Workers; the United Public Workers; the New York Association of Federation Workers; workers of the Jewish Federation; the Union of Office and Professional Workers of America (1937); and the United Service for New Americans.[17]

The idea behind the constant and historic activity of Jews in various social movements can be succinctly stated that Jews understood that "to survive, the world must change, and that to the extent we can, we must change the world...."[18]

Although there was no precedent for a Jew to be a head of a packinghouse union, Jews had been important leaders in unions since the end of the nineteenth century, when East European Jews arrived in large numbers.[19]

Since then, Jews have been an important component of the trade union movement. The relationship of Jewish labor leaders to their religion, however, has been conflicted and complex.

Ethically and socially conscious, ever willing to protest injustice, these millions of new Jewish Americans joined their non-Jewish counterparts in creating labor unions that transformed work in the United States. Some Jews became socialists or even Communists, but most were just unionists. They followed the lead of Samuel Gompers, a Jewish American immigrant from England who founded the American Federation of Labor (AFL) in 1886. His program of cooperative negotiation with employers became the basis of modern collective bargaining. More militant Jewish labor leaders also made an impact, and "strikes . . . were a valuable instrument of persuasion."[20]

Jewish Communists were influential in bringing Communist Party members out into the open from their prior underground status in which, as a strategy, they hid from government oppression. The Jewish Communists were, by far, more assimilated in American life than the other foreign groups; they had a more realistic appreciation of the decisive significance of a party leadership that would appear to be a genuine American product. They wanted to be part of a larger American movement, not merely the leaders of a sect of foreign-born Communists.[21]

Jews were disproportionally involved in the civil rights movement. Jews were among the earliest supporters and board members of the National Association for the Advancement of Colored People (NAACP); Jewish leaders helped support the Urban League, the Jewish-dominated International Ladies Garment Workers Union (ILGWU), and the Amalgamated Clothing Workers. Jews took the lead in organizing "our black brothers" for union membership. Kenneth Clark's segregation study had been commissioned by the American Jewish Committee; that organization, as well as the Anti-Defamation League and the American Jewish Congress, submitted amicus curiae briefs in support of cases arguing for desegregation. The Julius Rosenthal Fund provided $20 million for the establishment of rural southern schools.

Young northern Jews enlisted in the civil rights struggle and migrated South; "as many as 90 percent of the civil rights lawyers in Mississippi were Jewish and Jews were at least 30 percent of the white volunteers who rode freedom buses in the South, registered blacks, and picketed segregated establishments. . . ."[22]

Helstein was a Jew who ended up as the leader of a labor union. During his career as president of the UPWA, he championed liberal causes; steered his union to lead in civil rights and civil liberties, including the rights of minorities and women; and as we will see, was one of the earliest union leaders to support Martin Luther King, Jr., both financially and organizationally.

Helstein's labor leadership cannot be considered an anomaly. Helstein was preceded by three Jewish labor leaders.[23]

Samuel Gompers, born in a London slum in 1850,[24] led the AFL for 35 years from its founding in 1886.[25] The next Jew who became an important labor leader was David Dubinsky. Born in Lodz, Poland in 1891, he was elected president of the ILGWU in 1932.[26]

Sidney Hillman, another Jewish labor leader, was born in 1887 in a small Lithuanian village in the Russian Pale. In 1907, Hillman founded a union of the "Jewish needle trades, with its heart in the world of Jewish socialism and labor radicalism."[27]

Similar to other Jewish-dominated unions, the Amalgamated Clothing Workers had ambitious educational plans. Members were to be schooled in the English language and in the parliamentary procedures of trade unions. Jewish trade unions embodied the Jewish principles of "haskalah and tachlis; its pedagological amalgamation of a secularized messianism" bringing together "rebelliousness and assimilation."[28]

Hillman's advocacy of fringe benefits in addition to wages came to be known as the "New Unionism." During the Roosevelt administration, Hillman was appointed first to the National Labor Advisory Board and then the labor member of the National Industrial Recovery Board. He was instrumental in organizing the Congress of Industrial Organizations (CIO) in 1936. To elect Democratic congressional candidates in 1943, the CIO, under Philip Murray, created a political action committee and named Hillman as its chair.[29]

Were Jewish-Dominated Unions Different from Other Unions?[30]

Jewish unions were different from those prevailing in the United States during the early years of the century. In tone and quality, they resembled the unions established by European Social Democrats and anticipated the social unionism later introduced by the CIO. Although most American unions focused on immediate bread-and-butter issues and were likely to be hostile to heterodox ideas, Jewish unions reached out toward a wide range of interests, from social insurance plans to cooperative housing, educational programs to Yiddishist cultural activity. Especially in the earlier years of their insurgency, the Jewish unions were not merely bargaining agencies; they were also centers of social-cultural life, serving some of the same functions as the *landsmanshaftn*,[31] although with a much more enlightened outlook.

Chapter 1

Early Years

Helstein described himself as having "a middle-class background." His father came to this country from Eastern Germany when he was about 10 years old. At 15 or 16 years of age, his mother joined a sister living in Superior, Wisconsin. His mother's father had been a captain of a grain barge that went up and down the Nieman River. One of his father's early memories was of the pogroms in Kovno in Lithuania.[1]

Helstein was born in Duluth, Minnesota. His parents first moved to St. Paul, and a year later when he was 4 years old, to Minneapolis, where he grew up. He went through Minneapolis public schools and received a B.A. degree in English literature from the University of Minnesota.[2]

Minnesota's Jewish History

Why Would Any Jew Go to Minnesota?

Non-Jews were first drawn to the saw and flour mills. Iron-ore mines made the territories' minerals, timber, and agricultural lands a ready source of investment and employment. Gold was discovered in the Black Hills during the 1870s. The 1862 Homestead Act encouraged farm land ownership. Helstein's family history was consistent with the history of other Jews coming to Minnesota.

During the two-decade period from 1870 to 1890, the Minneapolis population rose from 13,600 to 160,738, and St. Paul's increased from 20,030 to 133,156. The first and most numerous immigrants were Scandinavian, but the largest single ethnic group was from Germany. Published history of Minnesota makes reference to many other ethnic groups but not to Jews.

The first Jews arrived from German-speaking lands in the 1850s and 1860s to trade in furs, to mine gold, to speculate in land, to open stores and small manufacturing ventures, and occasionally to farm. Most arrived in cities such as St. Paul, Minneapolis, or Duluth, and formed Hebrew congregations.[3]

In the 1890s, Jews had been driven out of Eastern Europe by the May Laws, Czarist decrees banning Jews from rural areas, placing quotas on Jews in higher education and the professions. Once in the States, a usual trajectory was to borrow a sufficient sum from fellow Jews to fill a backpack and peddle to surrounding farms and small communities. With his earnings, the recent immigrant would buy a cart and then a horse and buggy and finally would open a small downtown business. Next Jews would band together to meet in homes and stores until they could build a synagogue.[4]

During the 1880s, Eastern European Jews were assisted by the Industrial Removal Office, which sought to settle Jews away from eastern cities, often coming through Galveston, Texas, to the Midwest. B'nai B'rith (Sons of the Covenant) then found them jobs. By coming through Canada and entering by the Great Lakes, these Jews could avoid Ellis Island. A train to Grand Forks, 100 miles away, cost them a penny a mile. So they could say that for a dollar, they could come to America.[5]

Generally, new immigrants to large cities like Minneapolis or St. Paul would settle in downtown neighborhoods, near work and where rent was cheap. "St Paul had two Jewish districts, the West Side and the Capital City area. Minneapolis had its North Side" where Russian Jews (and the Helsteins) lived; Rumanians lived on the South Side. " '[S]ynagogues, kosher butcher shops and other stores catering to Jewish tastes, socialist meeting halls, and Hebrew schools' were available for Yiddish-speaking inhabitants."[6]

A problem for religious Jews in the Midwest was keeping kosher. For women in these communities, this was a constant problem. Sarah Thal, isolated on a farm in what is present-day North Dakota, found it necessary to discard dietary laws in order to feed her family because good health, under Jewish law, was more important than Kashrut (Jewish dietary rules). The Reform movement, which did not require its members to adhere to dietary laws, was more in line with American, particularly Midwest, conditions.[7] By the 1930s, one study showed that no more than 20 percent of Jewish women in Minneapolis kept kosher.[8]

Both Helstein's family and his wife's family were involved in Jewish affairs. Arthur Brin (1880–1947), the father of Rachel, Helstein's wife, was born Arthur Lewinsky in Chicago in 1880. After Brin's father died, his mother moved to join a brother in Minneapolis. There she married Samuel Brin, who adopted Arthur and changed his name to Brin. When Arthur was 16 years old, he took a job with a glass company, and in 1908, he founded his own company, the Brin Glass Company. Brin was active in Jewish organizations, joining B'nai B'rith in 1905[9] and serving as president from 1909 to 1912. He was active in the Minneapolis Community Chest. He served on boards of the Council for Social Agencies from 1922 to 1947; Jewish Family and Children's Services, other social and Jewish welfare agencies, the Minneapolis Talmud Torah (classes from 1 to 12), and the Round Table of the National Conference of Christians and Jews and was among the founders of the Minnesota Jewish Council and Mt. Sinai Hospital.[10]

Fanny Fligelman Brin (Rachel Helstein's mother), as a small child in 1885, immigrated with her family to Minneapolis from Berlad, Romania.[11] She graduated from the University of Minnesota as the sole female to win the Pillsbury Prize for oratory. In 1906, she graduated Phi Beta Kappa as the only female member of the debate team. Thereafter, she taught English in a Minneapolis high school and was active in the suffragette movement and in the Minneapolis chapter of the National Council of Jewish Women.[12]

She was later elected president of the National Council's Minnesota chapter, where she served from 1932 to 1938. In 1938, she undertook a peace-seeking mission to Berlin and Moscow. She was a founder of the National Committee on the Cause and Cure of War. She worked with Jane Adams, Carrie Chapman Catt, and other prominent women to promote world peace.[13]

In 1933, Brin was appointed by Eleanor Roosevelt to the Mobilization of Human Needs Committee. In 1934, with Eleanor Roosevelt and Labor Secretary Frances Perkins, she was nominated as one of the "ten outstanding women" in the world. She continued to be active in the Women's International League for Peace and Freedom as well as numerous similar organizations. In 1945, she served as nongovernment organization delegate to the organizing conference of the United Nations.[14]

For a 1994 "Helstein Family Reunion,"[15] "the Helstein story" was described as:

> no different from the classic urban Jewish immigrant experience ... pioneers who arrived among the earliest Russian Jews (1889) and for some reason selected just about the coldest place in America. And the next generations moved to remote towns where there were few other Jews. ...
> The history recounted of these small-town Jews shows that they lived Jewish lives, early photos showing the older men with beards, the younger men in business suits, the older women in black high-collar dresses, and the younger women in modern dress; seeking Jewish education for their children.

Marion Newman recalls her "grandmother kneading the dough to bake the Shabbat bread." She was told that her grandfather, the oldest of the children, came to the United States first and brought the others over. He founded the Talmud Torah in Superior. When her brother was 10 years old, he was sent to a *cheder* (elementary school) in Duluth because there was no Hebrew school in the small community where they lived. Going on family car trips and picnicking was a family tradition.

> I think the idea was to move to a small town, make a fortune and then move to the city, and you never got there. It became a way of living in a small town. There were 10 Jewish families in Brainerd [Minnesota] and we had our own society, and we gathered together for birthdays, anniversaries in different homes. And during the summer we would have a picnic and everyone would make a dish.[16]

Later, the Helsteins followed this pattern. The town in Michigan where they had "a [summer] house was Pentwater. . . . [W]hen we were children we went to northern Minnesota to the boundary waters (the boundary between Minnesota and Canada). . . . [W]e would get there from Ely Minnesota where we would get our provisions and set out to an island on what was called a 'duck' because it could be both land and water transportation."[17]

Minnesota's Jewish Community

In 1935, the University of Minnesota began a study of its General College students who "for one reason or another, were not likely to complete more than two years at the university," a study that surveyed "nearly the entire student population for the academic year 1935–36," six years after Helstein obtained his B.A. at the school. The study showed there were six male students for every 10 women; two-thirds of the students came from the Twin-City area and still lived with their parents. Their parents were mostly native-born Americans who had entered but had not completed high school; the fathers were mostly "employed in upper middle-class occupations" and were "salesmen, office workers, skilled tradesmen, department managers or owners of small businesses."[18]

"Small-Town Jews" Like the Helsteins

Most Jews coming to the United States ended up in big cities. "75 per cent of all Jews reside in thirteen of the largest cities, whereas cities with a population of 500,000 or less account for less than 4 per cent of the total Jewish population. While in large cities Jews comprise somewhat more than 5 per cent of the population, in the cities of 500,000 or less they comprise somewhat less than 1 percent." According to the same study, "there were two main reasons for Jewish migration to small towns. The first and most frequent was business, and the second was to join relatives who were already established and who could help. The median length of residence . . . was twenty-five years."[19]

Helstein's father worked all his life. Helstein's mother told Helstein that his father would court her "in a big wagon with four white horses that he used to drive with one hand. . . . I remember looking at her in complete amazement at the light that used to come in her eyes when she'd tell me this story."[20]

Helstein's sister, 13 years older than him, became his "surrogate mother" and had a great influence on him. Although his father opposed it, his mother insisted that his sister go to college,[21] selling their carpets to pay for tuition. His sister was the first person in the family to go to college. After she got her B.A. degree in 1918, she continued on to Columbia for a degree in history.[22]

"My mother used to talk Yiddish to me and I loved it and I've never forgiven my sister for wanted me to quit talking Yiddish because she considered Yiddish as somehow mean."[23] For Helstein, Yiddish was a very rich language.[24]

His mother kept an orthodox house. They ate only kosher meats,[25] and she kept different sets of dishes.[26] As a youngster, he could not go swimming or play games on Saturday.[27] Every Saturday from the time he was 9 years old, he rode an hour or more to the Talmud Torah on the North side until he was bar mitzvahed.[28]

"As I was growing up,[29] I had a strong feeling about this question of discrimination.[30] Part of it may be because I was Jewish and when I was a kid, the kids would go along yelling 'sheeny' and I'd be excluded."[31]

A series of incidents during his childhood and early adulthood helped form his views on discrimination and labor issues.

One incident took place on his way to school. There was a black man seated next to an empty seat. Helstein asked an older white woman standing near the seat if she wanted the seat, and she shook her head. Helstein took the seat and heard people muttering. Helstein had been brought up to offer his seat to older people. He understood this incident as discrimination against the black passenger.[32]

Helstein's father owned a small factory that made work pants. The first contact Helstein had with a strike was in his father's plant. The Amalgamated

Clothing Workers had organized the plant. At the time he was 11 years old, his father asked him to drive over to St. Paul, an hour and a half's trip, to pick up a scab and take him through the picket line. Workers would yell, "Scab!" at him. He didn't know what it meant at the time. Finally, Helstein asked his father:

> "You know, I don't understand this. Here's this guy, all the people who I would think his interests are identified with are out there and he's coming to work. . . . I can't comprehend it." My father said: "Well look, this is a form of class warfare." And he wasn't using the term "class" in the Marxian sense because he had never read any Marx nor had any interest in Marx. . . . He said, "That guy isn't any good. He's a traitor to his group." He said, "I wouldn't trust him" [My father] had complete contempt for him even though the scab helped him carry on his business.[33]

Helstein was first exposed to radical literature when his sister married a scholar, Stanley, who had a huge library, including first editions. So at 13 years of age, Helstein was reading Chekhov, Dostoyevsky, Tolstoy, Turgenev, Lenin's *The State and Revolution*, the *Book of Mormons*, and some Confucius. He read these books and then would talk about them with Stanley "half the night."

What he had always been told as he grew up was that he would be a lawyer "because from the age of four or five I had been making public speeches." When Helstein was 5 or 6 years old, during the World War I years, he was recruited to make "Your Flag and My Flag" patriotic war bond rally speeches across Minnesota. He had learned a piece called "Your Flag and My Flag" and gave it one day in class. The teacher was so impressed that she had him give it before the whole school. Then he began to appear at civic clubs, and the Great Army of the Republic took him all over the city. He got his mother to buy him a uniform." When he walked down the street "guys would salute me and I'd return it and I'd feel so important."[34]

"If you could speak in those days [it] just meant you could be a good lawyer. But I sort of pushed it away. I still went around making speeches, but I just didn't think I wanted to be a lawyer."[35]

In college, Helstein became interested in Old English, Beowulf and Chaucer, and decided he wanted to be a teacher of old English.[36]

When Helstein was about 18 years old, one of his favorite teachers, Mary Ellen Chase, after he had given a paper on Cardinal Newman's *Epilogia*, called Helstein into her office and told him that he had done a fine job. Then she asked, "What do you think you're going to do? I sense that you have ideas about going on and teaching English in college." I answered: "Well, I dream about that as one of my fantasies. I certainly would love to do that and I'm gonna try."[37] Then she said:

> Yes, I was afraid that that's probably what you had in mind. . . . I think you ought to understand that it's not a question of whether it's good or bad. It's a fact of life that it's almost impossible for Jews to get jobs on faculties in English departments in colleges around the country. As a matter of fact, I don't know of a single one.

Helstein reacted to this conversation:

> Well, that came as a great blow for many reasons: one, I had never been bothered too much by this problem. I was aware of it obviously. I grew up with fights with kids, but the level of anti-Semitism was always a very primitive kind of nuisance. It never seemed to be anything that could fundamentally affect my life in any way.[38] Of course, I must confess I was very naïve about it. Particularly in Minneapolis I should have known better, but I guess it was because I was so young.

Although there was apparently no anti-Semitism at the University of Minnesota, this was not true of Ivy League universities. Congress passed the Immigration Act of 1924, which reduced Southern and Eastern European immigration numbers from a yearly entry rate of 738,000 before World War I to less than 20,000 after its passage.

President A. Lawrence Lowell, president of Harvard University and vice president of the Immigration Restriction League, was the "outspoken leader of efforts to restrict Jewish immigration to America and the admission of Jews to its most prestigious institutions of higher education." Lowell supported the Immigration Act of 1924 aimed at restricting Jewish immigration, and in terms of Harvard, restricting their enrollment. He argued that such restriction would reduce rising anti-Semitism. He believed that "Jews lacked the necessary 'character' for Harvard and could not be true Americans until they gave up their 'peculiar practices.' "[39]

Led by Harvard's president, anti-Semitism was rampant at Ivy League universities. Jews were designated a special group by placing stars of David on their applications. Jews were divided among the seven student residences "in order to . . . spread the burden." English was not the only academic area in which Jews found restrictions in finding teaching positions. Selig Pearlman, a labor economist at the University of Wisconsin, advised Jewish graduate students in history to change their fields because "history belongs to the Anglo-Saxons." Major universities hesitated to allow Jews, many of whom were regarded as uncultured radicals, to educate the nation's youth about the nation's past. A 1937 report of the American Jewish Committee found it "very difficult these days for Jews to become full professors in the leading universities. . . . [E]xcept for Semitic studies, there were no tenured Jews on the arts and sciences faculty of Harvard, Yale, Princeton, or Dartmouth."[40]

Additional fuel was added to anti-Semitic fires by the brutal murder of adolescent Bobby Franks by Richard Loeb and Nathan Leopold. That all three, murderers and victim, were Jewish did not seem to diminish the "anti-Semitism throughout the nation."[41]

For a young man, Helstein had acquired considerable knowledge about anti-Semitism in Minneapolis and Minnesota as well as its political base: "Minneapolis, in addition to having a radical political tradition, was the most anti-Semitic city that you could find. A Jew couldn't belong to service clubs . . . get into the Lions, the Athletic Club or Automobile Club. . . . [A] very strong WASPish community . . . leaped over from Boston and landed in the Midwest. Minnesota was a very strange state, politically and in many, many other ways. Minneapolis had the largest Trotskyite movement in the country; it had a very big and strong Stalinist movement; it had the Coughlinites, the Silver Shirts were stronger there than any place else."[42] Helstein formed a political perspective on the problem:

> I grew up as these progressive movements started. There was a very close relationship between the LaFollettes in Wisconsin and the Farm-Laborites in Minnesota. Floyd Olson [governor of Minnesota] himself was a Shabbas Goy [a non-Jew who had learned Yiddish by living near or working with Jews and who did favors like turning on lights for Jews on the Sabbath (Saturday) when religious Jews were forbidden to do these tasks.]. He spoke Yiddish flawlessly in his political campaigns. Once a year he would come to the B'nai B'rith meeting and give an entire speech in Yiddish.

The Farmer-Labor Party, whose battle cry was "To Your Tents, O Israel," called itself "the party of the common people."

With this background, the warning given by Helstein's teacher "made a very strong impact on me. . . . Well, I'd had a tremendous interest in Chaucer at the time, and Middle English and I saw that slowly fading away from me; but the problem—what do I do?"

He did not find the prospect of going into his father's business particularly attractive.

I'm trying to make some decision on what to do. How especially do I do it in a way that it makes mine a meaningful existence in the light of these terrible problems. . . . So I finally decided that even though I had no special talent for it, didn't have the slightest interest in it, what I'd do is become a doctor, because somehow or other a doctor, in spite of himself, couldn't do anything but help people. Even if he wasn't very good at least he would help . . . [I]f I had been a Horowitz or a Heifitz or something then it would have been simple . . . .but in the absence of that a doctor seemed to be the best substitute. This reflected my family's strong drives toward a responsibility to the community. And the sort of thing that came out of the Jewish immigrant background, you know, and a moral responsibility to do good—not in the cynical manner that our friends in Reagan's administration would speak of it, but in many of those in the Democratic administration would, but really the sense that you had an obligation to help people.[43]

So Helstein decided to become a doctor. But he did not have the requisite college courses. He had to take a scientific language course. He chose French, which in its "scientific" form was "just deadly." He discovered that if he took an exam and got at least a B, he would get credit for a year's work. When he didn't pass,[44] "this was the final blow. . . . First of all I was tired of school . . . I said the hell with all this," and he headed for New York City, which he later realized was an attempt to break "my mother's apron strings."

In New York City, work was scarce. Helstein worked at a bookstore as a replacement employee when someone was ill; he entered a Macy's junior executive program for a few weeks and then an insurance company, none of which appealed to him.

During this time, 1929 and 1930, he got repeated messages from his father that his mother was ill. When he did return, he found his mother in a serious depressive state. It was the height of economic bad times, and his father's business was in bad shape. When he returned to take over the business, he was surprised to find that "certain elements" of the business interested him.

His father tried to teach him the fundamentals of the market system. But to him, that concept made no sense.

My father told me of the business: "What happened was that I bought some cloth, 10,000 yards of a certain kind of fabric that we were to use. . . . [I]t was about 11cents a yard. It was delivered about six weeks later but when it was delivered it was worth only 9 1/2 cents a yard and we had to pay 11 cents." I said to my father, "This is insane. What kind of a system works this way?

It's just crazy." And he said, "But that's the way it works." And I said, "Then it's crazy and anyone who lets it work that way is crazy. Either that stuff was never worth 11 cents, it was always worth 9 cents, or it ought to be worth 11 cents now." I said, "Nothing's happened to that fabric." "Well, he said, "People won't pay as much now as they would then." And I said, "Then they shouldn't charge you what they were changing then." Well, I didn't get anywhere convincing him. But I said to him at the time, ". . . [I]f I have inventories I want to have them under my hat, I don't want to have them on the shelves. I can control what's in my head but I can't control what's on the shelves subject to somebody else."[45]

From that experience, Helstein drew the conclusion that whatever he did, he wanted to have control over the rules that governed his life.

Helstein's Early Political Experiences

Helstein joined and started working with the Minnesota Young Democrats and became the group's chairman. Within 4 years, his group took the leadership of the party away from the old timers. They were all still in their twenties. "This was also during the period of the Farmer-Labor Party of Minnesota when Floyd Olsen was the governor. And in this respect I was not a pure Democrat because my sympathies were with Floyd Olsen who made that famous speech: 'I am a radical because I want to be.' A radical was one who goes to the root of things in our troubled society," a concept that embodied Helstein's early view of political life.

Shortly after Helstein began law school, in 1931, the contractor for one of Roosevelt's Public Works Administration programs[46] started tearing down the red light section of Minneapolis to build a new post office. After hiring the men to work for 40 cents an hour, the company proposed to pay them 20 cents in cash and the other 20 cents in wrecked materials. That's when the workers went on strike.

In reaction to this injustice, a group of law students, including Helstein, started picketing. The police were called and began throwing tear gas canisters at the strikers and the students. The students threw them back. Then they were arrested.

I called up my father and said, "I'm in jail." So he came down. Of course, he'd never heard of any member of our family being in jail. "How could it happen to a nice Jewish boy like you?" . . . My father said, "You know, I wish you'd find other ways of doing it, but if you feel very strongly about these things, you know I'm not apt to agree with you on many of them, but don't let that restrain or influence you. I'll do what I can to make sure you get an opportunity to express your views in whatever way you think is right. I just would be grateful if you picked other ways." Well, that had a big impact on me.

I was able to translate these things into political terms and I began to realize in a real way the prophetic quality of Judaism. I couldn't separate politics from being Jewish.

All those things, they seemed so irrational and unreasonable and indecent to me. It's very difficult for me to try and separate these things out. I think a very important thing in the direction I moved in, essentially intellectual, was my being Jewish. First of all, I had this sense of the fact that I was part of a persecuted people the world had rejected and had no place for them. And therefore it had to have a mission of some kind. And its mission was obviously to create a better society so we could end the need for these distinctions. I have felt over the years that that had a good deal to do with my relating to Judaism.[47]

Helstein's father died in 1932. Helstein liquidated the business, and in order to carry on at law school, he organized a "briefing trust" consisting of six students in which each one would read a case, type up a brief, and make six copies.

Often, instead of going to class, he obtained the notes from the best student. Using this method, he got As on his tests, conduct that earned him antipathy from his professor.[48] His life suddenly changed in 1934 when

... one of the guys that I worked with during the Roosevelt campaign ... came to me and said, "They need some people at the NRA [National Rifle Association]."[49] ... Well, you know this was the depression and I wanted a job real bad. Then I think they were offering $1,800 a year which seemed like the world with a fence around it.

I told him I'd love to do it but that I was almost finished with law school and that I wanted to get my degree. He said that he would try to work it out so that I could work part time, go back and forth until I finished my degree and then go on full time.

So that's what I did. At any event, I got all involved in the NRA because my job was to enforce the codes of fair competition as they applied to minimum wages. That really let me operate in the area that I was already beginning to develop an interest in. ... I had gone through this period in law school complaining because workers had no protection.

Now Helstein was in charge of operating the minimum wage provisions of the codes for the entire state, with a staff of 15 or 20 people.[50]

Helstein's employment in the New Deal federal government was not unusual. Most Jews were politically liberal and admired and supported Franklin D. Roosevelt; the New Deal; and his programs, which were making the federal government an active agent to solve problems of poverty and economic inequality. Jews entered the federal government as social workers; lawyers; or as Roosevelt's advisors, among whom were Sidney Hillman, Felix Frankfurter, and Henry Morganthau, to the extent that some critics called Roosevelt's administration, the "Jew Deal."[51]

Helstein very soon became an important addition to the agency. He recounts how the director of the agency became dependent on him for advice. She was called to testify before a congressional committee and asked him to accompany her.

> I'd never been to Washington. Washington seemed like a very exciting place in those days.... [The hearing room] ....had raised desks, very high, behind which the Senate sat in a semi-circle. The senators on the committee, all of them of course, were familiar to me. The two that I remember the most were King of Utah, who I think was the chairman and who had a W.C. Fields nose, which I'm convinced he got in the same way, and who was stupid and vicious, a real reactionary.... And the other guy was [Hugo] Black.[52] Black was enough to throw the fear of G-D in you—penetrating eyes. Sharp, too, were his questions.
>
> Anyway she [his boss] either just got scared or completely muddled.... She couldn't answer questions, she wasn't answering responsively. I kept whispering to her and at one point King told me to stop because I'd be in contempt of the Senate. I said, "Well, I don't agree with the Senate, Senator ... but that's my view and my prerogative." Jesus! The Director of NRA, who has to get his budget approved, was sitting back and he was just dying a thousand deaths. This punk was being so smart. And Black finally got mad at me. Up to that time I think he was enjoying the proceedings.... [Black] said, "You know, if this young man is going to testify I think he ought to be sworn. I think he's the one we ought to listen to." Well, we took a recess and at this point Rosenberg, who was head of the NRA, said to me, "Go get lost, get out of here, beat it quick. You're not under subpoena, she is but you're not. Get out of here, don't let me see you again." So I got out.

This hearing gave him "some insight then into how political mechanisms worked and what power meant and how it operated, who used it and for what purposes." Shortly thereafter the Schechter decision, "the chicken case," came down,[53] and "that finished the agency."

People in the agency asked Helstein to stay in Washington to work with the agency. Helstein was sent to Boston to do a special study on monopoly in the fish industry. But by 1935, Helstein was "fed up" with Washington. So he returned to Minneapolis, took and passed the bar, and was admitted to practice[54] in partnership with Doug Hall—Helstein and Hall.[55]

During the time Helstein worked for the NRA, he got to know people connected with unions in St. Paul. The Teamsters asked Helstein to help them negotiate their contracts. With 2,000 members, that was a big client. After that, a couple of other unions came to him, and it soon got to the point where Helstein did not want to handle any other kinds of cases.

For him, being a union lawyer became an integral part of his life. At night he went out organizing, and in the day practiced law or negotiated contracts. Shortly, he was a part of the Congress of Industrial Organizations (CIO) operation in Minnesota, where he developed a philosophy of law and social action.

> To me, the law, insofar as the labor movement was concerned, was primarily designed to provide you with a forum which you could use then as an organizing mechanism or which you could use as an instrument of power in the situation, but it was ancillary to the basic need of organizing and unifying workers.[56]

There was a lot going on politically in the late 1930s both on the national and local scenes. There was Roosevelt's landslide victory and that of liberal Democrat Frank Murphy as governor of Michigan. In addition, the LaFollette Civil Liberties Committee hearings exposing industrial espionage and other anti-union activity created a pro-union anti-industrial receptivity. By spring 1937, the Steel Workers Organizing Committee (SWOC) had negotiated more than 50 contracts covering more than 280,000 members. The *Jones and Laughlin* United States Supreme Court decision holding the National Labor Relations Board (NLRB) Act constitutional put to rest the hopes of industry that the New Deal structure would collapse.

But as Helstein noted, politically, "the tide was already turning against labor, symbolically made apparent by Roosevelt's celebrated 'a plague on both your houses' comment at a presidential press conference in which he castigated with equal force the intransigence of the companies and the militancy of the CIO."[57]

Roosevelt made this shift apparent by appointing NLRB members who were pro–American Federation of Labor (AFL), a union more craft oriented and more sympathetic to employer concerns.[58] In 1941, Roosevelt appointed Sidney Hillman co-director of the Office of Production Management (OPM). Hillman lobbied for an agency to settle disputes in war production industries, the National Defense Mediation Board (NDMB). With the infusion of dollar-a-year men and cost-plus contracts came huge profits, while labor, hamstrung by its no-strike pledge, saw the political pendulum swinging to industry's side.[59]

The "Little Steel Formula" that the NWLB decided in July 1942 provided a 15 percent wage increase to meet the rise in inflation, much less than the union demanded. The chairman of the NWLB argued that they could not grant a wage increase because corporations would demand a price hike and that would lead to inflation. Even more important for the union was the rejection of the union shop in favor of a maintenance of membership clause and dues check off.[60]

In an effort to restore the political balance, the CIO created the political action committee chaired by Sidney Hillman.[61]

During 1946, the major strike wave made an already pro-corporate Congress more receptive to legislation to restore "equality of treatment" to the labor scene—the passage in July 1947 of the Taft-Hartley Act over President Truman's veto[62] started a wave of anti-union legislation and anti-"red" witch hunts.

Chapter 2

The Origin of the UPWA; Helstein Takes the Helm

Organizing in the 1930s and 1940s

Before Helstein could enter the picture as the United Packinghouse Workers of America's (UPWA's) first general counsel and then president in 1946, workers had first to become organized in unions. Three factors explain workers' success in organizing in the 1930s and 1940s: (1) supportive government legislation, (2) the assistance of skilled union leadership, and (3) changes in the attitudes and behavior of rank-and-file workers.[1]

Capital dominated labor until the rise of the Congress of Industrial Organizations (CIO) after the Great Depression.[2] The breakthrough came when a Democratically controlled Congress passed Section 7(a) of the National Industrial Recovery Act, which encouraged collective bargaining. Pro-labor legislation was made possible by a bloc of ethnics (Poles, Italians, Irish, and Bohemians), Jews, and blacks who organized labor unions. These unions then provided the energy and votes for the resurgence of the Democratic Party. The Communist Party–backed Popular Front brought various groups on the left together and allowed Communists to enter the labor movement. In turn, Communists provided much of the organizing muscle for this political turnaround.[3]

Communists and veterans of earlier packing union struggles formed the nucleus of union activists; second, these activists were able to obtain the cooperation of Slavic, especially Polish, workers from the Back of the Yards neighborhood who brought community institutions behind the union; and third, black workers became actively involved in the Packinghouse Workers Organizing Committee (PWOC).[4]

Before organizing black workers, the activists had to convince both blacks and whites of the advantages of unity. Beginning in the 1930s, organizers consistently pointed out to workers that racial discrimination "was just one of those things that the company was using to make money off of both of us."[5]

The PWOC used the threat of a white boycott to integrate bars and restaurants in the stockyards area. It was at a bar on Ashland Avenue where the PWOC was founded. Taverns were often used as meeting places for departments or where stewards could collect union dues.[6]

During the Depression in the 1930s, unemployed councils, often led by the Communist Party, used direct action in black areas of Chicago, protesting police violence, engaging in interracial activities, and demanding jobs for blacks.[7] Social activities such as dances, picnics, summer camps, and sports activities in which both races participated broke down racist attitudes among workers.[8]

In November 1935, the Committee for Industrial Organization (CIO), headed by John L. Lewis, was formed. After several futile attempts to get the Amalgamated Meatcutters to organize the stockyards, activists turned to the CIO. The Amalgamated had been weakened by lost strikes. Lewis presented the Amalgamated in April 1937 with an ultimatum that unless they left the American Federation of Labor (AFL), he would go it alone. When the Amalgamated decided to remain in the AFL, Lewis formed the CIO.[9] The PWOC was recognized by the CIO on October 27, 1937, with the Chicago Steel Workers Organizing Committee (SWOC) district director, Van Bittner, as chair.[10]

PWOC's means of organizing gave birth to its later militant structure:

> Its first step in organizing a plant was to identify a core of indigenous leaders and form a plant organizing committee. This committee would then form a steward system, giving more and more workers responsibility for establishing a local. From the steward system grievance committees, co-stewardships, and sometimes educational directors and committees would be quickly formed.[11]

Because Armour had the most workers and the most repressive working conditions, the PWOC decided to make it their first target. Bringing Armour to the bargaining table and getting them to negotiate in good faith was a step-by-step process and required an enormous amount of skill and tenacity.

Although by October 12, 1938, the union had won an election and been certified as bargaining agent by the National Labor Relations Board (NLRB), Armour refused to recognize the union as bargaining agent. It was only after a number of struggles that the union won bargaining rights—a series of slowdowns and work stoppages over grievances; winning another election in November 1939 by a lopsided margin, the revenge firing of a number of union members, an unsuccessful attempt by Armour to support the company union as bargaining agent, and assaults on union leaders—that Armour reluctantly agreed to bargain.[12]

Although the National Labor Relations (Wagner) Act, Section 8(5), allowed unions to organize, required employers to recognize them and to bargain in "good faith," the provision did not require employers "to accede to the demands of the employees." So all the packers did was to listen to the union's demands. They did not bargain, did not make counter offers, and did not sign contracts. Instead, the company would make an announcement to the employees of its decision with no mention of the union, just as if the union did not exist.[13]

When in 1939 a strike against Armour seemed imminent, the federal government intervened to try to bring the parties together. Armour agreed to plant-wide bargaining but rejected bargaining for the whole company. Claims from the Amalgamated that that union represented a majority of the workers forced a November election that resulted in a clear victory for the PWOC. The resulting contract signed with Armour in 1940 codified "the series of small victories they had secured during the previous two years of struggle on the shop floor."[14]

In that contract, workers gained a "guaranteed thirty-two-hour week, survival or seniority rights for a year rather than sixty days in the case of a layoff, and a commitment to equal pay for equal work." By July, 1939, about two-thirds of the 128,000 packing workers in the nation were CIO members.[15]

By the beginning of World War II, the Armour plant under Local 347 had almost 100 percent union membership. In January 1942, Swift Local 28 won an NLRB-certified election. Wilson succumbed in December 1942 to bring all three major packers within the PWOC.[16]

Post–World War II Developments

During the war, union–company negotiations and settlements were under the jurisdiction of the War Labor Board. Because the union found little response from the Board to its complaints, the union relied on its tradition of shop-floor actions.

> Typically strikes were short job actions by a particular department, led by the respected leaders of the individual work group, union stewards, or at times local union officials.... The rank and file militancy underlying the job actions tended to turn the local unions and structures within the international into channels for sentiment from the base, rather than transmission belts for orders from the central office.[17]

Organizing Black Workers

Except as strikebreakers, before World War I, few blacks obtained manufacturing jobs in packing. The war opened up such jobs for blacks. By 1920, blacks represented 40 percent of manufacturing jobs. Half of these jobs were in packing, increasing to 60 or 70 percent in some companies. One difference between the experience of black and white workers was that while workers lived within walking distance of the plants, but blacks lived in segregated neighborhoods from which they had to take public transportation or drive to work. Because black workers saw the union as the base of their present and future well-being, black union members became the most militant and dependable union members.

Origin of the UPWA

By 1940, the PWOC wanted and determined to have its own leadership. The CIO threw a sop to the organization by appointing Van A. Bittner[18] as chairman of the PWOC. But Bittner was answerable to the CIO Executive Board. On a personal and administrative level, Bittner was seen as autocratic, refusing to disclose financial data, distant and often absent, making decisions without consultation.[19] He sought to counter opposition by gathering around him loyalists such as Lewis J. Clark.[20]

To calm the waters, Philip Murray appointed a three-man committee to investigate. After lengthy hearings, Bittner and his deputy resigned, and J. C. Lewis, a Mine Workers official like Bittner, and for the first time, a packinghouse worker, Lewis C. Clark, was named vice chairman.[21]

In July 1943, the PWOC conference recommended a constitutional conference between September and October 1943 and elected a committee to make arrangements and draw up a constitution. There were three groups seeking to influence the convention: the 1941 dissidents, the Communists, and the PWOC administration.[22]

At the October 1943 constitutional convention in Chicago, CIO representatives, including Allan Haywood, CIO vice president, "hammered out a compromise" slate: president, Lewis J. Clark; vice presidents, Frank Ellis and Philip Weightman, Chicago; and Secretary-Treasurer, Frank F. Roche, East St. Louis, Illinois. The political basis on which the UPWA was formed was an alliance of people in the middle allied with people on the left. They brought in Ralph Helstein to be the union's general counsel.

Helstein's route to that post followed the rapidly changing political fortunes of the times. Starting out as a practicing lawyer in Minneapolis, he was asked by the PWOC to help in organizing the St. Paul stockyards, one of the biggest in the country. Before long, Helstein had become general counsel for the Minnesota CIO. As a result of some of the union contacts he had developed, he was contacted by the Chicago offices of the PWOC to come to Chicago to be the PWOC's general legal counsel. Helstein describes the process as follows:

> As I recall it was in September or August of 1942. I was asked to handle a Labor Board matter for the Packinghouse Workers Organizing Committee in Water-loo, Iowa where they had an organizing drive going at what was then one of the largest packinghouses in the country, the Rath Packing Company.... So I went to Waterloo to handle the Labor Board case. [I]n all those cases ... we won the election. At some point after the experience with these cases in Chicago I was talked to by the officials of the committee. They ... asked me if I would be interested in moving to Chicago as the general counsel of the PWOC and just work out of that office. Well I found it very intriguing. I wasn't sure I wanted to leave Minneapolis but the prospects of operating in a bigger field—I was in my late twenties, early thirties at the time and I'd decided finally that this was the greener pasture from where I sat, that I couldn't turn it down for the comforts of what had been a very happy city for me to live in, so finally in October of '42' or early November ... I came to Chicago.[23]

First, however, Helstein called his wife, Rachel, to get her reaction to the offer. She recounted the experience as follows:

> I was very happy to think that he would be on a salary [laughing] because when he had to send a bill of $33 to the UE [United Electrical Workers], Honeywell union, having gone to all their meetings, and worked with them on the writing of pamphlets and striking, done everything, and at the end of that month he felt that he had to send a bill for $33, he suffered. Because they didn't have any money, and I thought well this really is going to be a different life [laughing] to have a wage. It wasn't a difficult decision at all.[24]

Part of the reason that the move from Minneapolis to Chicago was acceptable was that Rachel had attended the University of Chicago, where she had lived in International House on the Midway on 59th Street. They found an apartment in Hyde Park near the university. In 1951, they liter-ally built a glass house at 58th and Blackstone.[25]

> In those days [the house] was so advanced modern that the people just couldn't believe it. The neighbors were furious.... They were convinced

that it had to be a garage—well it stands on pillars you know. It's all glass and concrete. But we lived there ever since, raised our kids. . . .

I worked out an arrangement for my withdrawing from my office in Minneapolis although I continued to be part of it for a few months, maybe even a couple of years.[26]

The Call for the Third International Convention of the Packinghouse Workers Organizing Committee notified local unions of the PWOC that:

> a Convention will be held . . . in the auditorium of the Engineering Building, 205 West Wacker Drive, Chicago, Illinois, on October 13, 14, and 15, 1943. . . . The Convention will bring together the leaders of a democratic labor union. . . . The Convention is called for the purpose of adopting a constitution; providing for the election of officers; and to make plans for the future which will lead to the complete organization of the entire packing industry and their subsidiaries in the United States and Canada. . . .[27]

Helstein understood the factors at play within the union and his place that allowed him to perform his job as general counsel to the fledgling union. His first task was to help draft the constitution to govern the new organization. His role became not just a legal draftsman but a player in the political process:

> I found myself time and again caught between competing factions in the union. . . .[28] Many of them had a common end but none of them had any common understanding on how to get there or willingness to accept a compromise on people and individuals, who would be in the leadership. . . . But they did want an organization to be run by packinghouse workers. They wanted no glass workers, miners or clothing workers and this is what they had ever since they were set up in 1937. . . . They wanted . . . an international charter and they wanted to elect their own officers.

To start the process to becoming an international union affiliated with the CIO, a committee was appointed to work on a constitution, with Helstein a member.

> I worked very closely with that committee. It was perfectly natural that the lawyer would, but I had begun finding myself in another kind of role and I was to begin to cement, to mediate, to operate politically even though it was none of my damn business. . . . Whether it was part of my job or not it was clearly part of my temperament that I got very much involved in the

internal politics of the union. I began to work in the direction of bringing together the diverse elements from one end of the country to the other, making them sit down and talk to each other and insisting that they had to work out meaningful compromises because others now were waiting for the establishment of the international union. If that's what they wanted why this was the way it had to be done. And I got such disparate people, in those days at least. There was a guy like Tony Stephens out in Iowa, a guy like Herb March who was a member of the National Committee of the Communist Party. . . . I became the center of this and began operating on all these questions . . . that people like the union officials soon got in the habit of calling and talking directly to me instead of calling one of the operating people whom they should have called. Given my temperament I didn't do what I should have done and that is referred them to them. . . . It was clear that all they'd do was refer them back to me and I discussed this with Clark [union president] and the others. They said take the calls and give them the answers. They were perfectly happy not to be bothered. What it did, obviously, and this was not conscious on my part (I am most reluctant to say that there weren't some unconscious elements operating within me at the time but it clearly was not conscious), it did result in my establishing a much closer relationship with the average worker than I would have done otherwise.

Helstein's Election as President of the UPWA

According to Helstein,[29] the first time the question was raised about his being a candidate for union president was by Joe Ollman, District 2 director. Several months before the 1946 convention, as Joe was driving Helstein from Austin, Minnesota, to St. Paul, Ollman asked Helstein if he would consider running for president. Helstein said he "fluffed it off as ridiculous. I made it very clear that not only hadn't I considered it but I wasn't about to." Helstein suggested that Tony Stephens (District 3, Sioux City, Iowa, director) was the "logical candidate" and that "it is almost unheard of—a lawyer running for President of a union. To which Joe replied—'Maybe unheard of but you're the logical person and the only one who can pull this thing together—you've been doing the work.'"

Helstein does not recall the matter ever coming up again until he arrived at Montreal, where the 1946 convention was being held. The board got to Montreal about a week before the convention started. The idea kept resurfacing, perhaps at the initiative of Ollman. This talk made Helstein extremely uncomfortable because he roomed next to Lewis J. Clark, the current president, with whom he had to carry on business.

Every time I looked at him I felt embarrassed and I didn't know what to say.... My recollection is that that was Saturday night before the convention. I remember spending a sleepless night. They [the board members] didn't leave me until one o'clock in the morning. But I was thinking about what was on the other side of that door. I was really all tied in knots. The following morning I called Rachel.... I was not about to do this without her agreeing. I said to her this is apt to mean a totally different kind of life, in many ways more exciting and more destructive.... How do you feel about it? All she would say was that you have to follow your own instincts, judgment. Whatever you want to do I'll support but it has to be your decision.... I guess I wanted to hear what I heard because in retrospect, I can tell you the urge to do this was very great. I can remember the first time I had the gavel, the whole quality of that room had changed, the kind of thing I had always dreamt of doing so that there is no question that I unconsciously had the push and meanwhile I had the awful feeling about Clark, almost a sense of shame rather than anything else. I didn't think he was competent. I knew that there wasn't a delegate in that hall that would go out of their way for him.

But Helstein's nomination was anything but simple. Herb March, union organizer and Communist Party member, gave the following scenario:[30]

In the course of the 1946 strike, Clark was ready to capitulate in issue after issue. He was the CIO's man. He used to write letters how much he hated reds.... From 1944–46 he was President of UPWA. He was incompetent but in addition to that he told us that during the 36 strike everything that was done he checked with the FBI and worked together with them and he thought that was impressing us.[31] Well, when that report was made to the board, as far as I was concerned I was through with Lou Clark, and so were a number of other people. When he got through saying that in addition to the fact he made no contribution we said we gotta get somebody whose [sic] a labor leader, not a stooge.[32]

There were a lot of guys who agreed with some of the basic principles who were not communists. But in terms of organization, the only organized left was the CP [Communist Party]. Clark just played no roll whatever. He was not a fighter for anything. He was so incompetent that the roll that should have been played by the President was being played by Helstein. Clark said if we need brains he'd hire them. His whole attitude was sniping at the left, fighting the District One [Chicago] leadership; and District 6 (New York, Meyer Stern) and he was losing friends even in the district he came from.

Jesse Prosten [head of grievance processing] and I got ahold of Helstein one night a couple months before the convention and raised the whole question of Clark and the discontent that existed with reference to him. He knew about it. He tried to save the guy's ass from making mistakes now and then. And we had talked to the people from District Three and other people. They agreed that by golly we gotta do something about this guy Clark. So we decided to make a change. A number of us decided that we ought to go for Helstein as president. Now that was a new decision to make, taking a lawyer and making him a president of an international union.[33] The people who were young Communists felt the same way, that Helstein was a logical guy. They felt that Clark had been so derelict of his duties, and anyhow that Helstein had been doing the job that the president ought to do, without the credit for it.

We told Helstein that there's tremendous sentiment against Clark and we figure you can play a role because you're not associated with one group or another. And we do believe in democracy in the union and judging people by their performance rather than by their politics. You would probably be able to unite this union and we were for it. The only other possible candidate would be me [March]. I was identified with one side [the left]. What we wanted was a United Front of all people and we figured Helstein would be it

He said: "I'm a lawyer and my tendency is to compromise,[34] rather than to confront in situations. And I may slow the union down because of my tendency to compromise." We said to Ralph you know what we are and you can depend on us to ride your rump if you are making unnecessary concessions. We finally convinced him to run.

Helstein, in a 1981 interview, provides another version of his nomination. Before the Montreal convention "a guy had come to me—he was a radical. . . . I mean he had no affiliation—he wasn't a Stalinist or a Trotskyite—he was just a good American radical."

He came to me and said, "Ralph, you ought to run for President." I said, "Don't be silly. I can't run for president, can't have a lawyer for president, it's just unheard of." We were having lunch in a restaurant when he did this. I was on my way from Minneapolis to Austin [Minneapolis] where he lived. "Well" he says "that has nothing to do with it. It's about time the Packing-house Workers got good representation." As he kept pushing me and I kept pushing it off and I didn't pay much attention to it. Then at some point, I don't know how long before we went to Montreal where the convention was, he got in touch with Fred Dowling who as our Canadian director and a social democrat. I mean that was his politics, he was part of what was then known as the CCF [Co-operative Commonwealth Federation] . . . and between the two of them they cooked this thing up. . . . They organized the votes.[35]

According to Oscar Brown[36] who worked for the union in the early 1950s as a publicist and who later became a well-known entertainer, Helstein was very sensitive about his lack of worker experience.

> Ralph had never been in the union, I mean had never been in the plant, so he always felt, I remember he told me he felt somewhat isolated. I was in the situation [Brown had worked in a Swift plant for some months] where I could at least talk to workers every day. You know, hang out with them, get drunk, go to the parties, and I was right there, on the front. He was not that kind of guy at all.
>
> ... [I]t was an inadequacy in his whole perception of the union, he would have liked to have had the experience that you [the author] had, for example. He told you, you said, to do that [work in a packing plant] and that was one of the reasons that would give you a sensitivity that he lacked and you know, an acquaintance with the whole thing that he did not have.

The insurrection against Clark also reflected the union's democratic structure. As described by organizer Les Orear,[37] later the editor of the union's newspaper, *The Packinghouse Worker.*

> Well, you got to realize that we were structured very democratically, with a great deal of participation by the local union leadership. The district directors had all been appointed from the most active people in the labor community. We already had this feeling that our district director was one of us. And all of our local officers were trained in organizing campaigns. They were people in our plants. They were elected, there were no appointed officers. And our style was always to consult and have a meeting and convince people that this was the right course.
>
> So when we come to the contract negotiations, about to have a big strike and all this in '46', there's a delegation of two or three from every Armour local in the country, all are there in Chicago, and they are witness to what is going on.
>
> So they could see and evaluate. And they can see Helstein at work. So even the people who were in the so-called CIO caucus, the anti-communists, would have been happy to see Clark go. Their reluctance was to see the CP or the left people who cooperated with the communists, put their man in. Herb March said:
>
> Before the election, the national CIO sent in [Alan] Haywood[38] together with a whole core of people to defeat Helstein and to make sure that Clark and his group were elected.[39] And they put the pressure on with promises, threats, you name it. They approached some top leaders of the CP who came in and tried to tell us to dump Helstein and work out something else.

A Labor reporter from *Daily Worker* said you can't elect Helstein. I told him, you guys in New York don't know your ass from a hole in the ground about the situation here. We're going to do what we packinghouse workers think ought to be done so forget about it. He said, I'm speaking for the Party. I direct you not to support Helstein. I said, well, I'm an official in the Party too and I'm directing you to keep your nose out of our goddamned business.[40] The top guys of the CIO went to the top CP officials and told them that if you guys pull that sort of crap around here you'll see a reign of terror unleashed against the communists in the unions. When they told me that I told them, what do you think they been doing until now? What difference is it going to make?[41]

There was a bifurcation between top Communist Party officials "who devoted themselves to party work" and those "who devoted most of their time to organizing and running unions." The result of this division was "usually to build up a different kind of relationship to the party . . . than that of the political leadership. . . ."[42] When Herb March, Jesse Prosten, and other Communists in the UPWA had to decide whether to follow the party line or party orders, for the most part, they placed their loyalty to the union above that to the Communist Party.

When Helstein was nominated to be union president[43] and was about to speak, the objection was raised that he was ineligible because he was not a member of the union. Hank Schoenstein, treasurer of Local 28, countered that he could attest that Helstein was a member in good standing of his local. Clark withdrew at the last moment. This was followed by his nomination as secretary-treasurer. It all happened so fast and so unexpectedly. The plan had been to nominate Norman Dolnick (staff member) for that post but Fred (Dowling, director of the Canadian district 10) said, "We lost our guts. We felt that Clark would get so much sympathy from his withdrawal and his desire to bring about unity that he could just win" and denying him any role "would make it even worse."

In Helstein's later interview with Balanoff, Helstein stated:

"As a result of some of Haywood's maneuverings, he [Clark] at the last minute, withdrew as a candidate and I was elected without any opposition. He then was nominated for secretary treasurer. Now at the time I was elected we had intended to support Norman Riches who had been one of the people on our staff in Canada, working under Fred Dowling's direction. He was young, very personable, very attractive and quite competent. We thought he'd really fill the job very well. Norman [Dolnick] was going to be our candidate but the suddenness and the complete secrecy behind this maneuver of Haywood's, when Clark withdrew and then got nominated as secretary treasurer, just caught us completely off guard. Our immediate reaction was that would win Clark a lot of sympathy and might result in Riches' defeat . . . [U]nder the pressure of that moment there was no time to make decisions at all and check where we stood. We concluded that the safest thing would be to have Riches withdraw and let Clark take the job unopposed."[44]

[T]here is a piece written by a guy by the name of Ben Krause that appeared in the Saint Paul paper after the convention in which he analyzes the selection and he says it was the most astonishing group and coalition that anyone can imagine. On the one hand, you had the Trotskyites from Minnesota, on the other hand you had Stalinists from different parts of the country; you had some plain unionists; you had some very conservative; the social democrats from Canada, and all of them gathered around this lawyer and supported him.

When Gene Cotton, the union's general counsel, was asked about the importance of Helstein's election to its later development, he said[45] that "Helstein didn't have Jesse's [Prosten's] firmness and stiffness and drive and purpose, but on the other hand, that's what made him and Jesse into an excellent negotiating team." So if Ralph had a weakness, it was a weakness of someone who came from an intellectual background and who had all the hesitations and all the uncertainties of an intellectual. Although he was able to see a lot, see all sides of a question.

I asked Cotton, suppose Helstein hadn't been chosen to be head of the union? Do you think the fate of the union would have been substantially different? Cotton responded: "I think the answer is yes because as I now look back on what the alternatives were, what kind of leadership would have developed if it were not Ralph? There'd be a void because there were two possible alternatives, neither of which seem politically likely. One would have been Herb March [an admitted Communist] or somebody like that, and I don't think that was politically possible. This was not a Communist-dominated union. There was a very wide political spectrum."

The coalition that formed to elect Helstein[46] was like a political Rorschach test of the union. Helstein analyzed it later this way:

One of the things that brought people who Herb [March] represented and those Joe Ollman represented; those that Fred [Dowling of Canada] represented; and the real mavericks out of the packinghouse—conservative on most questions—was my performance in that January 46 strike when I pointed out to them that we could not be held to be in violation of the law until after the time for seizure went into effect. . . . Truman announced seizure of the packing plants because we were threatening to strike [for a wage increase.] And I recall saying to them, "We're going to tell them to go to hell...." Whether or not we can actually pull off a strike against the government if they once take over these plants is a matter that we can't really resolve, we don't know.... But there's nothing that says we can't threaten to do it. And, just see what happens. We can say that we're not going back to work.... If we ask them to fix a figure, we're not going to get it. What we want from them is simply a commitment that whatever figure the panel that they have set up gives us, they will put in effect.... Because in the case of the autoworkers, they didn't. And in the case of the steel workers they didn't. And they had to keep the strike going for I don't know how long before they got what the panel had said.... [A]nd the conservative guys were opposed to it—"You can't tell the government to go to hell," and I'm saying "no reason why you can't. You can tell them anything, the question is what you do, it's not what you say, now." ... I got a call from Pressman who was this left-wing attorney for the CIO giving me hell, telling me, "You can't do that. Murray doesn't like it." And I said, "Well, we're gonna do it."[47]

After getting agreement from the workers, Helstein held a meeting the next morning at the Amalgamated Clothing Workers Hall on Ashland Avenue in Chicago. All of a sudden the phone, perched on a piano, rang, and Clark, who was president, answered. And it was Clinton Anderson, Secretary of Agriculture, who had been appointed by Truman to conduct the plant seizure. Helstein said to Clark, to tell Anderson:

Either we get a commitment that whatever the [government] panel recommends goes into effect or he can seize the plants, but there won't be a God-damned person there to run them. Well, [Secretary Anderson] just caved completely. And he says, Okay ... I'll send you a telegram making it clear that I will personally see to it that whatever that panel recommends will be put into effect[48].... And, of course, to the guys on the board, that really made me a hero .... I had called this, and it was so clear ... You didn't need the Talmudic training that I had had to know that, it was obvious. By the way, it never hurt me to have it.

The strategy for us to do was to say we were not going back to work and to reconsider our position if we thought we had to and then I wrote that strong, nasty statement about the Truman administration. There were headlines ... in the Chicago Daily News, "Union Defies Govt.... Well. We got 16 /2 cents an hour and we'd gotten more if it hadn't been ... [for] that God-damn stupid Gorman who was head of the Meatcutters union made a public statement that the meat cutters would be satisfied with 15 cents."[49]

This victory was followed by others. Helstein made a second request for a wage increase based on a War Labor Board exception for "rare and unusual" cases. Furthermore, similar to the portal-to-portal pay miners received, Helstein sought the same for packinghouse workers who wore white coats while working and then had to shower because they were all covered with blood; they had to change clothes

> I introduced this thinking that this labor board gang would feel guilty and not only that but I knew so many of them on there by that time, I'd gotten sophisticated enough to be around Washington. I'll never forget one afternoon I sat with Lloyd Harrison and George Taylor and Nathan Witt [board members], and a couple of others, convincing them of why they owed it to us to give us this clothes-changing time. Well, Christ, we finally won that decision and like to have drove every company crazy because they didn't know where this was going to end. . . . At any rate, we got 12 minutes a day, well that was an hour's pay. . . . If I ever felt that people thought I was a hero, well, it was then.[50]

As Rick Halpern wrote:[51]

> Politically, [Helstein's] selection as UPWA president was a brilliant stroke. Since he had not come out of the plants, Helstein was not tied to any particular local or regional power center. He was neither associated with the CIO . . . nor identified with any political faction. Precisely because of his origins and independence, Helstein was able to mediate between the various factions within the union. Acceptable to all parties, he immeasurably strengthened the political coalition that lay at the heart of the UPWA.

In some ways, given Helstein's intelligence, cunning, and tendency to manipulate situations rather than to passively let them happen, the sequence of events just related that leads to the conclusion that Helstein was swept into office by events raised questions, at least for me, whether I had the whole story. After I had written the above account, Nina Helstein, one of his two daughters, gave me a copy of a letter Helstein had written to his father, dated June 18, 1946 shortly after his election. His father had raised questions about the advisability of leaving the union counsel job for the presidency. The letter reads, in part:

> I have no intention of relinquishing my job as counsel—I agree with you that would be undesirable. . . . I went to Montreal without any notion or ambition for this job. It appeared clear that Clark was going to be elected.

The people who opposed him, primarily on the basis of his incompetence (and properly so) could not agree on anyone else to run against him. In addition, they felt that I had really given the union what leadership it had received and that I was the only person who stood above the internal political squabbles of the union and [was] the one person who everyone respected. In that connection even those who were for Clark never attacked me—the only complaint was that I had never worked in a packinghouse. Under all the circumstances I felt that I owed it to my conscience and to the cause which has become the major factor in my life, second only to my family, to assume this responsibility. I had no illusions—as a matter of fact I think that I understood better than most what I was getting into. I know that the days ahead present grave problems and that society as we know it is in the midst of the labor pains of change—perhaps even in the process of giving birth to a new order. This means many dangers and perhaps unhappiness for vast numbers of people. Conscious of these things the easy way out would have been to say no and to remain in an obscure position where neither maintenance nor change in the status quo would have affected me much more than the rank and file citizens connected in some way with the labor movement. I could not have been happy that way—once the issue was raised. As the leader of some 200,000 workers I hope to be able to make some contribution to Roosevelt's "Rendezvous with Destiny" and [Wendell] Wilkie's, [a moderate Republican Party leader] "One World" a better world where all people can live decently and at peace. To the extent of my ability I have to keep faith with the things I believe in.

Because of the political times, this was not the first time a popular front compromise strategy was tried. The choice of Communists such as Herb March and Jesse Prosten to forego the presidency of the union in favor of a noncommunist was also found at the first United Auto Workers (UAW) convention in 1936. Wyndham Mortimer, a Communist and successful experienced organizer and strike leader, was the obvious candidate for union president. But some feared his Communist connections could result in the new union's being smeared. This was the time of the United Front during which the Communist Party wanted to preserve its relations with non-Communist liberal elements. Instead of Mortimer, the Communists supported Homer Martin, a liberal preacher from Kansas City. Mortimer became the first vice president. Such a strategy permitted the convention to both adopt the Communist program and permitted the Communist Party to dominate the executive board.[52]

After he was elected president, Helstein, continued throughout his tenure to act in the dual capacity of attorney and president. One instance involved the regular meetings of CIO attorneys, in this instance in 1947, soon after the enactment of the Taft-Hartley Act. Viewing issues from his position as union president, Helstein often looked at an issue differently from other union lawyers. In one instance, the question was whether unions should publish their constitutions and bylaws and file them with the Department of Labor, a proposal to which Helstein had no objection.[53] This and related legal issues show the uniqueness of Helstein's views and use of the law. It also gives a view into the puckishness and the passion with which he pursued his profession.

Helstein discovered that the reason attorneys for other unions objected to publishing their constitutions was that these other unions, particularly AFL unions, had never bothered to draft any constitution, had thrown them away, or did not want their membership to have access to them because their membership might challenge them under the rules.[54]

A further question arose on how to handle a wildcat strike. Lee Pressman, then CIO's general counsel, proposed a provision in the steel contract that said that if a wildcat strike should occur, every effort should be made by the international union to get the people back to work immediately. They would call them publicly to return, and if they were not successful, the union would publicly denounce them.

> Well, said Helstein, I was shocked by his position and I said so to them. . . . My position was that the purpose of the union treasury was for the union members and it seemed to me that when wildcat strikes occurred it was because people had some complaints. They weren't just striking for the fun of it, although there were clearly irresponsible strikes, but those weren't the customary ones. . . . It meant then that they were having trouble and it seemed to me that it was when. . . they needed their union most. That was not the time when you denounced them. . . .[55]

Helstein was in a minority position on the issue and such as clause did go into most union contracts. The UPWA was one of the few unions that never had such a contract provision.[56]

> I recall that the sugar workers negotiated a contract. They used to do theirs locally and they put this provision in. This was in the South. Well first of all they didn't know why they shouldn't, most unions had them. It was a customary clause in the New Orleans area. . . . I refused to sign the contract because it was in there. I got a telegram one day from one of the employers because there was a wildcat and simply crumpled it up and threw it in the

waste basket. I didn't even bother to respond to it. It was demanding that I order them back to work and of course I didn't. I called our local people and asked them what was wrong. They got it settled.

We got sued on a number of occasions and when we'd get sued we'd play with the law suit for a long time, or as long as we could, try to prevent it from going to trial. Then when we'd get into negotiations we'd include that as one of the issues in the negotiations. We did on one occasion pay damages. That was only once that I remember and then [we were] clearly wrong.... [T]here was no way we could have gotten out of it. I was so mad at the time that I wanted to send the money over in pennies but I got talked out of it.

In any event this is an incident that still sticks with me and I am convinced that this particular provision in the Taft Hartley Act, taken together with the union's decision to insert these kinds of provisions, made the unions in many respects an arm of the company as a disciplinary mechanism....[57]

Helstein was conscious of the ramifications of such a provision and could recall examples from labor history to support his position. Wildcats usually occurred as a result of legitimate grievances. When called to the company's attention, because of the lengthy proceedings, companies would just laugh and challenge the union to file a grievance. The only penalty was for the company to pay

> ... the same kind of money it was going to cost them anyway. By the way I used to often remind myself that this was one of the things that led the Wobblies [International Workers of the World] in the old days to refuse to sign contracts. They would not sign contracts, you know, and one of the reasons was that, by G-d, they weren't going to have their hands tied and let the companies be free to do anything they wanted to.[58]

Walter Reuther, then an official of the Auto Workers Union, had a completely different philosophy about wildcat strikes. In a dispute between the UAW and General Motors three months after signing the 1940 contract in the Fisher Body plant at Flint, Michigan, General Motors fired 17 militant unionists. The local struck its 13,000 workers. Workers at the nearby Buick plant struck in sympathy.

> Reuther ... rushed to Flint and got everyone back to work.... To Reuther, the Flint wildcat, no matter how justified, represented a threat to the larger and more stable relationship the GM sought to build with the corporation.... The UAW would ... fight for the shop steward system, for the thirty-hour week, for a big wage increase, even for union participation in company

governance. But wildcat strikes and stoppages were out. "I want to be brutally frank with you on this point," said Reuther, "... that unless you have a recognition and observance of these provisions [of the contract] then instead of having democracy, you have 'mobocracy.' When you fight for the right to have a democratic organization, you also take on the responsibility to function within that organization in a democratic manner ... because otherwise you destroy the very thing you are trying to defend."[59]

Helstein's position on wildcat strikes was supported by the most radical black group, the League of Revolutionary Black Workers, which called for the UAW "to fire Reuther and elect a black president" declaring the "wildcat strike [to be] an act of defiance, a clearly illegal action directed at the union as well as management. It occurs when the everyday tensions of industrial conflict burst into collective struggle. The workers, in order to express their power, attempt to stop production."[60]

> Helstein's election to president of the UPWA has been cited as an example "of a factional battle" that may provide a fluid situation into which ... a staff expert who had proved indispensable [may rise] to power as the reconciliation candidate. Union people often cite this case, President Ralph Helstein of the CIO Packinghouse Workers, either as the exception that proves the rule (that a staff expert can never achieve power), or as the horrible (or encouraging) example that shows that technical indispensability inevitably means power in the era of the managerial revolution.[61]

The UPWA was often accused of being Communist dominated. But largely because of Helstein's leadership, it was never expelled from the CIO as 11 other left-leaning unions were. It is useful to trace the substance of the "Communist" issue within the union.

Communists in the Early Organization of the Union

Communists and Communist-dominated organizations had been very active in organizing the packing industry. The Communist Party in Chicago had 630 members in 1928, 683 in 1930. By 1931, the number had grown to 1,963; in 1932, it was 2,513; and in 1934, it was 3,303 members, almost "one-quarter of the nation's Communists, second only to New York City. Nevertheless, most of these members remained less than a year."[62]

Communist party members were the most hardworking, most clearly directed and most militant of any political group, so it is not surprising to find them overrepresented in the early PWOC and later UPWA.

The charge was made by anti-communists that the union was controlled and manipulated by its Communist Party members. Les Orear,[63] a Communist Party member at the time, described how the Party related to the union:

You get certain people and they decide how they're gonna vote and then by the fact that not a lot of people vote, they're able to win. . . . I'm sure that Nielson [District One president and non-communist] was consulted. . . . I am certain that it certainly did occur where the CP dictated union policies but certainly not with us. There is only one time that I was aware of that [that the CP told us what it wanted us to do]. That was at a May Day parade probably in 1936 when they wanted us to participate in that parade. I thought it was OK . . . to have a Packinghouse contingent in the May Day parade.

Jesse Prosten was on the payroll of the union. The rest of the organizing staff was Martinez who was assigned to Wilson Local 25. He was the leader of Hispanic Americans. Joseph Kinch and Sigmund Wlodarcwyk were one of the people who were non-communist on the staff.

As early as the second PWOC election, there was a black district president from the pork side, deep chill, whose name I do not now recall.

At some point, Jesse Prosten felt, from the policy point of view, that there ought to be a change in leadership, especially Armour, so when Joe Bezenhoffer, who was white, retired from presidency of Local 347, it was Leon Beverly who was a black man, who took his place. Also he felt that when Herb March left that it ought to be Charlie Hayes [who was black] to take his place. So that whole switch would be in 48.

Very early, Jesse was sharp enough to see that. And I was quite surprised, at the statement he made because the packinghouse workers was almost 70, 80% white in its leadership at that particular time. During the war time, the Packinghouse Workers Union was one of the very few unions that had blacks in their leadership. But not that much, you know. It was dominated by whites. It was dominated by white Poles, by white Hispanics, and by Czechs. There was only one or two Jews there. Bezenhoffer was Jewish. And Yugoslavs and Bohemians, because that was the whole back of the yards area.

How much credit should we give to the Communist Party for getting the union off the ground?[64] According to Charlie Hayes, a black organizer, "The CP should not get the credit. It was the perseverance of the people themselves and some credit to the company for the way they treated people in the period when people all around—even the President of the US—said people should join unions . . . the segregation—there were no hotels I could stay in; I stayed at people's homes; white [workers] had it pounded into them—the only way we could get ahead was to stay together."

Why didn't the charges of communism make much difference? The people who were most vociferous in pushing that line, looking under every bed for a red—black folks didn't get caught up. We wanted to get free. We didn't care who helped us. The vast majority in organizing came from blacks and they would not be stopped by ideological warfare. Human dignity was what counted—just to be treated like a human being.

Negotiations as a Reflection of the Basic Union Structure[65]

Irv King, an African American partner in Gene Cotton's law firm, commented in an interview that the UPWA had a closer working relationship between attorneys and the union negotiators than did most other unions.

That was probably because Ralph Helstein was a lawyer and Charlie Fisher was one of the people who did a lot of the collective bargaining negotiations. Charlie was a graduate of MIT and was the son of a lawyer and therefore accustomed to dealing with lawyers, and so I think that, plus the personality of Gene Cotton [the union's general counsel], who liked the sort of hands-on approach to things accustomed the leadership to trust and to understand the usefulness of lawyers in the negotiations.

There was also sort of this psychological thing. I don't know whether it was set up exactly that way but there's a difference between you and me sitting face to face, you, management, and me, labor, and me having 50 or 75, workers behind me[as part of the union's negotiating team], for a number of reasons. One is that the employers realize the total unity of the workers when they're there and they see the live bodies, and these were by and large rank-and-file out of the plants. The union negotiators were skilled at this, Ralph Helstein or Jesse Prosten or Charlie Fisher, whoever was the principal spokesman or chief negotiator, would in effect turn the troops loose on the company, and some issue would come up and without giving a signal, it became a fine art. The people behind the negotiating table would start speaking, one after another, and they were in a position to say things that the negotiators couldn't comfortably say, but they had no inhibitions on what they could say, and this was very effective. . . .

It's a two-sided table with chairs, ordinarily more chairs on the union side of the table.

I remember in the old days of Swift or Armour, there might be 40 or more people who were rank and file just sitting there, leaning forward in their seats and ready to pounce at any moment but well behaved.

[One of the workers] would get up and if the company was taking the position on some issue, such as for example, hours of work, what could be the maximum hours of work in a day. A guy would get up and give his take on what an inhuman thing this is for people who are standing in the packinghouse pulling hides off of steers all day long and here you are sitting up in the air conditioned office and you're telling us that we have to work 12 hours a day, and you work eight and then go home. . . .

Then there's the welfare mother, perhaps, that's getting up and saying what it's like to work like that. And then another would get up and recite some experience he may have had, or she, women too a mix of men, women, black, white and Hispanic people. And then the union negotiators would take it up.

The people who did the actual speaking, and carried the heavy load on this were not the lawyers.

From the union side, there were the chain meetings (employees from plants of the same company) exchange information about plants, discuss contract changes; resolutions will be adopted by local unions, and suggestions made by the international office.

In the actual bargaining sessions, the local president is assisted by grievance personnel, economists, representatives of the international and at a later stage of the negotiation, lawyers. Local members attending can vary up to five or ten and often there is an attempt to get representatives from each department. Locals may often have fifty to seventy-five representatives. There may be speech-making that gives union members "an opportunity . . . to discuss the problems with which it is confronted, thus providing the company with a clearer understanding of the reason for the union's submission of a particular proposal."[66]

The contract terms must be approved by all chain delegates and then by a special conference of all local unions affected by the contract.[67]

Loyalty as a Virtue

For Helstein, there was no quality he held more firmly than that of loyalty. That characteristic was illustrated in 1952 at the time of the unexpected sudden death of Philip Murray, president of the CIO. Murray died on the way to a board meeting preceding the union's California convention. That convention was postponed to be later held in Atlantic City. The issue of loyalty arose in the choice of candidate for the next president of the CIO—Alan Haywood or Walter Reuther.

Allen Haywood was an old associate of Phil Murray's, out of the Mine Workers as was Phil Murray. He came with Murray from the Mine Workers. . . He had been vice president of the CIO for a number of years and our union over the years had had a good relationship with Haywood. . . . [H]e had been very helpful to us in connection with strikes, in connection with some of our internal fights, helping to pull our people together. He had raised a lot of objections to my election as president of the union but really whether he was doing it, as he said, because Murray thought it was reprehensible that a lawyer should become president or whether on his own he didn't like the politics that I represented and he felt more comfortable with other people who felt he could exercise more hegemony over, I'm not sure. I've always thought it was the latter, that I made him a little uncomfortable, and that he wasn't sure I could be controlled as easily as the others and that that was really the basis for it, but it was quite unimportant. We did feel a sense of loyalty to him.

And it really wasn't a question of our being opposed to Reuther because Reuther was obviously going to add up to more ability and quality. But Haywood had been there for a long time and the probabilities were that he didn't have much longer to go. It would have been simple enough to have worked out an arrangement where he would have filled one or two terms, that would have been it. But Reuther was insistent he was going to get in there....[68]

When they got to the convention, it became evident to Helstein that if Haywood was to win they had to have a plan to get other unions to back Haywood. With Mike Quill he worked out a plan that would at least "make a respectable showing." Quill for some unknown reason gave his group of unions the name, Small Businessmen's Organization. So as Helstein noted: "So here we are in Atlantic City at a CIO convention, the Small Businessmen's Association, caucusing within the ranks of the CIO."[69]

Finally at one point just before the convention was to start I sat down with a couple of people and we drafted a speech for Haywood. We worked until four o'clock in the morning. It was a pretty good speech, actually. He was all excited—sweet old guy. He got up to give it the next morning and Carey just pushed him away from the mike and took over and started running the convention, calling it to order. Haywood never got a chance to deliver his speech. He was just devastated but he just didn't know how to deal with [Carey], he never had, where another person would have stood his ground and said, look, I'm convening this convention, I'm acting president [which, of course is what Helstein would have done in his place].[70]

... I really came to understand what was going on the night before the election when I was delegated to try and work out a deal with the Reuther forces to make sure that Haywood wasn't ... pushed around.... And the person I started working with on this was Frank Rosenblum of the Amalgamated Clothing Workers. I was an old friend of Frank's. We had a very good understanding and I said to him, "You know, Frank, we've had this old relationship with Haywood. That's really why we're supporting him." He said, "Well, don't you realize why we can't support him? McDonald's[71] essentially a fascist and Haywood's completely under McDonald's domination. All that will happen is that the CIO will be pushed further right than it has been with Haywood in there. Reuther at least gives us a chance and that's why we're not supporting Haywood.... [I]t's not that we love Reuther so much but it's really McDonald who's the candidate here and we wouldn't support him for anything."

I should have been smart enough to realize that but I'd gotten all involved with this emotional problem of loyalty which I should have been, by that time, smart enough to have understood better.... It worked out in a way. I was being completely honest about this. I kept saying when guys would get up and make these speeches attacking Reuther, I'd say, "Look, let's be clear about this. We are not against Reuther, we are for Haywood. Now, let's just keep this issue straight." I did this publicly, did it in front of the press ... It was really the way I felt.... I wasn't playing politics with it because I didn't realize what was going on....

That night Rosenblum and I worked out ... a constitutional plan that would make Haywood executive vice president or something. It was to give him a status as vice president that was different from the others. And he would also be Director of Organization so that he would have some power that was constitutionally present and wasn't dependent completely on Reuther.[72]

Salary information on union officers is hard to come by, but the Wisconsin Historical Society archives show for the year 1948, in a document titled, "International Office," salaries are listed as:

Ralph L. Helstein, Pres. $7,000; Rubi Marovich, Secretary $2,800; Lyle Cooper, Research Director $6,600 (penciled in—no per diem)[73]; Mary Crites, Secretary $2,400; Harvey Mader, Attorney $4,200; Jacqueline Green, Secretary $2,700; Harry Schonstein, Wage Rate $4,000; ... Lee Simon, Farm-Labor $4,000 ... Lewis J. Clark, Sec-Treas $6,000 ... Frank Ellis, V. P. $5,000. There is the Office of the President, Education and Publicity; Office of the Secretary-Treasurer; Office of Vice President in charge of Organization and the Office of Vice President in charge of Grievances.[74]

When Helstein became the UPWA's general counsel and then its president, it was impossible to separate one from the other. Helstein spent every waking hour at his office or at home on some aspect of union business.[75] Although he never worked in a packinghouse a day in his life, he learned everything possible about the lives and concerns of the workers; about the history of the industry and the union; and about the union's earlier struggles, its internal schisms, and strikes won and lost. The importance that race and ethnic identity played in those struggles became well known to him. He used this history in planning strategy, in his convention speeches, and in urging and convincing workers that the policies he recommended were in their best interests.

Chapter 3

Jewish Leadership in the Union

Because during the years after World War II, politically progressive political parties and movements had disproportionately large Jewish memberships,[1] it is not surprising that a union that professed and acted upon ideals of racial and gender equality and working class advancement should attract Jews to its leadership posts. Jews who had prominent posts in the United Packinghouse Workers of America (UPWA) included, in addition to Helstein, Eugene Cotton, the union's general counsel; Norman Dolnick, staff member; Jesse Prosten, the union's chief negotiator and grievance head; Meyer Stern, District 6 Director (New York area); Herbert March, District 1 director; and Joe Levy, social director of District 1.[2]

Eugene Cotton

Eugene Cotton,[3] general counsel of the union and a confident of Helstein, was another of the Jewish non-Communist leftists around Helstein. According to Herb March:

> Cotton... [did not] depart from that general outlook during his whole career as a labor lawyer. His support for honest, democratic, militant unionism, opposed to witchhunting, redbaiting, were in the best traditions of unionism. He had a very positive influence in dealing with Helstein because Helstein was always under attack by the [CIO] brass in an effort to push him to the right. He [Cotton] played a very good role in the labor movement.

In several interviews, Cotton described his background and career. He had a very similar background to Helstein, which might have been one reason they got along so well.

> My father[4] came over here in 1905, a period of revolution in Russia. He was a socialist, a follower of Norman Thomas and had a whole coterie of socialist

friends. He brought home the Jewish Forward, and voted the Socialist Party ticket at all times. When I was eight, nine or ten years old he took me to party meetings where I heard [Morris] Hilquit and [Louis] Waldman.

My mother came over in the 1890s as a little girl. I was brought up in very much a Jewish family atmosphere. The food was kosher; there was Passover observance. My parents spoke Yiddish to each other most of the time. Even now I can stumble along in Yiddish, and read a Yiddish newspaper. So there was a Yiddish background and it was in general the atmosphere of the Jewish socialist movement and the Jewish labor movement in New York.

My father was a very firm atheist. So he would eat on Yom Kippur, his only problem was that he had to find a delicatessen that was open. My mother was not serving food at home. She cleaned out all the non-Passover things and moved in the Passover things. We went through all the rituals. My father had been brought up in an Orthodox family in Russia. He simply had tossed it aside and was tolerant of those who followed it, but for himself, he saw no particular value in it.

My brother and I both had very good records in school; he was valedictorian in elementary school so that he graduated at the age of 12; I skipped six times so I graduated elementary school at age of 11.

City College was just overwhelmingly Jewish and most of them were from families like mine. I didn't, at that point, have an idea of what I wanted to do. I was editor of the college humor paper called the Mercury. I became editor of the yearbook of the graduating class and editor of the freshman handbook. I could write fluently. I was in college at the age of 14.

I was a very talkative intellectually aggressive—when I wanted to do something, I was regarded as stubborn, opinionated, that sort of thing so that when I would argue with my parents over something, the maiden aunt on my mother's side would say, oh, he's going to be a lawyer, he talks so much; that was the extent of the discussion of what I was going to be. There was no specific point where it was said, yes, that's my occupation.

What made Columbia possible for both of us was that we both [he and his brother] got tuition scholarships for the three years; otherwise, we would not. I graduated in CCNY in 1933. The whole atmosphere was one in which education was a prime objective; it was taken for granted that come what may my brother and I would go to college.

Once my brother went to law school which was 1931—he was a senior when I was a freshman—I would go to law school too; it was sort of an easy way out; it was something you did when you couldn't think of anything else to do. It didn't cost anything to go to City College. I graduated from Columbia University Law School in 1936.

My radicalization really took place in law school. The whole family was affected economically in the sense that my father had a store. For a long time that had been running into some difficulties. By 1930, the fall of his income was very significant. We were barely just scraping through. He actually had to close the store just about the time I was in law school, about 1934 or thereabouts. There was a time when he was totally unemployed but then he got himself a job in a small steel fabricating plant, a hand assembly job, and he worked at that job until he was 83 yrs old till 1965, about the last 20 years. He was no longer as politically active but he voted for Norman Thomas as long as he ran.

In law school, there were two teachers who I felt particularly attracted to and challenged by Herbert Wechsler and Walter Gellhorn, who taught administrative law. If there was any kind of beginnings of political influence in my life it was the result of those two. In my first year of law school, I worked during the summer for Wechsler. In that first year, Wechsler and Gellhorn both became involved in preparing materials for the appeal in the Scottsboro boys' case.[5] I was introduced to Carol Weiss King[6] who was then running the International Juridical Association Bulletin, a monthly publication in the fields of labor and civil liberties. She was like a siren or pied piper attracting young lawyers into working with her. As I worked with Wechsler and Gellhorn I began to become aware of what was going on.

They were all Jewish. Just as on the law review, probably ten were Jewish. I guess I formed the idea that law could be put to great uses defending people who needed it—working for an underclass, promoting sensible doctrines of citizen responsibility. I began to think of law as a form for social progress; I don't think it was ever concretized. I did not think of myself at the time as becoming a labor lawyer. Witness the fact that when I graduated, I went immediately to the interviewing group of the law firms in the town whereas there were others in my class who decided to go to work for the New Deal.

For one year I worked for a Wall Street law firm, about 90 percent on one matter which is what drove me away from being a Wall Street lawyer. . . . [While a] large number in the class went to New Deal agencies, I didn't even think in terms of doing that. So the basic ethos, as I understand it, is not idealistic. It was basically people were there to make a living.

I think they all were looking at that time to getting a job. They would all like to get a job that was consistent with a developing social outlook, and the New Deal offered them an ideal outlook for that. Everybody accepted the fact that what was going on in Washington in the New Deal was social progress.

At the time, it was fairly well understood that there were firms to which you didn't go if you were Jewish and you didn't bother wasting their time and yours because at the time, they just didn't hire Jews. Therefore, those in the graduating class who were Jewish made the rounds of the Jewish law firms. I went to about three different law firms that I can recall off hand,

and got the offer from this firm fairly early on, so that I don't recall whether I had gotten any offers from any of the other firms, but their offer was high for the Jewish people. It was $35 a week . . . so I accepted that offer. This is 1936 dash 37.

I was strongly pro-labor. I was strongly pro-civil rights. Beyond that, I guess I didn't have any ideological framework in a sense. I was strongly pro-New Deal. I was strongly in favor of the kinds of government action that were being taken by the New Deal.

I had no doubt about which side I was on in terms of what the National Labor Relations Act meant. As to the background of what were then called Negroes and Negro problems, I was clear in my mind that I was horror-struck, stricken by the lynching, the literal lynch atmosphere, that is the history of lynching, the history of slavery, but at that time, there had not yet developed any real movement for what we think of as civil rights.

In 1937, the National Labor Relations Act finally passed constitutional muster. The law had been practically inoperative since its passage in 1935 because an agglomeration of major lawyers known as the Liberty League had simply tied it up. So in 37 that spawned a whole series of state labor boards. New York passed its labor relations act in 1937 and I went down there when they were first setting up their office to get a job there. That's the point I entered the labor field.

At the end of the fourth year there, the man who had been assistant general counsel during all those years, first hired, moved upwards, the job of executive secretary, and therefore the problem was to name a new assistant general counsel. I was called in by the then only Jewish member of the board itself, who felt that he could talk as one Jew to another to explain the predicament, and that predicament was that, while they recognized the logic of the situation, that the general counsel who left a year later was Jewish. The executive secretary who got moved up from assistant general counsel job was Jewish, and they would be ending up with the top three jobs in the agency held by Jews, and they didn't think they could face up to that. So they wanted me to understand that it was going to be necessary to promote somebody else, which they did. At that point I was ready to leave.

Out of the blue, I got a telegram from Washington from Tom Harris whereas he was at that time, assistant general counsel to the FCC in Washington, and this telegram to me was, would I be willing to take a job in Washington as special counsel to the FCC [Federal Communications Commission]. I knew him from law review in those days.

"So it came as a total surprise to me; I took the job. And I'm glad I did." The background as it turned out was that they were conducting hearings before the full FCC [Federal Communications Commission] on the subject of, newspaper ownership of radio stations, that it should be as a matter of policy, prohibit newspapers from owning a radio station in the same town for fear that you're establishing a monopoly on news broadcasting, and so they were holding hearings on that which had gone on for a fair period of time, several months by that time.

At that point I knew nothing about the FCC but this was clearly a good escape from the position I found myself in, so I went to Washington for an interview, was interviewed by both [Telford] Taylor and Harris, and they offered me the job and I took it.

Three or four months later I got a phone call from Lee Pressman,[7] whom I had never met and knew by name of course, asking me to have lunch with him, and he said would you be willing to come to work for me as assistant general counsel for the CIO? I learned later that he had gotten my name from Carol King, She had pointed out to him that she knew my job was running out and I was available, so he offered me the job.

He said the job would require imminent patience—you're going to be dealing with labor leaders, labor members who aren't particularly sophisticated in the law, or even in a lot of other things, and who will drive you to frustration, and exasperation. You've got to have infinite patience in dealing with them, and how slow things move, infinite patience in dealing with negotiations which drag on, drag on, but he said that would be the major quality. So I told him that I thought I had.

First of all, it sounded even more exciting than what I was doing, and second it would involve no physical hardship. Here I didn't know Pressman particularly, but at the same time, this talk about being where the action is, this was the CIO which was the focal point of all political, of all good political things, good labor things at that time. I just knew it was the CIO, and I knew it was an ongoing job and I think he must have outlined some of the general nature of the job, was being assistant general counsel by the way, not just the CIO, but also to the steelworkers, because Murray was both chairman of the steelworkers organizing committee, and president of the CIO. Lee [Pressman] was in both jobs, and this would be assistant general counsel in both jobs. A good deal of what I did involved shuffling later on back and forth between Pittsburgh and Washington to handle both ends of that responsibility. I had to do work for the steelworkers who's headquarters were in Pittsburgh.[8]

Later, Pressman left the CIO and I was offered the job by Helstein as general counsel of the UPWA out in Chicago in the end of 47.

One of my earliest cases working for the CIO involved taking a case before the War Labor Board, which involved a group of black trade unionists. Some of the rank and file were working with me in the preparation of the case for presentation. On the first day they were in it became lunch time. I took them aside and said let's go out to lunch and we all went out to lunch and I took them to a cafeteria in the neighborhood. I noted that they were kind of looking at me quizzically but I didn't know what was in their minds. I was fresh to Washington from New York, and while we're waiting on line—there were about four of them, I think; and a young woman, the hostess, while we're waiting in line to go into the cafeteria stands up to me and says, we don't serve Negroes here. And this was the first contact that I had personally in a sense of relating to this kind of discrimination in the capital of the country. . . .

I was horrified, but my reaction was not, well let's stage a sit-in. We had a job to do, so my reaction was, well, we'll find someplace else. We went out and managed to locate some place that would serve us.

Irv King, an African-American partner in Cotton's Chicago law firm said of Cotton:[9]

His ability to understand complicated legal issues and to devise arguments and strategies to accomplish what has to be accomplished in the face of legal obstacles, which I regard as being the great strengths of good lawyers. Or figuring out ways of doing, of getting something accomplished that needs to be accomplished, in the face of adverse law. I think he's exceptionally good at that.

He has a sense of humor, and he's very nice. He's an easy-going, easy to get along with and gets along with everybody. And I think he's sensitive to people, and I don't recall a single issue that I've ever seen him take what I would regard as a wrong position on an issue of any kind, legal, social, political.

He's very impressive in court, but he has a presence; his strength is just the power of his intellect.

C: Logic?

I: Gets right to the heart of it, of the matter, and he sees all sides, and he sees all angles.

Nina Helstein, during a dinner honoring Cotton,[10] said in part:

I want to tell you what I came to know about Gene through the 26-year collaboration between him and my father. I recall years of Saturday and Sunday afternoons when Gene would come over to our house. Armed with yellow legal pads, he and my father would engage in hours of war counsels. My father valued and needed Gene's thoughts and advice. The adjectives he used in relation to Gene's intelligence span brilliant to gifted with probably everything in between. He relied on Gene's judgment and was always confident of his integrity.

Herb March

Herb March's life and union career is a blueprint for understanding UPWA history.[11] March was born November 8, 1912.[12] He grew up in Brownsville, a working class immigrant area of Brooklyn and then "out in the country." As a child, his family went to *schul* on the High Holidays, but his father believed that organized religion was a "racket."[13] His father was pro-labor and became a steward for the postal station where he worked.

March was very well-read, reading among other authors Victor Hugo's *Les Miserables*, Dumas, and Dickens.

At the 15 years of age, March enrolled in the Brooklyn branch of the City College of New York. On the route he took home, there were Communist and Socialist open-air meetings. At one meeting of the Young Workers League, a Communist group, he was asked to sign a card. "I was just curious. I knew they were interested in having socialism; I thought there would be discussions. At the first meeting, they said, a revolution was needed." He thought maybe a revolution was needed, but a bloodless revolution. Up to that time, he had never read any Marxist writings. But he got hold of a book by Harold Laski, called *Communism*. Some unions were on strike; he was asked to help picket and pass out leaflets. In 1928 to 1929, at the age of 16 years, he joined the Young Workers Communist League.

March decided to take on a "party" name. He didn't want his father who worked at the post office or uncle who worked at the Navy Yard to be affected by the fact he was a member of a Communist organization. Originally, his name had been Falk, but that sounded too much like another four-letter word, so he changed it back to his grandfather's name, Finklestein, later shortened by his father to Fink. But Fink, in strike lingo, meant a scab, so Herb again changed it to March. He took the name of March because the month he made the change was March.[14] Similar to many Jewish political radicals, March's attitude toward his Judaism "was essentially negative, if not actually hostile."[15] March said:

> I went to work at all kinds of jobs, furniture and doll factories. It was mostly not unionized. About 1928 I was asked by the YCL [Young Communist League] to go to Perth Amboy, New Jersey and help their organization there. Then the depression came along. I just didn't think it was right for some people to be poor and some people to be so damned rich. I knew about unions and why people needed them.

We decided the best thing for us to do was to work on packinghouses. And we had a group of people, particularly among the Yugoslavs who worked in the packinghouses and the Russians, and some blacks, and what we did was we got out a packinghouse workers shop paper, which we distributed. I don't know what, probably called it the Packinghouse Worker.

The guys used to say about me. Herb may be a red, but whatever he is, he's a damn good one.[16] I was a fighter for the workers. They all knew that.

March's union activity took place in an era of labor goons and gangsters. He was the subject of several assassination attempts. "They shot me on the way home from the meeting (June 1939). I carried a gun for awhile. . . ."[17] He continued:

There was an attempt to knock me off during the Livestock Handlers strike. They fired nine shots at me and fortunately none of them hit me but I busted my nose diving into the pavement. What I did was I kept on hitting the brake of the cab and they're popping away at me. I hit a car, opened the door, rolled out and dove to the pavement, and the shots around me. They were standing on the running board of a V8 Ford at 51st and Ashland, a busy godarned place. And then I ran into a house and made a phone call. I told the guy—let me stay in the closet for awhile. The guy said OK. And after about five minutes and nothing happened, I called up the union hall to have somebody pick me up.

March's experience of violence was not unusual at the time for people engaged in left-wing union activity. Racial violence accompanied attempts to integrate blacks and whites. Union thugs tried to prevent organizing of rival groups, and police beatings of organizers took place. "In Chicago—home to Al Capone's underworld–labor politics frequently turned to violence. . . . By the late 1920s, gangsters entered a number of trade unions, making racketeering a profitable and violent characteristic of the city's labor scene."[18]

David Cantor,[19] who knew March in 1943 when March was District 1 director, described March as follows:

Herb March had a very famous reputation at that time as the guy to see in packing, very strongly pro-labor and very strongly progressive. He was a hero. He was absolutely revered. He was already a hero when I first came on [District One's staff], a strong square-jawed, very, very quiet and silent, a brilliant orator.

He was great in speeches. In mass audiences. Quite a lot of times at Armour Square, which is right smack in the middle of the stockyards, we used to have these mass meetings at noontime where all the workers would come out and the stewards would come out, and the staff would prepare banners and they would have loudspeakers and they would have this big raised platform on which Herb March would stand. Herb was great, because he appealed with the street type of language that the workers could understand. He was sharp, in being able to penetrate. His rhetorical devices were great. His articulation was great. The man had a bellowing voice. He was full of humor.

Herb was invulnerable. The man was a hero in the eyes of the working class and a hero in the eyes of the membership. He was the guy that could do no wrong. All the others were little people around a colossus, you know, and as such, a lot of his relationships with people was not that he didn't want to work with them, as that they didn't want to work with him. They were envious of him. This man wasn't a tin god, he was a real god. There was no question about his loyalty to the movement. He achieved a tremendous amount of victories. He was a brilliant organizer. He got more people into the union, he had an open door in his office. There were guys that would troop up straight up from the kill, with dirty uniforms and dirty, tracking mud and everything like that, walked into Herb's office.

The union brought him in as head of the negotiating team. Armour refused to recognize him cause they knew he was a tough son of a bitch. They knew that he could just pound it and just sit there and look at them and stare at them.

Herb was expelled from the Communist Party. It must have been early in the 50s because this is after Herb resigned as district director because of the Taft-Hartley Law and he was hired by Local 347 to be its organizer. The local established that office to give Herb something to do. So this went on for some time and the occasion arose that they were planning a new election of officers in 347 and there was some woman officer who was white, and the local CP [Communist Party] cell had decided that they were going to not re-nominate her, maybe recording secretary. Herb felt there was no occasion to drop her and they needed to keep a white person in the leadership in some capacity. Then the cell expelled Herb for white chauvinism. Herb went to the National Committee. This was at a time when there was a great push for black take-over. The National Committee of the CP reversed the charges, reinstated Herb whereupon he went out to California. I presume he then resigned form the CP.[20]

Jesse Prosten

Jesse Prosten was perhaps the closest of these men to the Helsteins and their intersecting lives. The interviews with Prosten cover his work experiences but provide precious little about his earlier life or his Jewish background.

Some information is provided by Prosten's testimony before Congressional Committees.[21] Prosten testified that he had been an international representative of the UPWA in the capacity of field representative for approximately 13 years. Before that he worked for the same union in New York and before that in Boston as a field representative for six or seven years. His education was grade school and a year and half of high school. He testified that he was not then a member of the Communist Party. He was asked if he knew several people who had testified that he was a member of the Communist Party, and on advice of counsel, he took the Fifth Amendment.

For additional information about Prosten, we must rely on my interviews with his wife, Ann, a fascinating person in her own right.[22] Ann Prosten was born in Brownsville (Brooklyn, NY) in 1912. Her parents, fleeing from pogroms, arrived in New York City from Odessa in 1907. She said:

> I remember the horror stories of my mother telling of the raid of the Pogromchiks on the Jewish ghetto, seeing her sister impaled against a fence by the spear of one of the horsemen who had ridden into town attacking the Jews.[23] That was the story my mother told when she lay dying. She was in a coma and it has haunted me for the rest of my life, that the one memory that came to her as she lay there was the memory of that terrible time. She actually was seeing her sister impaled again.
>
> My father's real name was Rosen, but that was a Jewish name, and when the Pogromchiks came through the first thing they did was check the town roster and go after the Jewish names. So he became Klutch. And I confess privately to people that was the reason I married Jesse. My maiden name was Ann Klutch. You could see how anxious I was to get married.
>
> My father was a member of the union, and that was always a very important institution in our lives because you couldn't get a job unless you were a union painter. But they also had corruption in the union in those days because the leader of the union was called Jake the Bum. So my awareness of unions was, on the one hand it was important to be a member cause that's where you got a job, and on the other hand, the guys who ran the union were not such hot people.
>
> At home we spoke Yiddish, and when they didn't want the kids to understand they spoke Russian, and I pleaded with my father to teach me Russian. I wanted to know what they were talking about. And my mother said, over my dead body (laughter). If she learns Russian she may go back there to that terrible country with the anti-Semites and they'll kill her. That was my

mother's reason for not wanting me to learn Russian. So my father just didn't want to fight with her, and I never learned Russian there My mother insisted that her children all go to Hebrew School, and I did go to Hebrew School for a couple of years.

Ann met Jesse at a demonstration in front of the Port Authority Building on the west side of Manhattan

He would have been hard not to notice because Jesse had red hair and a red mustache. We were marching back and forth chanting and the police came along and said okay. Into the wagon, and all of us were arrested. And it was in the night court when I noticed Jesse's absence, or noted that the red-headed fellow wasn't there. When the guy asked Jesse his name, he didn't want to give his real name. He glanced down and saw a Dickson pencil and gave the name of John Dickson.

Jesse asked me to come and have dinner with him one night, and we went to a restaurant on 2nd Avenue, where the meal cost 25 cents or 50 cents for the whole dinner. He ordered oysters on the half shell (Jesse was not kosher), and I had never eaten an oyster. He came from Coney Island, and he said, go on. Taste them. They're good, and I, to be polite, I thought they were revolting. . . .

Our lives were totally consumed by union activities. By what we were doing. Our associations were all in connection with union meetings and so forth. And at some point we began living together.

It was not one of those flaming love at first sight relations, as far as I was concerned, and I must say that Jesse was more [chuckling] more the aggressor in the situation. I had a crush on somebody else at the time, and I spent that first evening telling Jesse about it. He was just a friendly person, very sympathetic ear. He listened very carefully as I told him about this, about this guy that I was in love with. And Jesse was very sympathetic. And for me it was a gradual thing. It wasn't a head over a heels kind of thing. For Jesse it just seemed to be a very early on decision that he wanted to be friends, and he was very persistent about it. Never obnoxious, never offensive in any way, but he always seemed to be there. Wherever I was, he was there, and he just became a very good, dear friend, and it sort of became a gradual thing. I told my mother that I was living with a girlfriend.

Jesse was always an optimist. He never gripped. He never felt sorry for himself. For him, life was a beautiful adventure.

Jesse was born April of 1912, one month before I was born. Jesse had two brothers and two sisters. One sister, the youngest in the family, developed appendicitis and died of peritonitis.

He was born and raised in Brooklyn, and his family moved to Coney Island early on. His father was an engineer of some kind. His father left the family but he came back a couple of times to impregnate his wife. Jesse essentially was the male head of the family, and left school at an early age to find part-time jobs.

His mother was a very proud lady, a very lovely lady. She said something to me that I doubt many mother-in-laws ever say to their daughters-in-law when they first meet. She said to me, is he good to you? And it was usually the other way around. She'd had a bad experience with her own husband, and so she was more worried about how her son was treating his wife. I never forgot it.

I don't know at what point and how it was that he landed a job as a clerk on Wall Street. On Wall Street, Jesse met a couple. His first name was Dave and he had a Marxist view, and he was the first person who ever discussed anything political with Jesse as far as I know. Jesse must then have been in his late teens.

Then he got a job in Washington, some kind of a research job with the WPA.

But when towards the end of that one year, Jesse was told by a friend of the NLRB that some people in Boston were looking for an organizer for packinghouse workers in Boston, Jesse was very interested. That's really what he wanted to do. He wanted to be part of the industrial union movement that John L. Lewis had.

There was a lawyer at the NLRB who was a friend of his, whom he had met socially traveled to Boston and applied for the job. It was a local that was looking for an organizer for packinghouse workers.

First he organized the Boston meat market, small independents, who, at their core, were anarchists, who only a decade earlier had struggled on the Sacco-Vanzetti issue. . . . I wish I could remember their names. Now and then their names flash through my mind and then I lose them again. Never wrote them down anywhere. They were strong, ardent unionists, ardent for unionism, and I was baffled by my image of anarchists as being these wild, disruptive, unpredictable revolutionists who were just as soon kill you as look at you, and then encountering these sweet, lovely, gentle warm people, who had a dream of a society in which everybody loved everybody and everybody shared with everybody, totally contradicting the public image, and they taught Jesse a great deal. I think that's when Jesse came to his maturity in the labor movement. They taught him the pricelessness of solidarity, how important that was. They taught him, they demonstrated it. They were, they had solidarity in their own ranks. They didn't turn on each other. They didn't rat on each other. They didn't scab on each other. They didn't fight each other. They all knew they had a common enemy, and they stuck together, and they won. Their victories were due more to their own solidarity than to Jesse's great wisdom as a union organizer. But from that solidarity Jesse learned the most important lesson in unionism, which is the unity of the workers. And as somebody said, as we know, when Jesse left about six years later to go into the Army, most of the big packers throughout Massachusetts had been organized. Jesse had led in the organization. He was a member of the Packinghouse Workers Organizing Committee. He went on that payroll eventually.

This is from about 1936 to 42, 42 and that's when he went into the Army. In early 1941, they won union victories in Lawrence, and had a union hall there, and Jesse operated out of that union hall and organizing these workers. They had been so successful that they also elected the police chief in the town. Very friendly to the labor movement. One day when the strike had been on for some time, Jesse had a call, telling him to come to the offices of the National Labor Relations Board on Washington Street in Boston to meet with the employers, representatives of the employer to talk about the possible settlement of the strike. Jesse, with picketing workers, arrived at the offices of the NLRB, and found that nobody was there to meet with them. So they left. They came back downstairs and as they left, walked out of the elevator, three gunmen approached. One went for Jesse and smashed him on the head, and dropped him. He just fell to the ground, and the other two held the other gunmen, the two other men held these other two at bay until this guy had beaten Jesse up and then they all ran and left.

His colleagues picked him up and took him to the emergency room of the hospital, and they stitched him up there. I knew nothing about this. I thought he was in Lawrence. About midnight, somebody called on the phone, and said Ann, did Jesse get it bad? And I said, did he get what bad? And the guy realized that I didn't know anything about it. He said never mind. I said wait a minute, what are you talking about? And he finally told me that Jesse had been beaten up. I didn't know where Jesse was. But he came home and he had been stitched up.

And he had been back in his office for a day or so when he got a phone call, and the guy said, hey Red, how'd you like the treatment you got the other day? And Jesse realized he was talking to the guy who had beaten him up. And Jesse said, well how do you think I liked it? I didn't like it at all. And the guy said, well, you know you can do something about it if you used your head. Jesse thought very quickly at that point. He said, listen. I can't talk to you here. Call me at the union hall in Lawrence and maybe we can talk. And on Sunday, Jesse and the police chief of Lawrence were on two phones and the guy called Jesse. And I took down the conversation, shorthand, and the police chief was sitting on the other end, and the next day (chuckling), Mr. SM Packing had a heart attack. The strike was settled.

I don't know if anybody went to jail over it or what. And sometime not too long thereafter, I understand that one or two of the men who attacked Jesse were found very badly beaten up in Boston.

In 1943 Jesse volunteered for the army and was sent to Officers Training School. Shortly thereafter two of his brothers were killed in the war and he asked to be discharged to care for his mother who was now alone. When he was discharged, the union asked him to come back to work, and instead of him going to work in Boston, they asked him to come to Chicago out of the verge of becoming an international union. They were the Packinghouse Workers Organizing Committee.

In the meantime, the packinghouse workers were moving toward affiliation with the CIO. Jesse had acquired a reputation in Boston; he was a veteran in packinghouse organizing. The grievance department and organizing seemed to be separate at some point, but then it came together, and he began being in charge of negotiations. Ralph [Helstein] was certainly already there, and Jesse was always at his side. They developed a pretty close relationship, both social and working. We were there occasionally for dinner

I remember the Un-American Activities Committee was involved at some point around then. Jesse appeared. I wouldn't say he testified. I would say he defied them and told them to go to hell, and I have the check to him lying among the papers there for $9 (laughing) that he never cashed of course and it's lying there among some of his documents that I have. No, he simply invoked the 5th Amendment and never spoke. Other people did testify, including a man named Hackney, who borrowed our car one day and never returned it, and then testified before the committee that Jesse was a communist.

As the union moved toward a merger with the Amalgamated Butcher Workman, tensions developed between Jesse and Ralph. Eva Sandman described these relations in an interview:

Jesse Prosten was definitely Jewish and very emotional. Jesse was very critical of Ralph many times. Jesse was critical of Ralph because Ralph hadn't come up through the plant. Ralph hadn't come up the kosher way. He was a union lawyer and that's how he got to be president. There was probably some competitiveness there. At the time I was there, the packinghouses were leaving Chicago and Ralph was into negotiations with Armour and Swift, trying to help them do this in a way that would be best for the workers. He was trying to negotiate severance arrangements for the workers and training possibilities and so forth. And Jesse was very critical of all this. He thought that Ralph was selling out to the companies and that there ought to be a great deal more resistance. There were arguments that

I overheard ... [a]rguments that took place where other people could hear them. ... Jesse always thought Ralph was giving away more than he should be giving [during the Amalgamated negotiations].[24] And Ralph recognized that the world was changing, and you couldn't fight forces that he couldn't do anything about; you had to ameliorate; you could change the circumstances somewhat but just going out on strike wasn't going to do it—that these companies were going to move regardless. And Jesse didn't understand that; he was old school and he was much more rigid and he thought that Helstein ... was giving away the store. I think Ralph had fairly good relationships with people in management and Jesse didn't like that. He thought you should maintain a completely antagonistic attitude at all times. Jesse spoke Yiddish too because he came from the wrong side of the tracks but Jesse wanted to get away from that and I think that Ann [Jesse's wife] also fit into this. I think that Jesse relied a lot on Ann. I think she was angry at Ralph as well and that they were sort of a united front. She was a strong influence on Jesse.

David Cantor gave the following account of his experiences with Jesse while he worked editing the District 1 newspaper in 1943:

Jesse was almost like a chief of staff. Just remember, Jesse was the national officer assigned on grievances, and people who had first-step grievances are usually taking place in the plant itself. And the second-step grievances went to the head of the local grievance committee. Then the third-step grievance went past the local into the district office, and that's where Jesse steps in. So Jesse had to do with almost every local in the district. There were about 40 locals in the district, and so Jesse was a real grassroots kind of a guy.

Who was in a better position to know what was going on in the union, how to organize workers, how to keep them organized, how to build the union, how to build a labor movement, except the labor leaders themselves that were proven heroes. They were proven in their ability. They were proven in their work. They were on the firing line, whereas the members of the Communist Party were not. I mean, the leaders of the Communist Party in Illinois were not. It's ridiculous to say that they controlled them. The only thing that could be said was, that as the leadership were members of the Communist Party, that they probably had the most advanced outlook and the best ability by virtue of their work, as communists, to do a better job than most of the people who were so that, therefore, there's no such thing as a daily control. There's no such thing as a weekly or a monthly control. I remember that there were meetings held once, maybe twice in the basement of the union headquarters. Some of the leading members, and I was not part of it cause they never considered me as part of their core group, and what were they discussing? I'm not too sure that they were discussing any union affairs. I don't think the people were discussing union affairs were people who were ideologically united to make sure that they were in control. But did the Communist Party ever exercise a daily control? No. They weren't capable of doing it.

Because Jesse was a warm, open-hearted guy. He was not the kind of a cold type that Herb was. Herb was strong and silent, strong jaws. Jesse was a red-head, open, you know. And Jesse was the kind of a guy who used to walk around the hall. Herb would sit in his office all the time. Jesse was a street guy. Jesse was the one who went up to my eldest son when the kid was four years old. He would say, hi fella, how's my friend with the short pecker? That was Jesse. Jesse stood at that mantlepiece and flipped cigarette ashes into a fishtank, my goldfish. My daughter's goldfish died the next day. That's the kind of a guy Jesse was. It's hard to pin down Jesse. I know I saw him flick those ashes in there. I said Jesse, what are you doing? You're killing my goldfish. Oh, sorry.

Jesse was clearly not only respected in the Packinghouse Workers Union. He was respected all over. Dr. King used to defer to Jesse many times, Jesse also had a face with his two sons. Jesse used to live at 61st and Blackstone on the other side of the Midway, in an apartment there. And the kids got victimized by racism. Reverse racism. And they came to their father and they said, I don't want to deal with black kids anymore. And Jesse had a talk with me, and we visited, Miriam and I visited Jesse in which he said, he's got a problem. He has to move out of that neighborhood because the kids don't want to go to that school anymore. He's the kind who would recognize some of the problems far sharper than most people. And eventually he did move. He didn't rationalize it, he simply said his kids came back and told him, that they don't want to go to that school anymore, and so he and Ann Prosten were forced to move, and they moved over to 53rd and Cornell where the school wasn't so bad. But that's the kind of a guy Jesse was, you know. He resolved personal problems.

There's no question that I miss him, because he was my mentor. Whenever I had problems, I went to Jesse. I did not go to Herb.

Both Herb March and Jesse Prosten were open Communists. In that, they defied Communist Party policy to encourage clandestinity.[25] But in other ways, they were typical of Communists in the labor movement:

Communists were more willing than the average worker to face gross employer discrimination and even violence. [S]uch qualities as indifference to being fired, willingness to work night and day and courage to face threats of physical violence were prerequisites for successful organizers. These qualities the Communists possessed.[26]

Nina Helstein,[27] Ralph Helstein's daughter, talks of her relationship to Jesse:

Well Jesse was the closest [of all her father's friends], you know. I mean I remember Jesse since I was very tiny. He'd come in the house and swing me around and call me Duchess. I felt about Jesse like he was a guardian angel for me. It seems as though whenever I was in big trouble, Jesse was there. When I was 16 and I'd just learned to drive, I remember I was in the car, driving barefoot without my license. I was one or two blocks away from my parents' house. There was a dance going on at the high school, and I think I was trying to see it, and so I was driving with my head turned, and I went into a parked car. I mean it was just ridiculous. And the minute it happened, Jesse walked out, it was right in front of International House at the University [of Chicago]. And I guess a policeman was there, and I said, oh I don't have my license but I'm half a block from home; can I run home and get it? What a mess, you know. Anyway, Jesse appeared at that moment, and there he was, talking to the policeman and, it didn't surprise me a bit to see him. I just thought, well of course Jesse would be here now, cause he was in my life. And he said, don't worry about it babe, we'll take care of it. Don't worry about a thing. You don't even have to tell your old man. But of course I did. But he was just very comforting. I remember I was in New York and I was having a very difficult time. I was teaching in Harlem. It was really rough, and Jesse showed up one day and said, come on babe, I'm taking you out for soul food, and we went and had a corned beef sandwich, and he was just kind of there. I have memories of how he and dad worked together,[28] in the early days when they were like a team. They knew each other so well, and they worked together very, very well. I think they had fun with what they were doing. I remember them telling stories about things they did. There were grievances, maybe in Iowa? All I remember is that they went someplace and this [management] guy was talking about the problems, and they didn't know if they could help in this situation, that they had a bad year. Things were really tough and they'd like to help, but they didn't think they could, and I remember Jesse and dad saying that they asked for some time and they said they were going to meet with their people.

They waited quite a while and then they came back and said something like, we talked to our people about this and everybody is concerned. We understand you had a bad year. So we took up a collection, and they gave him some change. They said, here's what we were able to raise to help you out. They were just having fun.

As I read these interviews many years later, I can appreciate what extraordinary individuals these were. Each of them with forceful personalities, dedicated to giving workers and their families better lives through working together to organize a militant union. There was meaning in calling these men and women, "organizers," for that describes them and their dedicated lives. They were able thereby to give power to the powerless, and for a time, unleash political forces that scared the daylights out of the ruling classes. That these classes crushed these militants represents a loss not merely for these workers but for American society as a whole.

But, in addition, in listening to these voices, there is a humanity, humor, love, sanity, and a way of life that could have been and maybe someday will.

Chapter 4

The 1948 Strike and Its Aftermath and Women Workers' Advancement

Les Orear describes the motivations leading up to the disastrous 1948 strike. Orear shows Helstein's thinking; how he disagreed with the decision to strike; and how after Helstein was proved right, instead of vaunting his superiority, found a strategy to repair the damage and strengthen the union:[1]

Just prior to the strike, the Amalgamated Meatcutters and the UPWA [United Packinghouse Workers of America] had a mutual understanding that there would be joint negotiations in the industry at the expiration of their contracts. As I recall, in these joint negotiations, there was a joint committee that met in the same room with the companies, meeting separately but in touch with one another. The UPWA committee formed to guide our national negotiations had about 15 or 16 members, people from Iowa, Nebraska, New York and elsewhere.

The crisis came within about a week of the deadline for the expiration of the contract. Our national strike strategy committee got word that the Meatcutters had signed an agreement for a mere 9 cents an hour increase. Our strategy committee was in an uproar that those guys who were only a small part of the industry relative to us, thought that they could set the pattern, and we were damned if we were going to allow them to get away with that. The strategy committee's attitude was that: "We're not going to let the Packers think that the tail will wag the dog cause we were the dog here."

Ralph told me that he was dubious about the idea of holding a national strike of all the meatpackers; he thought it would be much more sensible just to isolate one of the big packers and concentrate on that as being the bellweather and let the rest keep working cause we were not on strike; we were negotiating. But he said that . . . local leaders from Iowa in particular, were so incensed at the idea of giving any quarter here. . . . These are people whose union tradition had been with the United Mine Workers . . . and so they were taking their cue from the tradition of the miners to strike everybody. No contract, no work. The contract expires, everybody strikes.

Helstein told Orear that the reaction he was getting was that the union should strike the whole industry. That would get the world's attention, and you can't let the packers play you off, one against another. So, being only recently elected, Helstein felt that he could not lay down the law. So he went along with it.

But as the strike dragged into the 10th week, there were grumbles of disaffection. The [union] president of the big Swift plant in Chicago let it be known that he would lead the strike-breakers back into the plant. The atmosphere was tense.

Finally, Helstein called the strike strategy committee together. We had to accept the nine cents [that the Amalgamated had earlier negotiated] and go back to work.[2] We still had a contract and so when we retuned to work, our steward system was intact. But we had all these people that had been discharged because of illegal picket-line activity, people who had been arrested. We returned under an agreement to grieve these discharges.

As a result of this strike, we ended up broke. First of all, our staff people went off the payroll during the strike, which is a tradition of ours. . . . Nobody got paid during the strike. We had five hundred people fired around the country. The Meat Cutters were raiding us. We went through fourteen elections in a period of just months. We had lawsuits all over the place. It was just a very rough situation.

[But] in plant after plant, department after department, people would go back to work and the foreman would say, I'm the steward here now, and our steward [would tell him] I've still got the whistle to call the people out on the stump. That was the thing. Our people still knew who was the steward. . . . This is a real tribute to their sense of ownership in the union on the part of the members. The members felt loyal to their organization. They had always been kept informed; there were no orders from the top. Everybody was part of the decision-making process. . . . Nobody is going around bad-mouthing anybody. We've all got a job to do and that is to hold the thing together. The first thing was to get back to work the people who had been discharged and [that was] Jesse Prosten's job as the head of the grievance department.

. . . We landed right on our feet. Because from the top down, from Helstein on down, there was no guy that was putting their tail between their legs. . . . We had our district directors, a good part of the national leadership; the strategy was to keep your chin up; keep moving; raise grievances, get back in the saddle as you were, take it in stride, not be overwhelmed and not give up. . . . We're still here, aren't we? We've got a contract. Now, let's go. We have negotiations coming up next year. We'll be back, won't we?

Yes, of course, we will. I think we had these little stoppages, these hit and runs. Then the company says, "You gotta put a stop to these stoppages, here." We said, we can't stop those guys, you know that. You can't stop them and I can't stop them, and I wouldn't if I could. He might not have said that but that was his style. In other words, Helstein was not a part of the philosophy of most CIO people trained under Lewis—my word is my bond—I have to enforce the contract. . . .

We're now approaching negotiations a year later—but before that, we are approaching the struggle of our lives. The Amalgamated Meatcutters-AFL [American Federation of Labor] is raiding every place they can so we're on the defensive, so we have to circle the wagons. To begin with, we were under attack. Those guys that betrayed us in the first place are now going to be like cannibals try to pick up something off the bones. That union that took the god-damned 9 cents, and forced us into a strike, are now going to be like animals and eat the local unions out here where they can pick something off. We lost a couple places in the South. Most of that was because of the civil rights issue.

Ralph conceded the notion that now we have to give people something to do. We've gotten them back in the plants, but we can't have people worrying about their sorrows and so on. We have to get everybody moving on something. Move on the civil rights issue. That's how the civil rights issue, the non-discrimination policy of the union and everybody had seen it carried out so effectively on the picket line—the black workers were absolutely steel. This is a very good issue because a) it's one that we have had in our constitution, in our contracts, b) our loyalties, our brotherhood is solid here, it's our work line because this is where the companies are vulnerable; this is how we all can reform our pay ranks, force movement on the part of the companies. . . . We negotiated every damned thing that we would ever have dreamed we would have gotten out of the failed strike.

How Come the Strike Was Lost?

The union appeared to be well-prepared for the strike. The national office issued a strike manual prepared by Herb March. Various committees were formed flowing out of the Strike Strategy Committee—Publicity, Finance, Recreation, Welfare, Transportation, Legal Aid, Commissary, Headquarters, and Picketing. Each committee was headed by a qualified person; for example, the Publicity committee by a journalist. The Entertainment committee provided singing at meetings, dancing, and children's parties, and the Transportation committee—nicknamed the "flying squad"—had 450 trucks and automobiles at its disposal.[3]

The Back of the Yards Council and Bishop Shiel supported the strike and raised money and maintained a nursery for children and a kitchen. The "flying squad" took pickets to and from their shifts. Every Sunday, Herb March did a half-hour radio broadcast discussing strike issues. The plant and refrigeration equipment was maintained. At 3 A.M. the day of the strike, Helstein and the international officers came to the union hall, inspected the picket lines at the gate, and held a National Strike Strategy meeting.[4]

Then why did the UPWA lose the strike? Although Congress of Industrial Organizations (CIO) plants were out, 34 Big Four plants that were non-unionized or represented by other unions, not affected by the dispute, continued to operate. Moreover, the strike lacked strong public support, and the President's Board of Inquiry sympathized with the packers' problem in having to settle with three "competing unions"—the Amalgamated, the UPWA, and the Brotherhood (a small "independent" union). The final coup was struck by the Amalgamated that settled for the nine cents, whereupon the packers refused to make any concessions to the isolated UPWA.[5]

UPWA-CIO Policy Caucus

"Internal strife within the labour movement seems to be as eternal as the movement itself."[6]

One month after the end of the strike, in June 1948, a "caucus" of anti-Communists met to support CIO policy and to oppose Helstein's re-election. Calling themselves the UPWA-CIO Policy Caucus, they charged at the 1948 convention that the 1948 strike "was ill-advised, ill-handled and misconducted throughout."

Helstein saw the Caucus from the following perspective:

[A] number of the group who had opposed my election as president in 1946 organized what they called a CIO caucus. We had in our ranks a number of people who were very pro-[Henry]Wallace[7]. . . . This was then used as a claim that we were not following the CIO policy. . . . Of course at that point in time we were already without resources to begin with [as a result of the 1948 strike]. . . . And this was a relatively small number of unions but of some size so that it made a difference.[8]

Helstein and Clark eeked out a narrow victory with 56½ and 54 percent of the vote, respectively. Thereafter, certain of the locals, under the aegis of this CIO Caucus, withheld their per capita dues,[9] the portion of the dues that goes to the international union.[10]

The formation of the "CIO Policy Caucus," an anti-communist coalition with the intention of ousting the Helstein administration, was reactivated by the strike. This group objected to communist Herb March, now appointed as field representative, from which he could run the Chicago district; as well as Les Orear and Jesse Prosten. This movement was energized by press reports during the strike of the "red-dominated" union as well as efforts in other CIO unions to oust reds, while their union seemed to welcome them.[11]

Local 28, the Swift local, that had the strongest employer benefit plan and where the militancy of the union was weakest, was one of the main locals in the Policy Caucus. In a handout dated September 13, 1948, the "Swift CIO Flash," called for a "closed" "Membership-Meeting" and charged that the "March Gang [was] trying to Seize Local # 28." After recounting that the local had repulsed an attempt by March to take it over, it reported that a:

> new thrust by the March gang has begun. This time it is not only Local 28, but they are bent on the capture of the entire UPWA International as well. As the new front emerged into view Local leaders across the country were astounded by the "Helstein" UPWA Staff Purge and the brazen departure of the International from any semblance of an attempt to follow the principles of the C.I.O or its policies . . .

Among the demands of the Policy Caucus were that the International "Conduct the affairs of the International Union in line with the policies of the National C.I.O . . . " and to replace the people "wrongfully" discharged.[12]

At Wilson Local 25, on August 25, 1948, there was an "Important Announcement" that "a new Independent and vigorous union was organized by a large and enthusiastic number of your fellow employees" named "United Packing-House Workers Amalgamated Independent Union. . . . They are pledged to a program . . . without loss of opportunity due to strikes called by selfish irresponsible so-called leaders who have proven themselves to be more interested in their soft well-paid CIO union jobs than they are in the welfare of the people who have to work for a living." A later undated handout (December 2, 1948, "Received, U.P.W.A.") leads off with the headline: "Let's get rid of the Communists."[13] The caucus had its roots in the Henry Wallace candidacy for president on a third-party platform. Wallace touched the deep resentment felt with Truman's perceived anti-labor and red-baiting policies. UPWA's tolerance of pro-Wallace activities were in direct conflict with CIO directives supporting Truman. In a speech to a District 3 convention in February 1948, Helstein said: "If the facts are as they are today, I will cast my ballot for Henry Wallace." That the UPWA administration seemed ready to support Wallace was evidence to the Caucus that the Helstein administration was openly defying the CIO and was Communist dominated.[14]

But the hard work of Jesse Prosten in getting fired workers back to work and the resignations of Communists Stern and March for the good of the union were ample response to charges by the Caucus that the union was a pawn of the Communist Party and that workers suffered as a result. By the end of 1948, the Caucus had expired.[15]

The 5th Constitutional Convention held June 28 to July 1, 1948, at the Sherman Hotel in Chicago was dominated by the aftermath of the strike. As a first order of business, the delegates adopted a series of measures that detailed the means of electing delegates, the votes to which each local is entitled, credentials required by delegates, voting for delegates, procedures for submitting resolutions, and duties of the secretary-treasurer in regard to record keeping showing adherence to these procedures.[16]

Bishop Shiel gave the invocation and spoke, after being introduced by Helstein, as follows:

> In the early days of the building of this organization, there was one person among others who stood out in his unqualified and complete support of the rights of man. He has been particularly devoted to this organization. He is His Excellency, the Most Reverend Bernard J. Shiel, Senior Auxiliary Catholic Bishop, Chicago . . . and I think we all know, the Patron Saint of the United Packinghouse Workers of America.

After the Invocation, the bishop said in part:

> In no other labor dispute in recent years . . . has any union been faced with greater difficulties, and no union has made such an effort as that of your president to impress upon the minds of the general public the issues involved in the strike, and yet it was met with almost complete refusal upon the part of the press to carry this story of the union. . . . As far as your president, my very good friend, Mr. Ralph Helstein, there is little that I can tell you that you do not already know. He has the virtues that I have mentioned and others, and he has made a great contribution to the labor movement of our country, and I know he will continue always to give of his best.[17]

Nevertheless, all was not bread and roses during the convention. Responding to recriminations and hard feelings expressed arising from the lost strike, Vice President Frank Ellis took the floor and stated:

> [Y]ou people were squabbling yesterday and trying to find a scapegoat for the strike. Who was the cause of it? Well, I want to tell you that I was one of them. I voted for it. I believed in it. I thought we had something to fight for. I felt that we would win, and I thought we had a right to strike in justice ... so if you want to blame somebody, blame me.... You lost. I lost. I am willing to take my responsibility. Are you going to take yours? That is all I want to say [applause and Shouts].[18]

This convention also produced an attempt to take on the anti-Communist question pointedly raised by the requirement that all officers sign a noncommunist oath. There was also substantial pressure from the CIO to "cleanse" the union of communist influence. The union responded by drafting and passing a "statement of policy." As Helstein described it:

> [A] resolution which it believes protects the basic civil liberties and basic rights of our entire membership and still serves notice that this organization is an organization of the Packinghouse Workers and it will be run by the Packinghouse Workers.... With all sincerity at my command, with all the hopes for a better world that we share together, and in full recognition of the fact that the great problem which trade unions have is the problem of always holding itself together, never permitting itself to be divided, I should like to see a unanimous convention adopt this resolution, and in that spirit in which these expressed hopes, with a vision of a better and greater life for the common people of the world, we submit this resolution to you.

Helstein then read the resolution:

Statement of Policy—United Packinghouse Workers of America, CIO.

In this time of crisis to the free institutions of our country we affirm our basic conviction that freedom just like peace is indivisible. Repression of any sort which attacks civil liberties is the weapon of reaction. We recognize and properly evaluate the present wave of witch hunt hysteria as the weapon of reaction and monopoly whose goal is to destroy the trade union movement.

Our movement is dedicated to the task of raising the standard of living of our membership, improving their educational opportunities and bringing to them a better life.... We believe that our nation can achieve these goals through our existing institution, and we reaffirm our unshakable faith in its processes. Those who for whatever reason attempt to influence our actions in other directions will receive no aid or comfort from us. We resent attempts to influence our actions, and we will not tolerate efforts by outsiders, individuals, organizations of [sic] groups who attempt to infiltrate, dictate, meddle or interfere in any way with the functions of our organization. . . . The surest way of protecting our way of life is to give our people a program for peace, progress and plenty that is superior to any offered elsewhere. Our union is nothing more or less than its membership. We realize that our primary task is to preserve its basic principles of keeping our ranks closed and solid and together march forward to our common goals. United we stand, divided we fall.

After adopting the resolution, the delegation "arose, applauded and sang." A further motion moved that the policy be printed as a pamphlet and "submitted to the rank and file union."[19]

Thus Helstein was able to draft a resolution to deal with the Communist issue in the tradition of the UPWA—that it was an organization of packinghouse workers that would breach no interference by nonpacking-house workers just as they had in rejecting interference by the CIO at the time of their formation.

The 1948 Convention victory gave Helstein the ability to do some "housecleaning" by "disposing of the services of many who have carried on factional activities." The union also made concessions to the CIO by downplaying the pro-Wallace propaganda, passed a resolution supporting CIO policy. "Seemingly trivial, this move, coupled with the collapse of a viable right-wing, helped the UPWA avoid the fate of the other left-wing unions purged by the CIO the following year. Even here, the UPWA found a middle ground, declining to interfere with the pro-Wallace activities of local bodies." Nevertheless, the union responded to internal anti-Communist elements at Swift, which, aided by the CIO, pressured the union to fire Herb March. This it did in January 1949. Even so, March continued as an organizer for Armour Local 347.[20]

The Firing of Herb March

March, first hired as a field representative by the international office, was fired by Helstein, bowing to pressure from the CIO. The result was a colloquy between Helstein and March that revealed a chink in Helstein's moral armor: March said to Helstein that "At worst . . . I'll go to work for my local. But the question is, what's happening to you? Where is your principle?" Helstein was criticized by many, including Saul Alinsky, his close friend, for his "craven" behavior. In his defense, Helstein said the action was necessary "to save the union." He claimed that he had to make concessions to the CIO. March was just "too heavy a load to carry."[21]

Firing March, a personal friend as well as a coworker, was a very difficult decision for Helstein. His wife, Rachel states the effect on him:[22]

Ralph had a great deal of respect for Herb. He was very bright, and well informed. And a strong leader. Ralph was very torn, but he knew that there was no other way to save the union. He didn't totally go, but he [March] could not be a member of the [UPWA] Executive Board. It was a hard time for Ralph. He felt very bad, he really did. Helstein's well-known resistance to the anti-communist crusade had some personal consequences.

March reflected on Helstein's action of firing him:[23]

Helstein made a big contribution to our union. He played a role of being a unifying force that enabled the unity of a broad membership of the union left to right. And he also helped to establish and helped develop a real democratic, honest organization. He pursued an excellent course, developing a relationship of the union to the community, and the struggle against discrimination in all forms—A progressive unionist in every sense of the word. Now, there was some argument if and to what extent he could have fought back against the rightward pressures from the national leadership of the CIO. And on that we had our differences. . . . I thought he made a mistake in agreeing to my being dumped. I think his motives were pure. I spent a night with him once after being out to California. We came to his house in Chicago for a visit and we talked till about three in the morning and he's telling me that [he's] fighting a rear-guard action against reactionaries that want to sweep this union in the wrong direction and that's the role he had to play . . . and then, of course, he was a guy who suffered a lot in his thinking. He said; "You know I'm afraid that being in this position and having the advantages that we have, compensation, and personal prestige, whether this is corrupting and sometimes I think that it is." [Helstein's] a very honest guy. He wasn't happy in the hot spot and to be a leader, especially one like the Packinghouse, you're in the kitchen when it's always hot. He suffered a lot from it.

But March thought that "Helstein could have fought a bit harder":[24]

If you were there, what do you think could have been done? If I were there and not publicly a member of the CP [Communist Party], I would have insisted that the principles of unionism be observed. I'd take the fight to the rank and file. I would do like Bridges did with the Longshoremen's Union. Bridges was not inimical to the Communists but he was never a Communist. When an issue came up, he'd carry it to the rank and file, let them vote. Bridges told me, you're going to be under attack, and he said let me give you some advice. Never take a political position in the name of the union unless you get the rank and file to adopt that position. That's the way I stood. If Helstein had done that, [he thought] the union would have been thrown out of the CIO. That's what happened to the Longshoremen. That might have happened.

I'm afraid they couldn't do that [throw the UPWA out of the CIO] with our union because we had a broader leadership in that various trends of thinking represented in the UPWA all along with an understanding that we all work together and tolerate our differences. That was basic. The leadership of the CIO didn't care anything about that, I know they didn't but it would be difficult for them to succeed in dumping the UPWA in that situation. The Bridges union was largely a West coast organization of longshoreman. That's it. Ours was a much broader organization. I think that the CIO would have backed down. Big issue, fire one guy, March. So what happened, they did. They didn't have to. For Chrisake, I knew of unions in the AFL, the Typographical union that had guys who were considered reds. Nobody died and they could have fallen back on that.

Couldn't Helstein have been more concerned with the splits within the union itself and this was sort of throwing you to the wolves? I don't know. I know that he didn't fight on it as he should have. I told him, I'm going to be in this union. You're not getting rid of me. I'll be around and I'll still be playing a role. That made it easier for him, didn't it? He wasn't causing you hunger. You'd still be on the payroll? I wasn't about to do any whimpering.

March pointed out that firing him was a choice virtually forced on Helstein.[25]

Helstein said we can't carry you; the pressure is too much to bear. He showed me some letters he'd gotten from Alan Hayward [CIO vice president and CIO's "hatchet man"], even a letter from Michael Quill who had jumped fence—he said, this guy March, he'll never straighten out. Finally, Helstein said, Herb, let me explain the situation to you. You have a problem. You want to go from point A to point B and it's a straight line, you somehow or other manage to go way out to point C, D, and F before you get to B. You won't take the shortest line without trouble. You're a controversial personality. In view of the fact that you're so controversial, we're not in the position to carry on with you as a member of the staff.

Helstein suffered for years and years over what he did.

> I [March] said, this one you're going to have to fire me. You're running contrary to your own announced beliefs on political freedom and the challenge of political dissidence in the market place of ideas. Those are the things you've preached about all these years. Well, you seem to have forgotten them.
>
> Helstein got most hell on this whole thing from Saul Alinsky. Saul told Ralph that that was one thing he did that was unforgivable and he would never forgive him for that. Alinsky was not a guy [who] would compromise on certain fundamental things.

The fact that the administration slate won showed that anti-Communism was not the issue it was within other CIO unions. "The ability of these leaders to 'deliver the goods' meant far more to most workers than their politics. We were part of the people we worked with," Jesse Prosten observed. "I was some fucking nut who was a Red as far as they were concerned, but I was the guy who produced for them." Moreover, most UPWA unionists understood the role of the Communists in organizing the union in the 1930s and their militant leadership thereafter.[26]

This point was put to its proof after the loss of the 1948 strike. Hundreds of the union's members were discharged. The fact the union was in noncompliance with the Taft-Hartley Act left the union open to numerous representation elections that put its survival in question. The union bounced back in large part because Jesse Prosten, the union's chief negotiator, secured reinstatement of almost all the workers fired during the strike.[27]

The Amalgamated tried to take advantage of the UPWA's perceived weakness, but as Helstein remarked, "We were able to call them pariahs for coming along and trying to feed on a corpse—well, some corpse it turned out to be."

Post–Strike 1948 Convention

Helstein, in speaking to union delegates at the Sherman Hotel in Chicago just after the union's strike defeat, at the Fifth Constitutional Convention, June 28 to July 1, 1948, came out with fists bared,[28] saying, "I want to state frankly and bluntly at the outset that we are meeting at a time when our organization faces one of the most difficult periods that has confronted it during its entire existence."

Helstein went on to state that he faced the future with "complete confidence," that the task of the union was to "produce a kind of program that will keep this union in forward motion," and in order to do that we need "to analyze our problems carefully, intelligently, objectively and act with calm and deliberation." He then reviewed the history of the formation of the CIO and of progressive legislation that followed. He stated that this progress was evidence

> ... that the people of this country were on the march, and that reaction was on the run. . . . But in the past three years there has been a constant attack on labor, and on civil rights of minorities. . . . The real issue is: will the people fight back? . . . If the United Packinghouse Workers of America is an organization worthy of existence it . . . must continue to fight for tolerance, for freedom of thought, and religion, for equal rights and opportunities for all regardless of race, creed, color, or opinion. . . . Yes, our strike was a hard one; but we still hold our heads high. . . . We neither ran away nor bent our knee.

Calling on the tradition and words of George Washington and Thomas Paine, Helstein concluded by, in Paine's words, to "once more reaffirm our faith, realistically understand our problems and fastening our eyes on the common goal of all men. . . . Freedom."

In the after session devoted to reviewing the strike strategy, Helstein addressed himself to some internal criticism of the strike. In rewriting history and revising his own early opposition to striking the whole industry, he stated:

> I was for the strike and in the strategy committee I voted for it, the membership of the union voted for it, and I do not agree with the point of view that we should not have struck, and that I don't think we should repeat here, in attempting to evaluate the strike the very same arguments that are being peddled in the A.F. of L. [American Federation of Labor] attacked from one end of this country to the other. . . . I think that one factor that motivated against us was the fact that our union, in striking the industry, was faced at the beginning with the open, not only the betrayal, but the active assistance of the A.F. of L. Meatcutters working to get extra production to defeat the strike.

He then said he had some proposals to make, including more intensive work in all departments to strengthen the union and support of the Wilson boycott.

Even with the demise of the CIO Policy Caucus, splits remained within the union, and anti-Communism continued to be a divisive element; Helstein sought to stifle this divisiveness. The issue emerged at the December 19 to 20, 1949, Executive Board meeting over the hiring of an organizer, Leo Turner, a white man who had worked for the United Electrical Workers (UE), a union that had been expelled from the CIO as being Communist dominated. The issue developed when Elsten, a board member, demanded that Turner be fired. Elsten based his charge on an affidavit he had obtained from Tom Fitzpatrick, a member of the recently formed National Committee to set up the International Union of Electrical Workers (IUE) right-wing successor to the UE. Turner had been hired by Tony Stephens, who argued that Turner was the best person for the job.

During the board meeting, Helstein stated: "I am raising the question as to whether or not the only evidence you have on this guy is that statement of Fitzpatrick's."

Elsten: That is all.

Helstein: And that satisfies you, does it?

Elsten: As far as I am concerned, yes.

Helstein: You think that without reference to any other consideration the fact that one guy says that he had a fight with a guy and that the basis for his fight was that he alleges that that guy went around soliciting membership in the Communist Party contrary to instructions he received from Fitzpatrick, from Fitzgerald and Emspak, and that he then quit the UE for whatever the reason may have been, and I don't know because . . . so far as I know I have never seen Turner and don't know what he looks like and wouldn't recognize him if he came in this door now, and you are satisfied with that kind of evidence, and the only objective statement in the whole thing, I am sure you realize, is his participation in this "free Earl Browder," and I don't know, Paul, maybe you signed one of those petitions for Earl Browder's freedom. I know there were a hell of a lot of them around in those days. I don't have the resources to check, either, any contact with the un-American activities of the committee or the FBI to check those things, so I don't know whether that is true or not.

Elsten: Assuming that he did, I know that there are other people on the Board who also signed some of those petitions and I don't happen to be one of them. . . .

By questioning Elsten further, Helstein learned that Elsten had gone outside the organization to the IUE without first seeking information from Tony Stevens, who would have been the person to whom he should have made such an inquiry.

Helstein reacted:

> ... Now, I happen to know that this talk about Turner, you see, was general during the Armour negotiations, and the Cudahy negotiations, and created a situation that made it more difficult for us to negotiate the contract, and I am getting damned sick and tired, if there is anyone who questions it, let's have it out now. ... and I know that the Turner thing was one of the businesses that went on during the Armour negotiations and created rifts between the people who came in here and made it more difficult to negotiate what were extremely difficult negotiations, made my job harder.
>
> Tony apparently made all the investigation [about Turner] that he thought was necessary. Maybe other people disagree. Isn't it a proper procedure to go to Tony and say, you are making a mistake on this guy, check with so-and-so, and you will get some additional information from him. Why is it that within our own ranks we have to have people who pay no attention to administrative procedures on this union and go out on their own and make inquiries? Why can't they be done through the established machinery and then if you don't get satisfaction you are free to take any steps you want. Why isn't that the proper procedure?

Chinander, to dispose of the issue, moved "this matter be referred to the organizational department for investigation and that they take whatever action they deem is proper, and that the question be brought up at the next Board meeting."

Mr. Nielsen, director of District 1, stated:

> On the motion, I would like to say when this guy was interviewed—I interviewed him along with Stephens—questions of policy were asked him point blank and he suggested that any time he didn't follow the policies as laid down to him by our organization, why, he could be fired. He was hired to do a job and these complaints that have been raised about him—I laid them openly on the table in front of him when he was interviewed, and I knew about this business about some of our people insisting the guys has got to be a packinghouse worker, and to me that is so much malarkey. You hire a man to do a job. I told you, in my opinion, he is the best guy we have on our staff. I think it is decidedly unfair to him, after these things have been laid on the table to him and the fact that he is doing a good job and who

turned down several offers of other jobs prior to being on our staff, to hire him and then, because a few wolves start squealing around the country that you are going to fire him because you can't stand the pressure I think it has gotten to a point where we have got to face these things head on. If the wolves squeal, all right. If the guy can't do the job, we fire him.[29]

The motion was carried.[30]

This incident made evident Helstein's attorney skills in cross-examination and that he could pull it off using worker's language.

Rebuilding the Union

Helstein later summarized the condition of the union at the termination of the strike:

> Our resources were depleted, were practically nil. We were faced with all kinds of litigation all over the country. . . . [A]ctions against members, injunction suits, suits for damages. . . . The companies were using us as an excuse to speed up production lines and demand more production. They felt they were in a position where they could really beat us over the head because of our inability to take any overt kind of action. And in the case of Armour they [the company] simply took the position that they weren't going to pay any vacations to any of the people for that year, claiming that the period they had lost during the strike had been enough to constitute a break of some kind so that they were not eligible for vacation. Well those are just some of the many kinds of questions that we started to face.[31]

Even though Helstein was president of the union, he continued to act as a lawyer[32] when that skill was called upon:

> [W]e had begun the business of getting our leaders back to work in the plants. . . . [U]nder the terms of the contract that was still in effect the companies were required to arbitrate these cases. Gene Cotton and I began dividing up the work and I was handling some and he was handling some. We started on a number of interesting cases. I think they were in Omaha and from our point of view they were not the best cases but they were the ones we got going on and we won practically every one of them . . . with back pay.

In the course of one of these arbitration cases in Moultrie, Georgia, in which the worker was accused of "slugging someone," the opposing attorney asked the worker if he had talked to "a couple of men." The worker replied, "No, I never talked to a nigger in my life." Most of the people on both sides were whites from the North. Helstein called a recess.

> I got the committee together with this guy and I said, "Now look, let me tell you something. This is not the kind of language that is permissible in this union. I don't care how you feel; that's your business. Maybe it's true you wouldn't talk to a black man, that's possible. But you don't call him a nigger. You're going to go back in that room and you're going to apologize to everybody in that room for that language if you expect that case to go on. Otherwise I'm going to go in there, and I'm going to withdraw it, and I don't care what happens to your reinstatement.
>
> Moultrie is very close to the Florida border and its one of the worst parts of Georgia, always had been and was then. We went back in the room, he apologized rather nicely, I must say. . . . He was sorry he had offended, he had no intention to offend any particular people. This was the way he had been brought up and the way he felt and he really wanted everybody to know he should not have done it and he was sorry that he did it.[33]

Not only does this show how seriously Helstein took the union's antidiscrimination policy, but his way of firm handling it produced an on-the spot conversion. Whether the worker made his statement sincerely or under pressure is not known, but there is little question that Helstein acted from his deep abhorrence at racial prejudice[34] and that he saw this as one of the tenets of the union's structure and culture. No one present—the workers, management, or the company attorney—could have any doubt of the union's seriousness in opposing discrimination and in enforcing the contract's antidiscrimination provisions. Moreover, Helstein was not averse to taking the risk that it would not come out the way it did.

One of the most significant victories for black workers of the UPWA was winning a clause in the 1948 Swift contract: "The company agrees that it will give fair and reasonable consideration to any applicant or employee regardless of race, sex, color, nationality or membership in the union."

The union had a history of black–white unity. As Eugene Cotton, the union's general counsel stated:[35]

> Part of dedication to black-white unity was due to CIO influence and although the union was never under the Communist Party, it was a union that in its early years had a very substantial left influence. It didn't deserve the reputation it had for being supposedly being communist led or dominated. Among the lower levels of organizing there was a substantial left influence which brought with it a position on the black-white relationship,

and the union also early on recognized in Chicago and elsewhere that there was a substantial black component of the working population. They were organizing and if they didn't have a sound attitude on that, the organizing would have been almost impossible. Right from the start, the official seal of the union had a black and white hand shaking hands with each other. One of the first assignments I had in 1948 was an arbitration proceeding in which they enforced against Swift in hiring—a test case. We heard reports in hiring of women [in which] bacon wrapping was recognized as a white domain. In the test case, they had a black and white woman come to the hiring hall at about the same time. The Black woman was told nothing was available now and the white woman, one of our union secretaries, was welcomed warmly and offered the job. The case was won, but more importantly, the companies were put on notice that the union was serious about the non-discrimination clause in their contracts.

Helstein and the executive board decided to rebuild around their black membership.

Within weeks of the strike defeat, the executive board arranged for Fisk University's Race Relations Institute to conduct a series of "self-surveys" of racial attitudes and practices among packinghouse workers.[36] Designed to involve the union's members and prevent the fragmentation of hard-earned interracial unity, the surveys also helped keep workers' interest alive. Queried about the rationale behind this program, Helstein explained, 'I felt there had to be something affirmative going on outside of an area in which the companies could screw us. . . . [We] started the program and our people suddenly had something that the union was able to do.[37]

An article by John Hope II, four years later,[38] sets forth the success of the antidiscrimination policies, of which he was the architect:

The Cudahy and Armour chains are in the process of eliminating segregated facilities in their plants, in the South as well as in the North. . . . Although these changes make the Southern plant practices vary widely with prevailing local patterns, the Union reports only one case to date of significant organized opposition, and this was overcome without compromise on the part of the local union leadership.

The survey consisted of a *Local Union Study*; reports by UPWA officials of locals throughout the country; and a *Rank-and-File Study*, a random sample of majority and minority membership in various cities.

After the completion of the first report, the union began an antidiscrimination program in the winter of 1950. Shortly thereafter, on the basis of the second report, the first intensive citywide action program was initiated in Kansas City. By convention resolution, a national A-D Department was set up under the direction of a vice president and with a small full-time staff.

Even in the union's pre-UPWA stage as the Packinghouse Workers Organizing Committee (PWOC), racial discrimination was made an issue. In a handwritten letter, dated February 23, 1943, from Philip Weightman, a black delegate and later vice president of the UPWA, to Sam Sponseller, appointed by the CIO to direct the PWOC, Weightman wrote:

> On the second day of our PWOC conference... the chairman said "I have been asked to tell all colored delegates to meet out in the Hall to have their pictures taken" because the Chicago Defender Newspaper asks it. "I, Philip Weightman, arose and said, Mr. Chairman, we have no colored delegates here. ...Nor white delegates. We are all P.W.O.C. delegates and Brothers."[39]

With its own house in order, the union now moved against discrimination in the packinghouse plants, placing primary reliance upon its collective bargaining contracts and the grievance machinery.

> [T]he efforts of locals and the field staff to eliminate discriminatory hiring practice has continued with a measure of success in plants in various sections of the country. Reports from all UPWA districts in the United States show that the greatest success has been achieved in the discontinuance of refusal to hire Negro women, lily-white departments, and of segregated plant facilities and services, including cafeterias, locker rooms.

Unlike other unions, the UPWA had a nondiscrimination provision in its constitution, which it used its contracts to enforce. In the South, discrimination in locker rooms was regarded as a contract violation; some locals in the South objected because the International was doing things that just were not being done elsewhere in the labor movement. One local in Georgia defected and went over to the Amalgamated. The UPWA said, good riddance and continued on with its anti-discrimination program.[40]

The poststrike victories and anti-discrimination efforts had a dramatic effect on membership morale:

> We had ... just taken a beating. And I think [the members] were really responding to ... that we were going to continue to slug this thing out as

long as was necessary. I think, in terms of the company, they had never expected us to respond with the same kind of militant spirit. They thought that the least that would happen now would be . . . we'd have our tails hanging between our legs. . . . But . . . we made it very clear to them that nothing had changed . . . And I think this in turn was felt by the people in the plant and they responded. And then we began to pile up these victories. They could see their leaders coming back to work, people who were fired. In the old days when you got fired . . . you were just dead. That was the end of it, you never got back to work. Well here they were coming back to work.[41]

Helstein was himself engaged in the civil rights movement.

Martin [Luther King, Jr.] and I became very good friends. As a matter of fact, I was on . . . the thing he called his research committee, which used to meet monthly with him in New York. . . . I would go to a monthly meeting in New York City at which we would discuss strategy and tactics. . . . I can remember one of them at the time when it was clear that he was going to get the Nobel Prize that I got into a terrible argument with some of his supporters over the issue of whether or not he should come back to a white tail dinner—a white tie and tails dinner—at the Waldorf Astoria or go to Harlem at a church where people would stand in the streets. And many of the blacks there infuriated me because they were buying this thing that was being promoted by the PR guy to go to the Waldorf Astoria for—and I just felt that was just the worst and the last thing that he should do. . . . I think I was right and he [King] finally agreed with me.

Andy [Young] used to say, "All we have to do is go out and preach." This was when they were coming to Chicago. And I kept saying to him, Look, Andy, Dick Daily is not Clark. He isn't going to hit you over the head. . . . he's just going to embrace you. When he embraces you, he's going to choke you to death.[42]

I can remember one time being in Birmingham, when they had a convention of the SCLC [Southern Christian Leadership Conference]. . . . I'd been invited to speak with labor spokesmen. . . . [A]fter I finished I started walking back. King and Abernathy and Andy Young were sitting together in back and Martin says, 'You're a preacher, man!' And I said, 'Martin, you're not complimenting me, are you?' And he said, 'Oh, yes! You really preach it like it is!' "[43]

. . . I wasn't prepared to accept simply the CIO token kind of thing which said, 'All people have a right to join the union.' . . . I said, you had to go further, and, if you had occasion to take a look at our constitutional conventions, you'd see that we had resolutions in almost everyone of them in which we made it clear that it wasn't sufficient to deal with discrimination in the plant; you had to deal with it in the community. Because whatever you were able to do in the plant didn't do the guy any good if he couldn't rent a house in the community where he wanted to live, at a price he could afford to pay. So you may eliminate the discrimination on rates or seniority in the plant, but if you didn't take care of these other questions—and so, we started trying to do that. . . .

As a matter of fact one of the most interesting experiences I had was: we got a call one day from our organizer in Texas, Fort Worth, and he practically got laryngitis, and could hardly talk. And so I say to him, "What the hell is the matter with you? I can hardly understand you." He says, "Well, Christ, there are almost a thousand people marching in the hall; I'm scared stiff they're gonna kill me. I said, "What do you mean they're gonna kill you? What's the problem?" And he said, "Well, you just told the company that they had to take down the segregated eating facilities, and they removed the wall." And I said, "Yeah, but what do you mean they're gonna kill you? No one is gonna kill you." He said, "Well, boy, they sure look like it." And he *was* [emphasis in original] scared, so I said, "Okay, forget about it. Don't do anything. Get the hell out of the office and go away somewhere." So I then sent out—we had a vice-president who was black and a secretary-treasurer who was out of the South, out of Atlanta—I figured these would be two good guys to send down there. They could talk to whites, they could talk to blacks. So they go down there and they come back and they say, "This place is terrible. It's impossible. You can't talk to them, they've got guns and knives, everything and there's a thousand people participating and we couldn't talk sense to them." So I said, "Well, we're gonna get that God-dawn thing down. There's going to be no segregated facilities in that plant. That's our commitment. And I called the company's vice president in charge of labor relations, and I said, "You and I are going to Fort Worth." And he started laughing, and he says, "Yeah, you've got some problems there, haven't you?" And I said, "Yeah, but so have you." He said, "What do you mean? I haven't got any problems there." I said, "Oh, but you have." I said, "You're either going to come to Fort Worth with me or I'm going to get on this telephone and I'm going to call every plant in the country of Armour's and tell them the way your living up to your obligations under our contract." I said, I think you are violating them, and I don't know why they should show up at work tomorrow." He said, "You can't do that!" And I said, "You want to try?" He said, "I'll call you back." He calls me back in a few minutes and I knew God-damn well he didn't have guts enough to take that kind of pressure. I would have done it. I would have shut down every God-dawn Armour plant over this issue. I would have been prepared to make this a national issue.[44]

So at the plant in Fort Worth Helstein brought together the union committee and the supervisory staff that Helstein believed "is behind a lot of this." Helstein could really be tough on workers, a kind of reverse kind of respect:

> [O]ne guy comes up to me and whispers in my ear, "You don't expect me to use the same toilet one of those guys use, do you?" I said, "Why . . . what's your problem? He says, "Well, they all got syphilis." I said, "Oh, really, are you sure?" And he said, "Yeah." And I said, "I'll tell you what I'll do. Let's go down in the public library and go into the medical section and get a book on syphilis and find out whether that's a racial characteristic." He says, "Oh, you're not serious!" I said, "I'm just as serious as I can be. There is no better way of dealing with such a problem of this kind than trying it out. So, he said, "Oh, well, I won't. No, no, no." And I looked at this for a minute and suddenly it occurs to me. I realized what his problem was and I said, "You can't read, can you?" He looked at me, he froze, he said, "How did you know?" I said, "I didn't know, you told me. You don't want to understand and one of the reasons you don't want to is you don't know how. It's not that you're a bad guy, it's just that your . . . life didn't give you any breaks. And you can't read and you can't find out, so you come up with stories like this. You better forget them, because they're not true. It's a lie. And you shouldn't spread them." And he walked away dragging his tail.

Almost immediately thereafter, a woman shows Helstein a gun she carries to protect herself in case "one of those bastards walks close enough to me so that the wind of his passing rustles my dress." Finally, Helstein stated to the group:

> "Let me tell you . . . we just negotiated a contract that gave you people benefits that you've never had before in your life . . . we've put you on the same wage rates that Chicago had . . . you got sick leave benefits, vacation benefits, insurance benefits, benefits that you never would have believed that you would have gotten in a packinghouse. . . . [They complained that other unions don't require this.] Our constitution requires this kind of behavior. You are either going to live by it or you can get the hell out of the union. Now these are the contracts benefits we negotiated, if you want them you want to stay in the union; if you don't want them, get the hell out. We don't want you! But this is the way it's going to be." And I turned to the company representative . . . "You tell him the way I told them. . . . Tell him that if any problems come up . . . you're going to hold him responsible. . . . And he did."

Helstein arranged with the labor relations company guy for changes in dressing rooms and eating facilities to take place just before a holiday.

There was a provision in the contract that if a worker did not work the day before or after the holiday, he or she lost the holiday pay. So knowing that if they walked out they would lose that pay, as Helstein said, "There's nothing like a buck." So "they worked, there were no walk outs. . . . We had an election in that plant a couple of weeks later in which there were two slates—one completely white slate and one a black and white slate. The black and white slate won two to one."[45]

How did the UPWA compare with other unions in terms of black advancement?[46] One study of a number of CIO unions concluded that with the exception of the United Auto Workers (UAW), even though unions had a constitutional guarantee of equality, they tolerated some segregated locals. "In the UAW, Communists and their allies in the center-left coalition fought for black representation on the" executive board.[47]

In the CIO, the decline of interest in racial equality went hand in hand with the CIO's purging of Communists.

At the fall 1949 CIO convention, CIO officials pushed through an amendment to the CIO constitution to enable them to purge Communists from their midst, and during 1950 . . . they subjected its Communist-led internationals to pseudotrials, threw them out, and went on to 'cleanse' virtually all the [other] unions in which Communist influence had been significant. . . . And . . . to the extent that the unions expelled had been the more militant and devoted advocates of racial justice, the cause itself lost much of its meaning and appeal.[48]

Often it was only the instance of Communists and their allies . . . that forced CIO bodies to address such "extraneous" matters as civil rights and civil liberties . . . "Locals with vigorous Communist presence in the UAW and Packinghouse Workers fought for the rights of African Americans within both the union and community." In fact, long after the anti-Communist purge, the UPWA's leaders, whose exemplary record of interracial unity was exceptional, still found themselves suspect because of their emphasis on racial justice, which some in the CIO believed smacked of Communist enthusiasms. CIO officials even withheld the organization's support from the UPWA's efforts to organize both black and white workers in the sugar and other food-processing industries.[49]

By 1950, in the UAW's Rouge River plant where 15,000 blacks worked, Communist leadership developed a program of racial equality, placing blacks in prominent union positions. [Walter P.] Reuther also supported other black causes and organizations. But after World War II, as the wave turned against Communists, their aggressive support for racial equality ran up against the masses of Southern whites flocking into the industry. White leaders who had previously supported black demands for the best jobs (tool and die) joined with these young white workers to form "lily-white" slates, and even the Communists caved in to opposition to civil rights. Such a choice was never posed in the UPWA.[50]

Ironically, UPWA's strong stand on civil rights may have been a factor in saving the union from the purges to which other "left-wing" unions were subjected. Reuther, normally a champion of purges of communists from the CIO, refused to support the CIO Caucus, rejecting its charges of communist domination. "A CIO committee, steered by Emil Mazey, impressed with the UPW's [sic] vigorous efforts to end racial discrimination even in the Deep South, found the top leadership" of the union "free from communist domination or influence."[51]

It is also worth noting the views in society in the 1950s about the relevance of attitudes toward race relations as establishing political identity, specifically as to the Communist issue. In the course of a hearing before the Loyalty Review Board an African-American federal employee was questioned "about her contacts with a number of alleged Communists, most of whom were officials in her union. They wanted to know her opinions on a wide range of contemporary political and international issues. And, in the line of inquiry . . . one of the loyalty board members asked, 'Did you ever write a letter to the Red Cross about the segregation of blood? . . . What was your personal position about that?' " The board member later explained that such an "objection to blood segregation is a recognized 'party line' tactic."[52]

Helstein commented on the reaction of the Amalgamated to the UPWA's civil rights program.

There is no doubt that our civil rights program bothered them. They were disturbed because they did not have Negroes in their leadership. As a matter of fact they went out and got a guy on their board, a completely inadequate guy, so they could say they had a black man on their board. No man of any stature at all . . . a nice enough guy. But that, I think, did bother them. I think it was one of the things that was upsetting to Gorman.[53]

Yet there were occasionally tensions and misunderstandings in the racial climate of the times. In fall 1952, while Richard Durham was working in Kansas City, Kansas, Russell Lasley requested the use of an automobile for him. Helstein, by response in a memo of August 30, 1952, responded, "I am sure that the same case for a car can be made out by any number of people connected with the International Office," pointing out that he had just rejected such a request from another employee, who was white, although Helstein didn't appreciate the difference at the time. In a reply memo, Lasley stated in part:

> . . . it is impossible for Negro representatives of our organization to operate in segregated and highly discriminated areas . . . without constant humiliation to them. . . . I am not going to direct Richard Durham or any other Negro representative to travel under these circumstances. It requires a cab or an automobile to even get a meal, and that applies to three meals a day, in these segregated areas. . . . As you probably know, white hotels in Kansas and Missouri refuse to house Negroes. We are obliged to either stay in Negro hotels which are rat-traps, or find housing in some individual home which is in an outlying region. . . . Your refusal to pay this bill [of $42.25] may be the easy way out, but it sure as hell is not the answer to this problem.[54]

Helstein had a solid philosophical base for his antidiscrimination policy, as expressed in a 1952 interview:

> It is not just enough to eliminate discriminatory practices in the plant, but we also have to do it in the community, because you can't work with a man all day long, get along with him, and you go one way and he goes another, and then pick up where you left off the next day. Sooner or later this was going to create schisms, misunderstandings, and problems, so that it was essential to carry on this kind of activity in the communities in which you lived as well as in the plant. I suppose that in an important sense this reflected the age-old fight within the American labor movement . . . between social unionism on the one hand and business unionism on the other. We felt the union was something more than just an economic movement, it also had to be a social instrument to bring about change and progress. The UPWA's executive board agreed that "we cannot protect our own ranks against the evils of discrimination if such evils are prevalent in the communities in which we live."[55]

Here, Helstein was following, almost word for word, his concept of the uses of law he expressed as a law student:

> Around 1955, Helstein approached Reuther during the merger convention in New York and told him "that I thought it was essential that we get a Negro on [the executive council of the merged union] and I thought the CIO ought to take the initiative. . . . The only one who was president of an international union was William Townsend who was black and who was president of the Transport Workers Union, red caps that located in Chicago. I indicated that would be satisfactory of if they wanted someone else and they'd be willing to take a black person, there was Lasley who was vice

president of our union. And he started giving me this business about how you don't pick that way, you do it on the basis of merit. I said, "Oh Walter, come on now. Just look at what you've got there. . . . [Y]ou know you save that for somebody else." Well he kind of fidgeted and got embarrassed.

Reuther was "pushing" for Hartung of the Timber Workers Union. But at the last minute the AFL slated Phil Randolph. So Reuther told Hartung he wouldn't be nominated and "Hartung was madder than hell. . . . I went up to Reuther afterwards and I said, "You know, Walter, you could have saved yourself a lot of headaches." He said, "Can you imagine that, how unreasonable Hartung was?" Like it was all Hartung's fault, you know. I said to him, "Oh Walter, knock it off." It was a perfect response of the quality of a politician Reuther was. . . . [56]

The local union of the UPWA got the packers to hire blacks in the Cudahy Omaha office in 1955 and Armour in 1956. As pressure "we used pickets, we distributed handbills; we tried to focus public attention on that situation."[57]

Jimmy Porter, a black worker who worked at Rath Packing in 1954 was interviewed about the effectiveness of the union's antidiscrimination policies:

Our union was affiliated with every organization that was fighting discrimination: NAACP [National Association for the Advancement of Colored People], Welfare Rights, Urban League. When Dr. King came on the scene our union, all over the United States, had to contribute a dollar per member to the well-being of that organization. In some places that went over like a fart in church. It just was not accepted, and we had a lot of people withdraw. . . . We'd hold regional meetings, and once a year we met nationally as a Human Rights [Committee] through the district, and once a year we met nationally. . . . They knew the expectation from Helstein and Lasley and the rest of them.

The reason a lot of them had to do it, you had to report it. . . . Your district director was going to have to account for what you'd done. We had field reps. Every time he came in, he made a report on your ass and you were gonna hear it. They had such strong directors here on civil rights, [Russell] Bull, then [Dave] Hart. If you didn't do it he was on your ass. That made a difference, hell of a lot of difference.[58]

Charlie Hayes had served as field rep from 1949, for five years. But there was an increasing feeling developing that many members were black—why not have a black person head up the district? We reached an agreement that the mantle of leadership should go to a black—and Harold Neilson, the present white director of District One, agreed. Hayes was elected as one who had a level head, a good following, acceptable to most folks, white or black, that's how it started. Helstein didn't think it was a good idea. Harold had done a good job; he shouldn't be pushed out, but he went along with it. Following is resolution passed by the district electing Hayes as Director of District 1.[59]

The resolution electing Hayes read as follows:

By "Resolution Projecting the Endorsement of the Candidacy of Brother Charles Hayes for the Office of District Director, District No.1, UPWA-CIO," Charles Hayes was nominated for District Director, District 1:

WHEREAS: At the coming international Convention of our Union to be held in Sioux City, Iowa, the office of Director of District No. 1 will be open for election; and . . .

WHEREAS : Our International Union has within its composition of membership 45% Negro members and only two Negro members on the International Executive Board and the election of a Negro Packinghouse Worker in this District would help to bring about a better reflection in the composition of our International Executive Board, and; . . .

WHEREAS : Brother Charles Hayes has a fine record as a militant, able and courageous trade unionist and he is quite capable of filling the office of District Director; and . . .

NOW THEREFORE BE IT RESOLVED that this regular monthly membership meeting of UPWA-CIO Local No. 25, being on Thursday February 25, 1954, go on record endorsing Brother Hayes for the office of District Director, and that this Resolution be sent to all locals in UPWA-CIO District No. 1, asking them to support and endorse the candidacy of our own Brother Charles Hayes.[60]

Consequences for Helstein's Stand on "Red" Issues

Helstein's stand on Communist issues resulted in personal consequences in that these reasons were cited in the Illinois Senate's refusal to confirm Helstein for a place on the state Fair Employment Practices commission (FEPC). By a vote of 30 to 24, a straight party vote, Republicans in the Senate refused to confirm Governor Otto Kerners' nomination of Helstein and Earl B. Dickerson, a black lawyer, to the commission.[61] Earlier an attorney for the Illinois Manufacturers Association testified that men who held executive positions with the UPWA refused in 1959 to answer questions whether they had ever belonged to the Communist party at a hearing of the Un-American Activities Committee.[62]

The *Chicago Tribune*, which was right-wing and antilabor at the time, referring to Helstein as the UPWA's "perennial candidate,"[63] reported the Senate's rejection of Governor Kerner's nomination of Helstein to the FEPC because of Helstein's support of Herb March, a member of the

Communist Party's national committee and head of the Young Communist League and other left wingers. As Pat Gorman, Secretary-Treasurer of the Amalgamated Meatcutters and Butcher Workmen, said in 1959:

> ... the facts are there and I can't see how Helstein can deny them. He was commenting on the fact that more than a score of officials of Helstein's union had invoked the 5th amendment at hearings of the House un-American Activities committee. Gorman confirmed a widespread impression when he said at the time that plans for merging his and Helstein's union had fallen thru in 1956 because of the extent of UPWA's leftwingers. Thru the years Helstein has consistently denied that there was any substance to the often repeated accusations that the UPWA was heavily infiltrated by Communists, even when the charges were brought by such an insider as A. T. Stephens, a union officer of more than 20 years seniority and a former vice-president. However, the conduct of numerous subordinates in the union and the nature of Helstein's public disagreements with union leaders such as Gorman and Ruben Soderstrom, state AFL-CIO president naturally give rise to questions about his judgment. . . .

The article went on to criticize Governor Kerner for appointing Helstein "who, after the war was ended, sought to continue the war-time price controls that were wrecking the legitimate meat business, and thereby destroying the jobs of thousands of packing house workers whose interests he was supposed to protect. Fortunately, Congress rejected his bad advice."[64]

More of an editorial than a news article, the newspaper assembled a number of unrelated assertions that had nothing to do with Helstein's qualifications to serve on a commission whose mission was to fight racial discrimination. The paper did not mention the positive actions Helstein and his union had taken in this field nor it did mention that Stephens' assertions had been investigated at the beginning of that same year and rejected by the AFL-CIO nor that Pat Gorman's AFL-CIO had been particularly deficient compared with the UPWA in the very field the FEPC was concerned with. The fact that Helstein had been such a fighter in the area of discrimination no doubt was the real factor weighing against his and Dickerson's nominations to a commission that was more window dressing than a serious attempt to end racial discrimination.

George Meany, president of the AFL-CIO, in 1962 blocked "the energetic" Helstein's nomination to the AFL-CIO council to replace L. S. Buckmaster, former president of the United Rubber Workers Union, "on the grounds that his union was still 'tainted with communism.' " A few months later,

Meany again prevailed at a meeting of the Executive Council to fill a vacant post for which Reuther again futilely nominated Helstein.[65]

Reuther's efforts to get black representation in the upper ranks of the UAW were stymied by lack of interest and outright opposition by his boss, George Meany, by opposition from Southern delegates and by white racists in his union. The fact that his militant anti-Communism had eliminated Communists from leadership positions meant that there were few militant unionists who had racial equality on the top of their agenda. Top-notch black candidates for executive board membership were rejected because they were "too controversial" and "not team players."[66]

Helstein spoke at open housing conference in October 1961, stating that the "Government has the prime responsibility for 'creating the open society where all people will be treated as first class citizens.' '. . . Helstein was the principal luncheon speaker at a day long meeting in the Congress hotel, sponsored by the United Citizens Committee for Freedom of Residence in Illinois. . . . ' " Helstein continued:

> The civil rights issue is an emergency issue, and the breakthru [*Chicago Tribune* style] in the wall of discrimination is essential if we are to be a growing democratic America. . . . Every human being has the right to first class citizenship, and, in the fight to obtain this, the role of government is crucial. . . . A review of history shows that the law in the past was used for the creation and retention of segregation. The government must see to it now that it creates the open society where all people will be treated as first class citizens.[67]

In November 1961, A. Philip Randolph, the only Negro vice president of the union, was "rebuked" by the AFL-CIO executive council for urging the union to "adopt a policy of expelling affiliate unions that practice discrimination." Randolph was censured by the AFL-CIO council for making "incredible assertions, false and gratuitous statements, unfair and untrue allegations" in his charges that the AFL-CIO has been lax in fighting for civil and employment rights for blacks. George Meany, AFL-CIO president, Randolph said, "has adopted a policy of gradualism and tokenism" in dealing with discrimination in the labor movement. He insisted that Meany should call for the expulsion of any union found guilty of discrimination, the same action taken against unions involved in corruption and "Communism." Ralph Helstein was scheduled to speak at a meeting that night at McCormick Place to a "mass meeting which will formerly open the second national convention of the Negro American Labor Council," group organized and chaired by Charlie Hayes.[68]

In March 1962, tensions arising from the appointment of Helstein to fill a vacancy on the AFL-CIO's executive board, among other issues, rose to the point where Reuther, president of the UAW, threatened to resign from the council. This issue aggravated "the intense dislike between Mr. Reuther and George Meaney. . . . " According to Meany, "heads of the former C.I.O. unions have the unrestricted right to pick whomever they want from their ranks to fill vacancies on the executive council created by the resignation or death of men from their own group but that those chosen must also be acceptable to the council." Meany "has declared Mr. Helstein unacceptable because of the packinghouse union's left-wing past."[69] The denouement came in October 1963, when just before the AFL-CIO's convention in New York City, "Meany won as everyone knew he would" when John J. Grogan, president of the International Union of Maritime and Shipbuilding Workers was nominated to the council by the council's nominating committee. Reuther and some others who had supported Helstein abstained.[70]

And in July 1963, Helstein attended a convention in Chicago of the NAACP in which President Kennedy's civil rights program was criticized as "inadequate." A resolution demanded supplementary legislation that "would include sanctions against unions that discriminated against Negroes" and the creation of "a fair-employment practice commission, with adequate authority to compel attendance of witness and production of evidence and for the enforcement of its decrees." Among the speakers in addition to Helstein was Herbert Hill, the association's labor director, who accused unions "of giving only lip service to White House pleas for ending discrimination." In later statement, Hill specifically left out the UPWA from this condemnation.[71]

Irv King,[72] the African American partner in the Cotton law firm, described the antidiscrimination effort of the union as follows:

> Now the union had very strong anti-discrimination stance, almost from the very beginning with the handshake symbol [a black and white handshake]. . . .
>
> But in terms of the overall, the way that the union operated, I think that the program was highly successful. And you saw it in many ways. You saw it in the people who made up the delegates to the conventions, if you interacted within the conventions, the people who sat in the bargaining meetings, they were all fully mixed racially, and by gender.
>
> This UPWA was one of the old industrial unions, and you had a major part of the organization, organizing impetus for the whole union, coming out of Chicago on the South Side, and you had people there who were working in those plants that were activists in unions and in other things, and probably the political orientation may have had some effect on it too.

Some of the leaders, the left. the leadership, and the rank and file, may have had some effect, and again the top leadership of the union, believed that this was, the right thing to do, not only morally, but could understand the practical necessity and the power that comes from united forces.

This has some, a practical base as well. There's a lot more blacks coming into the union.

I: And if it had a practical basis, and people realized that power, that power required this kind of common working together and so on. And at all the conventions of the international union, this was made clear that segregation or racism would not be tolerated, that there was a civil rights committee which was a very high status committee at the conventions, and came up with resolutions on issues in this area. And the union brought in speakers who were, for example, Dr. King spoke up in Minnesota as I recall at one of the conventions. And this was a conscious effort to sort of preach this message.

Minutes of the A. Philip Randolph Institute from September 19, 1966, list Ralph Helstein as one of the attendees. During a discussion on "Crisis in the Civil Rights Movement," Helstein

stated that we need local grievance committees to work at the implementation of civil rights legislation. The Freedom Budget[73] is essential, but there is another question. What do you do at the local level, in terms of organizing the communities? The Freedom budget is not enough, there must be something more. Civil rights leaders need to look at themselves and ask themselves if they are doing the kind of job that needs to be done in mass movements. At a meeting in Chicago on fair housing, no effort was made to reach people on a logical basis.

Under Helstein's leadership the UPWA engaged not only in civil rights activity but in outreach to farmers though cultural activity that was reminiscent of the 1930's WPA worker activity in the South:

Helstein embraced the idea of the musical skit, the group that the UPWA paid for to go to the county fairs in Iowa.[74]

This all occurred in the early 50s because that group followed the 48 strike. The whole project was to repair our image among farmers in Iowa. There's a whole article in Labor's Heritage about it. I have tapes of the performance. It's clever, clever. Clive Knowles was the guy who wrote the skit. These were young performers who came out of some place in Pennsylvania. So there's things like that Helstein was pushing, this whole AD commission, anti-discrimination policy; the black community embraced that; Helstein had been so successful in bringing home the bacon at the bargaining table that all the white guys placed their faith in him. Anything he'd say, he's gotta be right. You could depend on his wisdom, his choices were viable.

Both the UPWA and the Amalgamated had antidiscrimination policies, but for the UPWA, antidiscrimination was a significant national policy that was implemented at all levels. The Amalgamated was not discriminatory at the national level, "but because of its retail heritage it had a smaller percentage of black members. For many years before the 1960s, major food stores did not employ black people in meat departments of stores with predominantly white customers."

According to Roger Horowitz, who wrote extensively on the history of the UPWA:

> The initiatives of the UPWA in the 1950s against racial discrimination provide an especially sharp contrast with other AFL-CIO unions. The formal commitment to racial equality on the part of most labor organizations did not translate in a challenge to the discriminatory customs of the plants under their jurisdiction; indeed, there is considerable evidence that CIO-affiliated unions often fully participated in the replication of those practices. The unions whose racial policies were more similar to the UPWA's were generally expelled from the CIO and unable to survive the 1950s.
>
> The UPWA's civil rights initiatives took place in a hostile environment in which racism and racial segregation remained commonplace. While the union could not displace racist attitudes generated by forces outside its plants, it could and did build on the material necessity for an interracial alliance among workers to provide an alternative set of values which stressed the essential equality of all races."[T]his community of our union," Ralph Helstein told a race relations institute in 1949, has "established folk-ways and mores and customs and methods of life that perhaps do not conform to the normal pattern existing in this country today." Helstein emphasized that the union was committed to these "customs" because they are "absolutely essential in terms of the betterment of the membership of our organization."[75]

Bureaucratic Organization[76]

Les Orear described the internal organization of the UPWA district One (Chicago) office as follows:

> I remember there being one secretary, in the big room adjacent to Helstein's office. There was also somebody who made travel arrangements. Her name was Rose and she sat about 30 feet away from Helstein's office much closer

to Butch Hathaway's office at the end of the offices. Hathaway was the secretary-treasurer. He ordered supplies. Charlie Fischer was not in the Common Room. The Common Room was a generally larger room, the book keepers, Hathaway's secretary. Hathaway had an office of his own, a corner office. The Common Room was the large unenclosed area around the north side of which there was a line of offices that was used by the finance people, the comptroller and the auditor and so on, and then there was Hathaway; he had the corner office, the northeast corner office. And there was some space in which Hathaway's secretary sat. And there was Helstein's office and there some more space and then there was Stephen's office at the end. Then there was another room leading off of the main hallway that led to the elevators. There was another room in which Jesse and Fischer were located, and then the next one down the line would have been the research people. And that's all I can think of.

On the west side of the main hallway where the elevator bank was located, facing west was the vice-president in charge of programs, Russ Lasley and his assistant, his secretary, at the south end of this area, and then there was my space and my assistant sat at the farther side, and my secretary sat behind me. But all this changed over time. Dolnick was the editor of the newspaper.

I was the assistant to Tony Stephens vice-president of organization. Dolnick was in the publications office was across the hall, on the west side of that main room. After he left, then the publications office was set up on the other side. . . . I had just been dumped by Stephens—I think because of the events that happened at Highlander school because I had crossed swords with the guy who was running the program department [Dunham]. I was out and Helstein found something for me to do. I could go and help this new editor to find his way around. This fellow from New York City only stayed a couple of months. It was my job to give him some guidance but then he left to return to New York City.

Charlie Fischer—he was a tall out-going person. He had been a captain in the US Marines and you know he was a person of command. He was a charming man, a good speaker. Fischer was the kind of person who had contact with the industrial world. Helstein was a thinker, manager, supervisor, answered telephone calls, smoothing out ruffled feathers, giving advice. As far as I know even though they had very different personalities they got along. . . .

It may have been some occasions when Helstein would call me in and said we have to get something in on this—there must have been such times but it was not a central part of our relationship. I'm sure that I needed guidance at times and I needed to be informed but I insist he was not a hands-on operation in the newspaper There may have been times when there was a policy he wanted approved in the newspaper—of course, but it was not much. Maybe there were times when I said I needed guidance but he never summoned me to tell me this is what we are going to do other than there was going to be a conference and this guy and that guy and the other guy but it was not a matter that I want you . . . . There was nothing like Monday morning when I would come in and he would say here's the marching orders for the week, not at all. If I needed some advice, I could go in and get it. He knew that I knew what to do, that my instincts were correct. It [the newspaper] was not the mouthpiece of the president. The president did not write a monthly column. If there was some idea I wanted to try out on him, I'm sure that must have happened. That was his general leadership style. He let me get on with it.

Helstein as Negotiator

According to Norm Dolnick, who participated in negotiations with Helstein,[77]

Ralph was a master negotiator. There was a quite impressive team when Gene Cotton, Jessie, and Ralph confronted a management. Those negotiations should have been recorded. Brilliant (laughing). I mean they'd have kicks, and their interpretations and their firmness. I saw a marvelous example. It was in 1947 in the nation-wide Canadian strike. It was in the third weekend; it was really weakening; and I was there for three months and worked with those guys; and finally there was a meeting with the Swift company, which was the largest of the packing plants. Fred Dowling [Canadian director], a very intelligent man, but he was weakening. I could see it, exhaustion, and he was conceding, and I called Ralph that night, told Ralph, you better get up here [Toronto] fast. I think Freddie is showing signs of weakening. Freddie is starting to back off and I think there's still go a little farther we can go if we just toughened up a little bit. So Ralph said I'll be on the next plane. And Freddie was surprised when Ralph walks in. This was the instance where Ralph accused these guys [management] of insulting him and he exploded. I remember his winking at me. I kind of thought Ralph was going to have an apoplexy. I got concerned about his health. Ralph says back off. I think what happened was that Ralph really got mad. And as long as he got mad, just what the hell, keep it up? Cause he watched them react. I think it sort of evolved as an act. After a while he watched these guys, they were just so horrified, they were terrified. He said well, I want to keep this up, and it worked. Another time, they send me and Frank McCarty up to this meeting; they send us out there. You go get beat up (laughing). So I went out to more or less to dramatize this whole assault on union guys and you know I wasn't married then, so it was 47 because I dated this city editor. And we had a date, and I got some good stuff in the paper (laughter).

But we went in negotiations. Ralph came down to settle this thing. And I went to take notes. And the company said, no, we will not negotiate with that man here, pointing to me. And Ralph looked at the company, they made it a big issue; they're trying to decide how he should run his bargaining for his committee, and Helstein said, well you know, I am very proud of this man. This man got national publicity, the best PR man in the country, and national awards, and he's too good for me to have him leave. So I became an issue, and these guys were frightened of their national reputation cause I was this big guy from somewhere and Ralph kept me and used me for that, and I sat there and he got some concessions out of them for that, and settled the strike. He improvised. Ralph used me to his advantage. See what I mean, cause he was flexible. You pick up ideas. And he scarred these guys on my national reputation (laughing).

In the sixties there was rife anti-Semitism among many blacks. The rise of Black power brought the rise of with leaders like Malcolm X saying that "all those Jews in the civil rights marches and going down South—you know why they did it? They do it to take the heat off themselves. They've got a bad conscience because they live on black dollars."[78]

By the mid-1960s polls showed 47 percent of blacks had anti-Semitic Beliefs against 35 for whites.[79] If these beliefs were true of blacks in general why did this problem never arise in the UPWA where a large part of the membership, particularly in large cities like Chicago and Des Moines were black, and where the leadership consisted mostly of Jews like Helstein, Prosten and Cotton. There was no anti-Semitism for the same reason that Prosten gave that members didn't care that he was a red. All these Jews produced for their members. Besides, every black could see that the union actively fought discrimination and advanced blacks in and our of the union. To my knowledge the issue of the leaders' Jewishness was never raised in the union and probably very few members even knew who was Jewish. Member's individual race, religion or creed was a non-issue in the union, but politically each of these were political issues of equality, nondiscrimination or assertion of rights.

That in the UPWA the fact that much of the leadership was Jewish was subordinated in the eyes of the black workers, who in the words of Prosten, didn't care if the leadership was red, green, Jewish, or blue as long as they produced better lives for them and their families. It was clear to all that these union leaders gave their lives to the union. They lived the lives of their workers, they mixed with the workers, they ate with the workers, they went to the same bars, all of which developed into a mutual respect. There was no aristocracy as there was with the Amalgamated.

Chapter 5

Helstein Under Fire and the Anti-Red Period

Helstein Under Fire

As a young general counsel to a newly formed union, Helstein was matched against multimillion dollar packinghouse industry lawyers. He was soon called on to prove himself. In June 1945, he settled an arbitration case with Frank Green, vice president in charge of Industrial Relations for Swift & Co. Part of that agreement included "a release of any other claims we might have." Helstein questioned the meaning of the phrase, but Green mollified him. A couple months later, Helstein got a call from truck drivers in Indianapolis about what they thought was a pending claim. When Helstein called Green saying he thought these claims had been settled, Green replied, "Well, you know that agreement in June . . . we agreed to drop all pending cases and that obviously included all grievances. . . . [Y]ou'll learn, young man. In this game, you'll learn. You have to pitch curves occasionally, and you just got struck out on a curve."

Helstein replied: "[L]et me tell you something, Green. I'm young, you're right, and I have to learn and apparently I'm going to have to learn the hard way with you. . . . I'm learning and I understand that knowledge is power and you will never finish paying for this. This is going to be the most expensive curve you ever threw."

As Helstein predicted, the occasion arose when Swift wanted something from him. Swift, for tax purposes, wanted to attribute a retroactive pay increase to the tax year 1945. But to do that, Green needed a stipulation from the union. So Green prepared the stipulation and sent it to Helstein. Helstein held the stipulation until the day it had to be filed, at which time he received a frantic call from Green:

"'You know, I've got to get this done today. Time's running out.'" Helstein said, "'Yeah, I know Frank, isn't that too bad?' And he said, What do you mean?' I said, 'Frank, does the word Indianapolis evoke any memory? Now before you say anything try to control yourself.... [D]on't ask me to get anything signed for you until you are prepared to do a number of things that I have in front of me that you should have done a long time ago. Now the only thing I can tell you finally is that I have been brought up in the fine tradition of American baseball.... In American baseball each side has a pitcher and both of those pitchers can presumably throw curves.' And I hung up the phone."

The phone rings right away and he calls back and says, 'I'm coming right down there.'" Helstein then drafted a series of stipulations covering the Indianapolis case and several other unsettled matters. "Green came to the office steaming. That stipulation meant perhaps a million dollars to Armour so he signed my stipulations," and Helstein signed his, adding, "'I hope we learned to understand each other better, Frank. You know I haven't been around too long yet but with teachers like you it doesn't take too long to learn.'"[1]

An earlier test came at the 1944 convention in Omaha scheduled at the Fontanelle Hotel, their first convention as an international union. "The delegates were coming in from all over the country so everybody wanted to make sure it went off right and relatively easy and that sort of thing."[2] Remember, this was 1944, long before the civil rights struggles but not before Helstein and the United Packinghouse Workers of America (UPWA) were concerned about their members' civil rights.

One of the delegates, Philip Weightman, who was slated to be vice president, was black, and the hotel refused to register him or to allow him to eat in the dining room. Helstein felt doubly injured, for Weightman and for himself because he couldn't have a meeting lunch with him there. Helstein insisted to the union s' executive board that they go to the hotel manager to point out that the hotel had promised lodging and hotel facilities and that many other members were black, and they couldn't be expected to dine elsewhere. Helstein then said they had to move the convention. The board said that was impossible. Helstein replied: "I just don't believe it's impossible and even if... it means pitching a tent and holding it outside I don't think you can permit this character to get away with this."

Thus to Helstein, this stand by the hotel was not only an insult to blacks but a personal affront to his belief of fairness and how you treat others. He felt these things personally, which explains his anger, not usual with a lawyer pleading his client's case.

Helstein argued that although the convention attracted 500 or 600 delegates, the Omaha union chapter, the second largest in the country, had a union hall that would seat 300 or 400 people. So the convention site was moved to the union hall. As the delegates came in, the union explained what had happened. The only complaints were from a few Southern delegates. Helstein wrote a statement for Clark that the convention adopted, its first strong antidiscrimination resolution. This statement reviewed the way discrimination had divided the union in the past and how the packers had used divisiveness to prevent organization.

Helstein argued that the union had to support its newly adopted constitution. After all, it had the following preamble:

> We recognize that our industry is composed of workers of all nationalities and many races, of different creeds and political opinions. In the past these differences have been used to divide us and one group has been set up against another by those who would prevent our unifying. We have organized by overcoming these divisive influences and by recognizing that our movement must be big enough to encompass all groups and all opinions.[3]

Helstein's election preserved the center-left alliance in the union and created vital breathing space for the Communists at a time when many other Congress of Industrial Organizations (CIO) unions were moving to isolate them." Herbl March commented that the diversity of political views "made for an unusual union. The Packinghouse Workers became a union under Helstein—for a time at least—in which there was tolerance for all sorts of viewpoints, a democracy in a true sense."[4]

The Anti-Communist Period: The "Old Red Question"

The early 1930s to late 1940s has been called the "Red Decade" when

> American capitalism was challenged by a "powerful and pervasive radical movement" built and led by Communists. . . . [D]espite the supine and craven obedience of the Communist Party (CP) officials and functionaries to the dictates of the Soviet regime through every tortuous twist in its line, Communist unionism during the Congress of Industrial Organizations (CIO) era was "the main expression of native, working class radicalism in the United States. . . ." [U]nions with Communist-aligned leaders represented about 1,370,000 unionists, a quarter of the CIO's total.[5]

One of the first times that the issue of "reds in unions" came up was early in the war period. Together with other anti-union measures, many of which later resurfaced in the Taft-Hartley bill, on December 3, 1941, Representatives Howard Smith and Carl Vinson introduced a bill that "denied Wagner Act benefits to unions with Communist officers." These measures were only defeated because of the start of the war and by labor's no-strike pledge.[6]

David Cantor, a one-time UPWA employee and Chicago activist, describes Communist Party influence in the union. Communist Party programs were intermingled with UPWA programs and policies:

> You would be involved in programs to fight discrimination. If there was somebody burned up in substandard housing, you might have a picket line down at the Chicago Housing Authority to protest that. We were always involved in some kind of activity, plus you'd go down to the County Fairs[7] and set up booths in order to have improved relations with the farmer who was told that he couldn't get higher prices because of the workers in the plant, and workers in the plant were told that they couldn't get higher wages because the farmers were charging too much. So our efforts were to bridge the gap and at least acquaint the farmers with what we were going through. So we would go on down to these places in rural Illinois and set a little booth in there. . . . And of course, our root concern was the bread and butter issues of the workers in the plant.

In summing up the importance of Communist Party members in the early organizing attempts, one labor historian writes:[8]

> . . . [T]he legitimacy of the Communists within the CIO rested upon their vital role in the formation of the new unions during the 1930s. . . . [T]he Communists were able to give their trade union work a strategic coherence that won them recruits and influence throughout this period. By the mid-1930s, they were the largest ideological group from which the CIO drew its shop-floor cadre and union organizers. In the maritime, electrical, auto industries, Communist dual unions emerged into the CIO, and party members easily moved into influential posts as the new institutions grew in size and power. In the steel and packinghouse drives, the Communists were for a time virtually indispensable to the success of the day-to-day struggle in the field.
>
> In the whole 40,000 employees of the Yards, card-carrying members of the Communist Party were a handful—about 20 or 30. However, there were a lot of communist sympathizers, people who had gone through the struggles of the Unemployment Councils; people among the various nationality groups who belonged to the International Workers Order; a Ukrainian group, a Polish group, a Lithuanian Group. So the left represented perhaps 15% of the members.
>
> There was at first a feeling of powerlessness, that the union can't win, so we'll just sit back and see. And the reverse of that was the need of only a small victory; it didn't have to be much. The turning point was the signing of the first memorandum of agreement.

Kelly, Chicago's mayor, had no idea of the surge of organization among industrial workers. Kelly was opposed within the Democratic machine by Courtney. When the split took place, we opposed Courtney because he was lined up with the worst elements, little more than goons, so we got into the primary campaign and were very effective. Two wards in white community and two in black. Our union played the biggest role in the election. We delivered and all politicians responded.

Kelly had police out there to be neutral which meant police allowed strikers to hold back strikebreakers. And then in negotiations, stockhandlers were not going to sign a contract. Kelly told them they were getting water from the city at a reasonable rate and that situation didn't have to continue. The Union took up issues in two areas, in economic areas and discrimination.

The Union entered into relations with units of the Catholic Church and Back of the Yards Council. We had a bunch of young people in the union, young communists, and sympathizers who said something had to be done for the youth, so the young people organized a conference that involved the YWCA and the settlement houses. They developed a united organization to campaign around the National Youth Administration [NYA] for a youth employment project to build a ball field at a spot where the railroad-owned property which had been vacant for years. This approach seemed to stimulate people, including [Saul] Alinsky, who approached the union to see if we would like to make the organization larger, not only young people. Also we had to overcome a situation where the church was conservative, Republican, playing a negative rule; we eventually changed it. On the black side, we worked closely with the Urban League and the NAACP [National Association for the Advancement of Colored People].

In the plant, from inception we were concerned about discrimination—we took a grievance about a star on the employment card to indicate a black worker. Black girls could work anywhere except sliced bacon and chipped beef. We changed that. Workers were very sensitive about use by employers of discrimination. The concept of black and white unity was well understood by workers. Surprisingly there was minimal opposition. Black people came to the white-area union hall. By and large integration was generally accepted in the community. We sent kids to the Catholic Youth organization's summer camp. We got Bishop Shiel to write a pamphlet urging people to oppose discrimination.

By and large the leadership was of left persuasion. The overwhelming majority of members supported us on basis of performance. I had many members tell me, Herb, I know you're a damn Communist but you're a good man and a fighter. I don't think anybody ever questioned my integrity and my honesty; even my enemies. I think I was popular with the rank and file. Except for the Dies Committee, the church never raised it.

Helstein Takes Over

Helstein assumed command of the UPWA just when the labor movement was entering a period of profound crisis. Truman's attack on the United Mine Workers in November of 1946 and the launching of a campaign to revise the Wagner Act marked the start of an economic and legislative backlash against organized labor that culminated with the passage of the Taft-Hartley Act in June 1947.[9]

The Taft-Hartley Act created all kinds of problems for unions. Sections 8(b)(4) and (7) retarded organization of industrial unions. Eugene Cotton, general counsel of the CIO-affiliated UPWA, noted that Section 8(b) in the CIO packinghouse union "virtually eliminated strikes for union recognition."

> ... the UPWA could not picket the butcher stores and supermarkets and other wholesale and retail outlets of unbranded products of struck plants, and UPWA members in those establishments could not support the strike by refusing to handle the products, that UPWA workers in plants in supplying the struck plant were forced to scab on their fellow union members because they could not refuse to work on products being sent into the struck plant. The introduction of the entire body of union unfair labor practices in Section 8(b) (consistent with the "balanced" revision of Section 7) meant in effect that the shield of protection of employee rights under the Wagner Act was reversed to become, instead, a line of cannons pointed against labor.[10]

The passage of the Taft-Hartley Act in June 1947 not only imposed legal restrictions on the trade unions but also symbolized a shift in the relationship between government and unions during the 1940s. The Taft-Hartley Act codified many key policy goals of business leaders and state industrial relations managers that had started in the early 1940s. This movement started with the no-strike pledge when major industrial unions cooperated closely with the government to maintain industrial and political discipline within their organizations. In conjunction with the anti-Communist currents then sweeping the working class and stiffening employer resistance, the anti-Communist clause represented state action that opened the door to inter-union raiding.

According to Cotton, the injunction provisions of Taft-Hartley had severely damaging effects on all unions but were "devastatingly evil" as implemented against the relatively low-paid, largely unskilled employees in the packing industry: "And the anti-labor provisions of [Taft-Hartley] [notwithstanding the 1931 Norris-LaGuardia anti-injunction law] were to be enforced not merely by the long drawn-out procedure of complaint hearing . . . but, far more devastatingly, by virtually mandatory, quickly issued court injunctions against unions."[11]

The wartime alliance between the United States and the Soviet Union gave way to the Cold War, allowing anti-Communism to emerge as a powerful divisive force within labor's ranks. Again, the UPWA responded to these twin obstacles in a way that distinguished it from other unions. It neither capitulated to the onerous requirements of the Taft-Hartley Act nor succumbed to the considerable pressure brought to bear upon it to purge the left and lend support to the Democratic Party.[12]

Why did this left-right shift occur? The war had a cataclysmic effect on the political realignment of immigrants in the United States, moving them from left to right. The invasion by the Soviet Union of Finland and the Baltic states and Nazi collaborators in Eastern Europe, particularly in Lithuania, Poland, and the Ukraine made them virulently anti-Communist. Walter Reuther, who himself had earlier worked in a Soviet factory and may have at one time been a member of the Communist Party, in August 1940, at the UAW St. Louis convention, sponsored a resolution "condemning 'the brutal dictatorships, and wars of aggression of the totalitarian governments of Germany, Italy, Russia and Japan,' " after which delegates voted to bar from union office any member of an organization declared "illegal" by the U.S. government.[13]

In part, Helstein was able to resist CIO pressure to join the anti-Communist chorus because the union had a liberal base. Like Helstein,

Vice-President Frank Ellis[14] [was] strongly liberal in politics and insistent on the protection of the rights of unpopular minorities. Even after the war the Communists shared with others in the UPWA many points of agreement: militancy in negotiations and on strike action, racial equality, and a variety of domestic political issues such as price control, FEPC, social security and so on. The left wingers were, moreover, demonstrably good union men. . . . Finally, the invocation of 'unity' by the Reds always was persuasive within the union.[15]

As one commentator who surveyed the political leanings of CIO unions wrote:

Communists or close Communist sympathizers controlled twelve of the CIO's thirty-five affiliates by 1946; . . . the United Electrical Workers (UE)

... the West Coast International Longshoremen's and Warehousemen's Union (ILWU), and the National Maritime Union (NMU). Other unions "with close Communist ties or conspicuous Communist leadership were the Mine, Mill and Smelter Workers, the Packinghouse Workers, and the New York-based Transport Workers Union. . . . In the [CIO] national office, the publicity director, Len DeCaux . . . and union's chief counsel, Lee Pressman, consulted closely with the Communist Party." But in their conduct of union affairs, for Communist party members "the union took precedence . . . over the Party."[16]

Certain policies during and after the war, particularly the Party's support of the "no-strike pledge" and speedups and the growing distrust of the Soviet Union, allowed union anti-Communists such as Walter Reuther, elected president of the CIO in 1946, to initiate anti-Communist measures. At the CIO's convention that same year, a resolution was adopted declaring that "we resent and reject efforts of the Communist Party or other political parties and their adherents to interfere in the affairs of the CIO. This convention serves notice that we will not tolerate such interference."[17]

This CIO anti-Communist policy took its impetus from the 1940 election of Philip Murray, selected by John L. Lewis to succeed him to the CIO presidency. Even though the left saw Murray as a "priest-ridden tool of the anti-Communist clergy" they believed Murray was the best alternative, which says a lot about the other candidates. On the eve of the CIO convention, "in a series of back room meetings," to avoid a total ban on Communists in the CIO, the left accepted "a compromise anti-Communist resolution." Passed without any debate or opposition, "the resolution stated that the CIO rejected . . . any policies emanating from totalitarianism, dictatorships and foreign ideologies such as Nazism, Communism and Fascism." Furthermore, it stated that "the dictatorships of Nazism, Communism and Fascism' [are] inimical to the welfare of labor, and destructive of our form of government. . . ."[18] In effect, the left accepted the proposition that Communism was just another form of totalitarianism and that Hitler and Stalin were in the same boat. It was ironic that Communism, once thought to be the antidote to Nazism and Fascism, was now seen as its equivalent. Communists accepted this result because anti-Communists threatened to bolt the CIO for the American Federation of Labor (AFL) if the resolution did not pass. Lewis worked out this compromise and reportedly threatened to follow David Dubinsky and Max Zaritsky back into the AFL, and in his speech, Lewis had reportedly said, "Dubinsky, Zaritsky, and so forth" in a particularly anti-Semitic way. Dubinsky thought that this was part of a campaign by Lewis to label the unions opposing him as "Jewish controlled."[19]

The "main propositions" that formed the anti-Communist doxology has been stated as follows:

> (1) the Communist party is not an authentic party. . . . It is, in fact, a "conspiratorial and revolutionary junta," and seeks by means of duplicity, chicanery, false fronts, and underhanded strategems [*sic*] to subvert the democratic order. Through systematic infiltration it captures a wide variety of private organizations—notably the labor unions—in order to impose policies alien to their purposes. This is a conspiracy that cannot be tolerated without its leading to the stultification of liberal society. (2) The Communist party alone among American parties past or present is controlled by and subservient to a foreign government. . . . (3) Every member of the Communist party is an agent of its purposes. Every member works under works under an "ironclad discipline" to carry out the Party's dictates and directions. . . .[20]

This is the ideology that dominated both political parties, Congress, most labor leadership, and most liberals from the early 1940s through the McCarthy period and led to the hysterical reactions to the "red scare" that followed.[21] The reader can determine whether the "reds" in the UPWA fit this measure and what Helstein's reactions to this challenge tells us of him.

Communist Influence in the UPWA and Other CIO Unions

In 1947, 12 members of the Communist Party board were indicted for violation of the Alien Registration law of 1940, known as the Smith Act, which prohibited the teaching and advocacy of the violent overthrow of the government by force and violence. Trials began in January 1949 and lasted until October 1950.[22]

The executive board, likely the work of Helstein, in 1947, issued a "Statement of Policy" denouncing "red baiting," stating that "Repression of any sort which attacks civil liberties is the weapon of reaction . . . whose goal is to destroy the trade union movement," at the same time asserting that "Those who for whatever reason attempt to influence our actions in other directions will receive no aid and comfort from us. . . . We shall make our own decisions free from all outside interference." This declaration passed by acclamation at the 1947 convention,[23] asserted not only freedom from Communist control but warned others who might try to influence UPWA policies, such as the CIO, that the UPWA was its own man.

There was a certain ingenuousness in asserting this issue on both sides. The assumption is that unions are run democratically by the actions of a majority of its members. But that is not how organizations, unions or not, act. As one commentator concluded after a study of unions and other organizations:

> [T]he bulk of the membership of unions, as in other private associations (e.g. members of the American Legion, American Medical Association, etc.), are relatively passive and indifferent, willing to entrust much decision-making to their officials. It means that day-to-day participation in union affairs is, with rare exceptions, confined to a small core of active members.[24]

There remained problems, both internal and external, in the 1950s and 1960s before the "old red question," as Helstein put it, was laid to rest. Helstein described how Arthur Murray, president of the CIO, came to the 1950 UPWA convention and stirred things up:

> [A]mong other things I made a speech in which I made it clear that the union was going to keep its channels open and that we had room for everybody, irrespective of their opinions. And Murray's way of dealing with this was not to attack it straight on out but sort of pat me on the head and say what a fine boy I was and how they could always rely on me. And I wasn't turning my back on them, I was just as anti-communist as everyone else, that kind of thing. It created the kind of situation where I felt compelled before the convention was over to just respond and say, not withstanding anything he said, this was the way I felt. We had had a fight, the usual fight about amending the constitution to bar communists. But again we had gone through the business of creating other issues that made those people pressing this anxious to make bargains because we always had votes. In the final analysis that's what counted.[25]

Murray initially appeared to take a firm stand against the oath. At a convention of the American Communications Association, he was quoted as saying that at a meeting of the CIO's Executive Board:

> I was unwilling to file an affidavit that I wasn't a communist. That's a matter of principle. I do not know why the Congress of the United States should require me to do that, as a citizen. I think the Congress is very presumptuous, because I think I if they do that to me about the question of communism, they could do it with it with any other citizen about any other kind of question. . . . I shall not attempt to explain the manifold reasons . . . which I attach to that principle.[26]

But soon after, Murray did sign it. Other than the United Mine Workers under Lewis, all succumbed to the need to comply to be eligible for National Labor Relations Board (NLRB) elections.[27]

Helstein then sets forth the political balancing act that showed his sophisticated political acumen:

> [W]e were able to work out generally these problems without ever conceding to the demand for amendment and never really pressing our advantages. We could have pressed them and there were those in our own ranks who felt we should. On the other hand I felt it was just as important to make sure that even those whose views I thought were terrible—I looked on them as not willing sympathizers with McCarthy but really representing, even though they didn't realize it, but they were caught up in this general national hysteria and never understood really what the issues were. I think I felt they were fearful people but I was convinced they had a right to be heard and to make sure they had their opportunity. . . . We managed to go through it and finally in '54 we finally brought it into the convention hall and debated the issue and put it to rest.[28]

But this battle continued first with Murray,[29] and then when he died in 1952, with Reuther.[30]

> And we just fought it out with him. We refused to give him an inch. That's when he turned to me one time in exasperation and said, "You know, Ralph, there isn't your intellectual peer in the CIO. There isn't anything you want that you couldn't have if you'd just straighten yourself out on this issue." And I said, "Walter, let's understand each other. First, I don't view this as a very great, great compliment when you tell me I don't have any intellectual peer in the CIO. If you would have said it about other places it might be a different matter but not here. Secondly, there's really not a single thing that you're in a position to give me that I really want except to be able to be left alone so this union could run its business as part of the labor movement and make its impact on the labor movement as a whole. . . . We are not going off on purges. Now you may think that's the right way to do it, we don't. And you're just going to have to let us handle our business in our own way."[31]

One study, based a variety of sources, including Federal Bureau of Investigation (FBI) files released under the Freedom of Information Act, concluded that in 1948, the Party had 59,000 members and 16,500 in the CIO, "less than 1 percent of the total CIO membership that year."[32]

At the 1949 convention, the CIO expelled two "Communist-dominated" unions and in 1950 expelled nine others, a total of 17 to 20 percent of its membership.[33]

At the 1950 convention, CIO officials put increasing pressure on Helstein to pass an amendment to the UPWA constitution to ban Communists from holding union office. In opposition, there was a resolution introduced on internal unity. Helstein, at this juncture, made the following remarks setting forth his philosophy of leadership on the Communist association issue. His position was not only different from the majority of labor leaders at that time but he was also able to elaborate his views in a manner that showed the interests of union members to follow such a policy. For Helstein, such a policy as he outlined was "a sample of democracy in action":

> We have differences of opinion and they get expressed. That is the way it should be. Out of those differences we formulate certain policies. At the time we formulate them we have no way of knowing whether we are right, whether we are wrong or whether we are somewhere in between. None of us had a crystal ball to look into but history will record eventually the accuracy or inaccuracy of the position that we may have on any given issue. Once we have acted in the convention, the highest body of our organization that becomes the policy of our organization. Our union has consistently and steadfastly held to the basic principle that we exist for the benefit of the worker in the plant, the stockyard, the soap factory and the sugar mill. We have consistently and steadfastly held to the basic principle of American Trade unionism that the way to achieve our objective is by uniting these workers in the packing plants, the stockyards, the soap factory and the sugar mill so that we can use our collective strength in the improvement of the hours of work, the wages and all the working conditions in the plant. Unity has been our watchword. It is not an empty catchword but a living reality. There are cynics who may sneer as I say that and point to differences that have existed and still exist and probably will continue to exist, you know, but it is exactly there that the singular strength and power of this union of ours lies, in the fact that we can have these differences and not only benefit from them but still go forward as we have and as we will. We have succeeded in that because we have not allowed ourselves to be deterred from our main highway. We have grown with and benefited from these differences because we've held firm and sound to the basic premise of trade unionism, that the grievance of one worker in the plant is the grievance of all the workers in the plant, that the struggle of one plant or one department is the struggle of all of us. Therein lies our strength, in the fact that we are many and we act as one. When we stop doing that we stop being a union. Yes, we have met this test because we have asked of all our members

only one thing, that he or she join in the common fight for the benefit of all of us because this common fight is for the benefit of all of us. We don't ask about their color. We haven't asked about their political opinions, their religion. We know that from the time a labor movement first came into being employers have tried an infinite variety of tactics to divide their employees. We have proven we can stand firm and united and hold to these basic trade union principles, the principles of freedom and democracy. And we have proven that we can do it even in a growing national atmosphere of hysteria. In this convention hall you've heard specific and very gracious approval given to the policies and record of your union and its officers. . . . I hope that what has happened in this convention has been proof and an acknowledgement that it is possible to steer such a course of consistent and honest trade unionism and still not be called a red. . . . [W]e, in our day to day work and our week to week existence, have proven that a union can devote itself wholeheartedly to the wage problems, the grievance problems, the working conditions of its membership end not become divided by issues unrelated to our performance as a union. Therein lies our strength and therein lies our power.[34]

Eugene Cotton believed that Helstein's fortitude on this issue was crucial to the union's success and stability in the face of continuing challenges:

I was always proud of the UPWA—I think they were a very unique organization. I attribute a large part of that to the leadership of Ralph Helstein. He was not only a dedicated and basically principled in civil rights, but also in civil liberties, that is, the protection of the rights of freedom of speech. At every convention I was at, he made it plain that everyone was invited to get up and speak on the floor and he invited disagreement with him because he felt that that was the best way for him to be sure that his decisions were thought out and responsive and he often delivered frequent lectures on the significance of the first amendment. I think it became pretty well ingrained within the union. There were wide ranges of political differences within the union and [Helstein believed] that civil debate was the way to handle this. So the fact that Charlie [Hayes] and others were called up before the Committee and having been members of the CP didn't make any significant wave. Charges had been made within the union and debated within the union so it was almost, so what else is new? Whatever views they might have, it won't become a political issue and it didn't.[35]

Cotton put the left influence in the union in perspective with its mission:

Not anyone was all left and not anyone was all right. In fact, there was no real strong right in the typical political sense. . . . Part of dedication to black-white unity was due to CIO influence and although never under the Communist Party. It was a union that in its early years had a very substantial left influence. It didn't deserve its reputation it had for being supposedly for being communist led or dominated. Among the lower levels of organizing there was a substantial left influence which brought with it a position on black-white relationship, and also early on recognized in Chicago and elsewhere realized that there was a very a substantial black component of the working population. . . . [A]nd if they didn't have a sound attitude on that, the organizing would have been almost impossible. Right from the start, the official seal of the union had a black and white hand shaking hands with each other. One of the first assignments I had in 1948 was an arbitration proceeding in which they enforced against Swift in hiring—a test case in hiring of women. Bacon wrapping was recognized as a white domain. The union had a black and white woman come to the hiring hall at about the same time. The black women were told nothing was available now and the white woman, one of the union secretaries, was welcomed warmly and offered the job. The case was won, but more importantly, the companies were put on notice that the union was serious about the non-discrimination clause in their contracts.[36]

As the following comment makes clear, Helstein's stand was in clear contrast to the position of almost all union officials and the vast majority of the left:

Few Democrats and liberals were now willing to defend their former activities and associations. In fact, in an effort to prove themselves completely "loyal," such liberals frequently outdid right wingers in attacking Communists and other critics of postwar American policies.[37] By the mid-1950s, apart from Herb March, and a couple more, most had dropped out of the CP.[38]

The pressures under which Helstein worked in the late 1940s and early 1950s were immense and constant. The attack on labor was based on "internal security." The rational was stated as follows:

Unions were central to the nation's economy; under Communist influence they could wreak immense harm, especially in vital defense industries. Communists were perceived as being incredibly powerful and invariably disloyal. "A single Communist," so former Congressman Fred Hartley [co-sponsor of the Taft-Hartley law] explained, in a position of power within the labor movement could act under the direction of Russian agents so as to seriously hinder the country's ability to defend its people and wage war against its enemies.[39]

The effort to "drive Communists out of the labor movement" involved congressional committees, the FBI, the NLRB, Subversive Activities Control Board (SACB), and almost every other federal government agency. Labor was a target of congressional committees from the start. The House [of Representatives] Un-American Activities Committee's (HUAC) first hearings in 1938 and 1939 charged Communist influence in unions, and in following years, other committees continued that line of investigation. More than 100 hearings dealt with the problem of Communists in the labor movement between 1946 and 1956. Criminal prosecutions, broken strikes, internal union purges, and the dismissal of individual workers often followed. Serving subpoenas during strikes involving left-wing unions became the pattern throughout the McCarthy period.[40]

To understand the courage of Helstein's stand, it is necessary to consider the wall of anti-red government legislative and administrative attacks on workers. Apart from the "self-cleanings" by the CIO and AFL and by state agencies federal programs included the industrial personnel security program, the port-security program, the Loyalty Review Board and more than 200 loyalty security boards for various government agencies, the Attorney General's List (1947 to 1955), the Coast Guard Army intelligence, the FBI, the Immigration and Naturalization Service, the Internal Security Division of the Justice Department, the SACB; Congress (the Alien and Sedition Act (1940), Labor-Management Relations Act (1947), the Internal Security Act (1950, which among other things authorized concentration camps for the internment of Communists in the event of a "national emergency"), the Port Security Act (1950), the Witness Immunity Act (1954), and the Communist Control Act (1954).[41]

This broad attack on the left ended the labor-left coalition, largely supported by Communists and their allies, and thus stifled the drive to obtain the kind of social democratic welfare state that existed in Western Europe.[42]

The same can be said of women's and blacks' advancement.[43] It is a tribute to Helstein and his staff that they were able not only to resist these attacks from the right but to also maintain the social democratic vision throughout this period.

Congressional Investigations

From the late 1930s to the early 1960s, the UPWA was under constant harassment from congressional committees, including the Committee on Un-American Activities, which held hearings on communist penetration of labor unions. The UPWA was subject to such investigations in 1939,[44] 1952,[45] 1954,[46] 1959,[47] and 1965.[48]

During the 1954 hearings, while testifying, Herb March stated what he believed was the real intent of the hearings. After a colloquy between the interrogator, Representative Francis E. Walter, about March's taking the Fifth Amendment, March commented about "this committee, which isn't friendly to labor. . . ." He continued:

> Well, if you are so interested in labor, I don't see why you come into a situation where the union has had its contract cancelled by a company throughout an industry at a time when the union and the company are engaged in a very serious wage and contract dispute and enter into a mess such as this for the purpose of casting reflection upon the union and weakening it in its struggle with the company. . . .
>
> My friend, if you were so concerned about whether or not this would harm our union, the least this committee could have done would have been to contact some of the officers of this union and ask them whether we had any feeling that an inquiry of this kind at this time would have any reflection on the fight of workers for higher wages.
>
> Mr. Walter. We would have done that but for the fact that we don't confer with Communists or ask their advice about anything.

Mr. Tavener, the committee counsel, asked March if he had testified at the hearing on November 18, 1939. March replied: "You are referring to the hearing that took place . . . 3 days before we had a labor board election in the Chicago Armour plant?"[49]

Ralph Helstein wrote a letter to the committee that was read into the record at the beginning of the hearing. Dated May 1, 1959, he wrote:

> We represent . . . over 100,000 employees in the meat packing industry and others in related industries. . . . Before our union was very old . . . it was faced with a fundamental choice of procedures. It could have embarked on a program that might have led to bitter internal conflict, diverting energies urgently needed for the task of providing economic improvements for the packinghouse workers. Our membership developed a different program. . . .
>
> There was never the slightest question or possibility of yielding control to a Communist group or any other ideology. But we felt that the challenge of Communism could best be met not by a civil war certain to blunt the union's collective bargaining effectiveness, but by demonstrating that a positive democratic brand of unionism would produce results, thereby defeating the attraction of Communism by undercutting its ground.

Our union has, over the years, established its position on Communism. . . . Our union has adopted as official policy the AFL-CIO Ethical practices Codes. No member of the Communist Party is or will be permitted to hold elective or appointive office in our union . . . If there are in our ranks persons with a Communist past, their present adherence to the democratic principles of our union represents a victory of democratic philosophy over totalitarianism. . . .

A rejected and disgruntled former officeholder [apparently referring to Tony Stephens] has been engaged in an effort to revive the long dead issue. . . . Finally, your hearings happen to come at a time when we are about to enter upon negotiations with the major packing companies, as the current three year term of contracts throughout the industry approaches expiration. Pressing problems of plant shutdowns, mass layoffs, technological unemployment, inadequate pensions and severance pay clauses, and many others claim the attention of our members and leaders. . . . Under these circumstances, you will understand, I am sure, the feeling of many among our members that your hearings may, without any intention on your part . . . create a misleading public impression of our union. . . .

Chairman Walter read into the record a reply, stating in part: "There is no intention on the part of [the committee] to interfere in any way on either side, with any negotiations between the union and employers. In this connection, I wish to point out that these investigations are in no way directed at the UPWA, as a union, or at its officers as such."[50]

Both Helstein spoke or wrote a bit tongue in cheek. The hearings alleged that the UPWA District 1 Chicago District was honeycombed with present or past Communist Party members, including Les Orear (director of the department of publications), Leon Beverly (field representative), Sam Parks (director of the Anti-Discrimination Department), Jack Souther (secretary-treasurer of District 1), Joseph Zabritzki (president of Local 25), Charlie Hayes (director of District 1), Rachael Carter Ellis (secretary to Charlie Hayes), and Leo Turner and Jesse Prosten (international representatives),[51] among other lesser figures.

The Taft-Hartley Non-Communist Affidavit

Signing the Taft-Hartley non-Communist affidavit, as required by section 9(h) of the Taft-Hartley Act,[52] was a prerequisite for participating in the services of the NLRB, including elections to be recognized as a bargaining agent. Signing such an oath, however, was contrary to the ideals of the UPWA and the ideas and ideals of Helstein. But the compliance of the

Amalgamated and the waffling of CIO leaders on the issue left the UPWA isolated. The issue again opened up left-right fissures. Right wingers, led by Philip Weightman on the UPWA national executive board, argued that failure to sign the non-Communist affidavit threatened the survival of the union. Leftists such as Herb March, Frank Ellis, and Joe Ollman answered that the union's only defense lay in the strength of the organization's rank-and-file structure. Joe Ollman warned that far from offering protection, compliance would weaken the union and render it defenseless against future attacks. Helstein supported him, arguing that the delays and restrictions incorporated in the NLRB process made the use of government machinery an impediment to organization. The better course—albeit the more difficult one—was to resist. "Those unions that do not comply, that take this thing the hard way," Helstein concluded, "are the unions that are going to be in a better position to survive than the ones that comply and operate under any illusions that they have any protection from this nefarious piece of legislation."[53]

Nevertheless, Helstein, seeing the handwriting on the wall, finally took the centrist position that compliance might ultimately be necessary. In the interim the membership should be made to understand that the meaning of Taft-Hartley was that "the government of the United States was now on the side of big business." He stated the union's negotiating position: "we are never willing to admit that the company's last offer is really their last offer," this same strategy applied to the union's opposition to the Taft-Hartley Act.[54]

Immediately after the CIO voted in late 1947 to leave to its affiliated internationals the decision about signing the affidavits, the UPWA's international executive board voted by a narrow margin to comply with the statute and with section 9(h), requiring all four top officers to sign. To protect March, the board voted to make him Chicago district director, then voted that district directors were not officers and therefore not required to sign the affidavits. But in December the Department of Labor determined that the UPWA was out of compliance unless all Executive Board members signed the affidavits, namely Herb March and Meyer Stern. Both men had refused to sign or to resign. Unable to resolve this dilemma, the board referred the issue of whether the district directors (all board members) had to sign to be decided at the union's next convention. Following the disastrous 1948 strike, the board decided it was vulnerable to raids from the AFL's Meatcutters' union, so the board voted for full compliance.[55] This meant that March would either have to sign or be fired.

This matter was resolved when Meyer Stern resigned from the Communist Party and signed the affidavit, and March sent the union an undated "Statement of Resignation,"[56] published in the *Packinghouse Worker*:

My loyalty to my union, its traditions and its membership, my uncompromising attitude towards the yellow dog affidavits of the vicious Taft-Hartley law, and my political convictions which I find impossible to betray, compels me to tender my resignation as a member of the International Executive Board of the UPWA, CIO.

He went on to criticize the board's decision to give up "our democratic rights to choose our own officers to the union-busting Taft-Hartleyites . . . as a violation of our constitutions [*sic*]."

But because both "a large percentage" of the board and the membership have concluded that the way to preserve the union is compliance, he said, "I have no intention of allowing my post on the board to block the will of the majority." He resigned to avoid internal conflict when the union needed all its strength to survive. He stated that his membership in the Communist Party was well known and that his membership and beliefs strengthened his ability to build the union. He asked: "Are we going to surrender the right, not only in the International Board, but in the union districts and locals to freely elect officers of our choosing? . . . Will it be the Communists today, the [Henry] Wallace supporters tomorrow, the Negro people and other minority groups the next day? . . . Compliance will not make our union 'safe.' The only answer to the Taft-Hartley Law is to be found in united, hard struggle for its repeal. . . . Enemies of our union . . . will undoubtedly say I am resigning because we did not win our strike. . . . [R]egardless of my rank or title, in the plant or out, I am going to remain an active member of this union and will fulfill any responsibility the union sees fit to place upon me." March finished with a ringing: "Let us go forward, united, militant and clear-minded in our devotion to our progressive principles. We can and will defeat the attacks of the Packers and their agents. We will keep our union strong and progressive."

The decision to fire (sacrifice?) March[57] to stifle the CIO's red charges presented a moral crisis to Helstein. March and his wife never forgave Helstein, and Norman Dolnick believed Helstein didn't fight hard enough. In theory, Helstein could have fired Jesse Prosten, but if he had, "the local unions would have killed him, cause Jessie was a negotiator par excellence and they knew it, and Jessie was more international. Jessie was through all the country, Herb's only regional, so Helstein could sort of throw Herb to the wolves, to the national CIO. Helstein really suffered as a result of this; he agonized but he felt that he was absolutely forced to act to save the union."

Helstein was so disturbed by these events that he contemplated resigning.[58] He wrote to a confidant that "I don't think that fundamentally the problem has to do with affidavits at all." Rather, "the Taft-Hartley law is designed for the purpose of forcing conformity on the American people and making it difficult for anyone who dissents from expressing his views." After several weeks of reflection, Helstein opted to go along with the board's decision and submitted his own affidavit.[59]

After the 1948 elections, the CIO's president, Philip Murray, denounced pro-Soviet labor leaders, conducted "hearings" to prove that certain labor leaders were in thrall to the Soviets and from 1948 to 1950 expelled 11 unions identified with Soviet policies. Such anti-red policies were accompanied by raids on the expelled unions and the dismissal of numerous red-tainted organizers and local union officials. The result was the decline of CIO membership from a peak of 5.2 million to 3.7 million by 1950.[60] Expelling these "Communist-dominated" unions from the CIO had its ironic side because at the time of its formation in November 1935, the AFL, its mother organization, "suspended" 10 international unions on charges of "fomenting insurrection and dual unionism."[61]

Which CIO unions were in the "Communist political camp" was a question studied by the Research Institute of America. The organization labeled a union "left-wing if it had espoused causes or taken positions as revealed by the *Daily Worker.*" According to this criterion, 18 unions, including the UPWA, fit this category, although the author considers the UPWA's ranking to be "uncertain and shifting." Other authors have described the UPWA as "Communist dominated," "a flagrant case of continuing Communist influence," or a union "controlled by Communists or close Communist sympathizers. . . ."[62]

After the conviction of the leaders of the Party, the government went after "secondary" leaders. On the street level, party headquarters and party meetings were attacked by mobs, and the trials and congressional hearings showed that the Party was "honeycombed" with informers; the Party reacted with "suspicion and paranoia." Internal witch hunts[63] resulted, one aspect of which were charges of "'white chauvinism.' Long-time Communists suddenly came under intense scrutiny for evidence that they held the slightest residual prejudice against African Americans. The campaign, which lasted roughly from 1949 to 1953, seemed in part an exercise in self-hatred . . . using the 'white chauvinism' accusation as a club."

Again, the UPWA responded in a way that distinguished it from other unions. It neither capitulated to onerous requirements of the Taft-Hartley Act nor succumbed to the considerable pressure brought upon it to purge the left and lend support to the Democratic Party.

Why Was the UPWA Not Included with Other Expelled CIO Unions?

Myles Horton, director of the Highlander Folk School and hired as the UPWA's educational director, recounts an attempt by the CIO to intimidate Helstein on the Communist issue:

> I'd set up an educational program for the Packinghouse Workers Union and, beginning in 1951, they used Highlander for their training workshops. That union had one of the best programs of nondiscrimination of any union in the United States, so we had a lot of things in common. At their next convention Allan Haywood, who was the chief spokesperson for the CIO at the time, said that if the Packinghouse Workers union didn't put in an anticommunist clause in the bylaws, they would raid the union and break it up. It was pretty tough talk. Ralph Helstein . . . stood firmly against that demand. He and I spent a week at Highlander talking the issue out. Ralph wanted to know what my position would be if the Packinghouse Workers tried to write an anti-communist provision into the by-laws. I told him I'd resign as educational director. We had already refused to draft such a statement in 1950 at Highlander, and I wouldn't work for an organization that did. Ralph was the kind of a person who wasn't afraid to stand up to the kind of challenge the CIO was making. We called their bluff and we were the only union refusing to ban Communist officials that wasn't kicked out of the CIO.[64]

Subsequent research studies, after the anti-red period passed, have led most scholars to conclude "that Communist unionists, men and women of radical conviction and egalitarian passion, were willing and able, and determined, in practice, to put workers' interests ahead of the zig-zag and momentary 'party line' of the CP's officialdom. The unions created and sustained by Communists and their allies . . . were among the most egalitarian, the most honest and well-administered, the most racially progressive, and the most class conscious."[65]

Admitted and active Communists such as Herb March and Jesse Prosten as well as Charley Hayes and Les Orear proved repeatedly that they were dedicated unionists before they were Communists. To them, the class struggle of Communism represented the championing of the working class through their union activity against capitalist employers. The politics of the Soviet Union had little, if any, influence on their day-to-day activities.

The main reputed object of anti-Communist purges was that Communist-dominated unions were inherently undemocratic—ruled by a tiny clique dedicated to the policies of the Soviet Union rather than to the union to which they were members.[66] How do we determine if a union—specifically, the UPWA—adheres to democratic principles—that is, provides a vehicle for its members to implement their union desires and needs? One researcher specifically concluded on this question:

> A democratic union's political system must combine three basic features: a *democratic constitution* (i.e. guarantees of basic civil liberties and political rights), *institutional opposition* (i.e., the freedom of members to criticize and debate union officials and to organize, oppose, and replace officials through freely contested elections among contending political associations, such as parties (factions), and an *active membership* (i.e. maximum participation by its members in the actual exercise of power within the union and in making the decisions that affect them).

By this measure, the reader will have to judge how the UPWA measures up. Meanwhile, taking into consideration, with reference to Helstein, what David Dubinsky said at the founding convention of the International Ladies Garment Workers Union (ILGWU), "In my union, we have democracy too—but they know who is boss!"[67] The word, "boss" would have been repellant to Helstein, for which he would have substituted "leader" with all the qualities of educator that went with it.

The authors of an anti-Communist book *Union Democracy* (author, date of publication, and publisher not cited) assert that

> Communists have a corrosive effect . . . on trade union democracy . . . Communist ideology does not tolerate the existence of an organized opposition. These antidemocratic goals seem to pervade any intra-union dispute to which the Communists are a party. . . . Local 600, as in the UAW as a whole, not Reds but the UAW's international leaders, who were advocates of a liberal or social-democratic "ideology," as well as their Activist [Catholic activists], were the ones whose actual political practices had a "corrosive" effect on union democracy; they were the ones who would not tolerate and sought to destroy organized opposition from the left.[68]

Critics of left unionism confound the party and its union members. Even where Communist Party members doggedly followed the party line on Soviet foreign policy, when it came to union policy, they usually did what, based on their union experience, they thought was best for their union. The union careers of March and Prosten vividly illustrate this conclusion. No Communist Party UPWA member was ever accused of following the Soviet line to the detriment of the union. Even the CIO Policy Caucus, in its brief existence, only accused March of failing to follow CIO policy, an ironic accusation, as the CIO represented an up-down bureaucracy.

The effect of the Taft-Hartley Act affidavit was to uniformly force conformity on the whole labor movement.

By August 1948, . . . 81,000 union officers, including officials of eighty-nine AFL affiliates and thirty of the CIOs already had sworn and signed the affidavit. . . . By July 1957, some 250 international unions were in compliance . . . and about 21,500 locals (involving affidavits by another 193,500) . . . at shop-floor level nearly 200,000 trade-union leaders had formally sworn that they did not belong to the CP or believe in its doctrines.[69]

These numbers do not tell the story of the innumerable struggles and energy expended on decisions on whether to sign the affidavit, the hard feelings, the suspicions sown, the loss of solidarity built over years of working together with workers of different persuasions but with the similar objective of improving workers' lives. Add to this the loss of admittedly the most active, devoted, hard-working, and honest union organizers and officials, resulting in a shock to the union movement from which it has never recovered.

How can one explain these anti-Communist eruptions in one union after another? What moved the actors? The big majority of American unionists— high, medium, minor officials, rank-and-filers—want to have their union considered a respectable enterprise. They want to be accepted as responsible citizens who adhere to the nation's ongoing traditions and precepts, and are uncomplicatedly loyal to the government. Worker and official alike have this in common with the general run of the middle class: their belligerently asserted Americanism is a compound of the same shibboleths and platitudes derived from an adherence to predominant values of our society. . . . Until recently they were locked in desperate battle with employers and were themselves bespattered with accusations, thrown at them by local dignitaries and government officials, of illegal trespass, disloyalty, even Communism. So on the one hand they build up resistance to the thunders of official public opinion which they defied before and may have to defy again, and on the other hand, they seek to compensate for their equivocal status by eager displays of political conformity and community-mindedness. Despite labor's growing self-confidence, there remains a strong element of an earlier feeling that workers constitute a minority group that requires alliances if it is not to be trampled upon. ... Hence, when anti-Communism became part of the American creed, it was a matter of course that it would be embraced by the unions. ... Communists had to be eliminated because they compromised reputation for political orthodoxy. ... But as experience was to show, while the crusading was on, in most situations all of them would work in unison because they had a common enemy and purpose, and they were moving with, not against, the political current.[70]

At its Fourteenth Constitutional Convention in New York City in May 1958, the UPWA adopted the "AFL-CIO Ethical Practices Codes," of which Paragraph 4-III reads as follows:

No person should hold or retain office or appointed position in the AFL-CIO or any of its affiliated national or international unions or subordinate bodies thereof who is a member, consistent supporter or who actively participates in the activities of the Communist Party or any fascist or other totalitarian organization which opposes the democratic principles to which our country and the American trade union movement are dedicated.

A subcommittee of the International Executive Board was charged with the responsibility of investigating and reporting to the Board on all situations in which there is reasonable grounds for inquiry into questions of compliance with any of these codes. ... In order that we may determine whether any question of possible violation of this Paragraph exists in your case, we ask you, on your honor as a trade unionist, to answer the questions on the attached page and return it, signed ... in the enclosed, stamped, addressed envelope.[71]

As we will see in Chapter 8, there was a specific reason—charges by a former UPWA officer, Tony Stephens, that the UPWA was communist dominated—that led to this strange development that, on its face, seems to go against steady opposition to such an anti-Communist declaration.

Organization in the South and Communist Charges

Organization in the South was generally less successful, with the UPWA winning only one-third of NLRB elections as against two-thirds elsewhere. Difficulties arose from provisions of the Taft-Hartley law that gave more rights to employers, from the NLRB that was slow to process complaints, restrictive state laws, and "hostile" public officials. But the greatest obstacle was resistance found in small towns, prejudice against unions and blacks that sometimes manifested itself in violence against organizers.[72]

Dowling proposed a resolution that would have required the executive board to fire or investigate people who were "connected to anything" of the kind of organization many other unions were adopting. Helstein kept arguing with him against such a resolution:

> This is a power that you propose to give me. I will not and cannot exercise it. I am unwilling to hold this office with that kind of burden put on me when I'm expected to carry it out. If, therefore, it is adopted I will resign. I simply cannot live with this, I'm not willing to do these kinds of things. I don't believe in purges and won't do it.

Helstein was able to negotiate a resolution that was submitted and unanimously agreed to by the International Executive Board and the Resolutions Committee:

> We affirm our opposition to all forms of totalitarianism including fascism, communism and any other authoritarian group. We affirm our faith in the democratic process. We therefore subscribe to the rule of the majority and will oppose any activity within our organization on the part of communists, fascists, or any other groups designed to destroy our democratic process in order to further their objectives.[73]

That resolution was one he "could live with" because it "said what I essentially believed."

Herb March, "a member of the National Committee of the Communist Party" spoke, and Helstein said he thought "it's worth repeating what he said (in part), stating that he wanted to express his "sharp disagreement and opposition to it":

> If there are any among you who think that by the adoption of this resolution our union will attain some measure of respectability in the eyes of our enemies and will avoid being red-baited and attacked, then disillusion yourselves. McCarthyism tolerates a no way approach and will not allow our union to be at rest from its attacks until such time as the union ceases to fight for the interests of its workers. Only at that time, in their eyes, will this union attain any sort of respectability.[74]

Apart from the civil liberties issue at hand, Helstein "felt that what I had to do was, at every cost, keep this coalition that we had together because we stood for progressive things. . . . And I could not permit this break with Dowling to get either wider or to get permanent. I had to find some way of bridging it."

> Otherwise, as I saw it, the extreme left wing could go on and do anything they wanted to do as far as I was concerned just so long as the union could stay on this progressive course it had followed. We could be for things we believed in because we believed in them, not because we were worried about some communist menace. And I realized that to do this meant keeping these channels of communication open. I was not prepared to give in on that. . . . That's why I was opposed to constitutional amendments, because to me that was a clogging up of the democratic processes and it would have been permanent.[75]

This was one of the most concise statements of Helstein's governance philosophy. Whether intended to or not, it represented a response to March's warning. His use of the editorial "we" is ambiguous in that it is unclear whether "we" means the union, "our group"—the people he consulted with such as Stephens and Bull—or himself.

Chapter 6

Organizing Puerto Rican Workers

Helstein's organizing efforts in Puerto Rico reveals how he approached an area about which he knew little, his means of acquiring knowledge, and his relation to the people from whom he required this knowledge, as well as how he reacted to a new culture, its customs, food, language, and empathy for this unusual land. The union expended an enormous amount of time and energy in the campaign to organize Puerto Rican sugar workers.

At the time that Helstein went about organizing sugar workers in Puerto Rico, the following events were taking place.[1] On August 5, 1947, the United States Congress passed the Elective Governors Act, allowing Puerto Ricans to elect its own governor. On November 2, 1947, the first popular elections for governor of Puerto Rico took place. Luis Muñoz Marín was elected, with 61.2% of the vote.

Marin had campaigned for economic reforms and structural changes in the political relationship between the United States and islanders. Marin and other political leaders considered agricultural countries to be under-developed and industrial countries developed. Manufacturing was seen as the means by which Puerto Rico could develop economically. As a consequence, the government launched an industrialization program known as "Operation Bootstrap." Under this program, the island was to become industrialized by providing labor locally, inviting investment of external capital, importing the raw materials, and exporting the finished products to the U.S. market. On July 4, 1951, a law gave Puerto Rico the power to establish a government with its own constitution. On July 25, 1952 the New Constitution was approved by voters in a referendum, and Puerto Rico was proclaimed the Commonwealth of Puerto Rico.

In March 1952, Eugene Cotton, the United Packinghouse Workers of America's (UPWA's) general counsel, spent two and a half days in the country "to see a sugar mill and observe some field operations outside the city" of San Juan, the capital. Cotton was assisted by David Sternback, a Congress of Industrial Organizations (CIO) representative. Cotton subsequently sent a 14-page memo to Helstein, dated March 3, 1952, titled, "Inside Puerto Rico—for Two Days" in which he set forth the people he met and the purpose of the trip: "to get my bearings on the legal problems which we will face." The report had sections on "The Island," "The People," "General Economic Situation," "Employment and Wage Rates," "The Politics of the Island," "Labor Organizations and Labor Laws," "The Organizational Relationship with the CGT (General Confederation of Workers [Spanish: Confederación General de Trabajadores])," "The Organizational and Contractual Situation in Sugar," and "Legal Problems."[2]

In July 1952, a detailed report, a "Supplement to Officers' report (eight single-spaced pages), was made to the Executive Board (author not indicated), titled "Puerto Rico":

> Since the Convention, and based on commitments previously made, the President and the Research Director [Lyle Cooper] went to Puerto Rico for the purpose of participating in the hearing before Industry Committee No, 12 established by the [U.S.] Wage and Hour Division, whose function was to recommend a new minimum wage rate for the sugar manufacturing industry. . . . It is important that we understand that Puerto Rico offers an opportunity not only for a substantial increase in membership to this International Union, but for a tremendous contribution to the lives of the people of Puerto Rico and to the economy of the island as a whole. If one were to think back on the conditions in the packing industry in about the middle thirties, and multiply the problems that the workers in the industry faced at that time by about six, one might be able to appreciate some of the difficulties faced by the people of Puerto Rico. We have, therefore, an opportunity for tremendous contribution, which will return not only increased membership and the revenue that flows from it, but perhaps more important, a devoted membership which, under proper leadership, can be expected to fight militantly and intelligently in promoting their own interests.
>
> Racial integration, on a basis that could present us with a goal to work toward here on the mainland, is accepted without question on the island. The principle of trade unionism and the need for it also have general acceptance. The major problem is to show them how to do it.[3]

In appreciation of Helstein and the union's efforts to organize Puerto Rican workers, on June 14, 1952, Armando Sanchez, director of the Puerto

Rican union Sugar Syndicate, sent Helstein a letter that was as sugary as the sugar cane in the fields:

> The Sugar Syndicate has asked me to express its profound gratitude for your very brilliant work on behalf of the workers who operate the sugar mills in Puerto Rico. We are aware that without your intelligent intervention the Committee would not have recommended the 75 cents an hour. Your commentaries and the extensive contents of your magnificent presentation were a decisive contribution. . . . This was the biggest victory achieved by the sugar workers in the last fifty years. For this reason we all recognize, and accept, that without the cooperation of the packinghouse workers in this struggle we would never have gained this extraordinary triumph. . . .[4]

Sugar refining [workers] joined the union in 47 or 48. They had been chartered as an industrial union by the CIO. There was an internal fight over which union they would be affiliated with and the UPWA won the election. In the 48-49 "red fight" this Louisiana affiliate was one that gave the most trouble. As members of the CIO Policy Caucus, they originally refused to pay per capita dues but eventually they straightened out.[5]

According to an interview of Helstein by Elizabeth Balanoff

> Puerto Rico has a tradition that is substantially different from the mainland's tradition in terms of labor organization. They think of the "syndicato" as embracing workers from all kinds of fields not just one particular industry. Nor is it limited to any particular geography if you remember the island is approximately 35 miles wide and 125 or 140 miles long. . . . In 1952, the first time I went there, most of the foodstuffs were being imported from the mainland, rice from Maryland, for example. Rice was the basic commodity of their diet but they still had to import it. . . . Obviously, they had such a low capita income. . . . But in any event sugar was traditionally a product of Puerto Rico. . . . Now in all this the United States occupies a very interesting role because in the '30s during the first Roosevelt administration a Sugar Act was passed . . . What it is to limit the importation of sugar into quotas, once being met, that's all that country could send in. It had to be raw sugar, a very small quota of refined sugar of any kind. That's because we have a lot of refineries in the mainland.
>
> As a result, the majority of the people who worked in sugar were working the sugar fields and the "syndicate azucar" . . . is what the union that affiliated was called. This was made up principally of field workers—the men who actually planted the cane and tilled it and cut it, harvested it and then it would be ground on the island and then shipped to the mainland as raw sugar, but ground sugar, not the cane sugar.

There was a dispute in the Puerto Rico union leadership, and one leader, Antonini, in the 1940s, came to the states where he entered into a relationship with the CIO. But at some point, the union needed assistance that only an international union could give. This was at the time the UPWA had won an election among sugar refinery workers, so Alan Haywood [CIO vice president] suggested they affiliate with the UPWA. Helstein met with Antonini and an associate.

> I agreed at the time because I was touched by their problems. . . . I had been told what wages they were being paid, you know thirty to forty cents. Even the people who worked in grinding mills were getting fifty cents an hour . . . and there was a wage and hour hearing scheduled to be held in the fall of 1952.[6]

Helstein agreed to come down for the hearing. He came to know "a man by the name of Olivarez, who at the time was the Research Director of the planning Board."

> My meeting with Olivarez was very fortuitous for me because I think he probably had a better comprehension and a more refined sense of the economy of the island and what its implications were than anyone I ever knew over the years there. I developed a habit when I'd be going back, the first thing I'd do when I got to the island was to call him and either have lunch with him or get away with him somewhere I could spend a couple hours. Then I'd go away feeling I knew what was going on all the time I'd been away from the island. . . . There were three things that I had to be familiar with. One, I ought to get some feel of the history of the island; two, I ought to get some clear understanding of the economy of the island; and third and of special importance would be an understanding of the sugar industry, how it operated, what its problems were.[7]
>
> I had three fortunate breaks in this situation. One, we had a research director by the name of Lyle Cooper, a man of tremendous capacity and understanding. . . . He'd give me things and put them in a form that he knew I could observe easier so I had that available to me. Secondly, there lived in . . . Hyde Park. . . . Victor Perlov who had written what was then thought to be the definitive book on Puerto Rico. . . . And Rex Tugwell [who also lived in Hyde Park] had a comprehensive understanding of not just the economics of the sugar industry but also its political economy . . . as a [former] governor of Puerto Rico. He had also been head of the United States Molasses Company. So he had it from the government, management and having been president of the University of Puerto Rico, from a scholarly point of view.[8]

Helstein describes the union leadership in Puerto Rico, where, ironically, a lawyer as union leader was normal rather than exceptional as in
the United States.

The head of the union was also a member of the legislature. It was as a union
leader that got him the nomination of the Populaire Party. But the man who
put him there was Ramos Antonini, speaker of the house. Antonini "was a
Negro, a brilliant lawyer [and] a leading figure of the island. He had gotten
involved as a lawyer with the labor movement and helped it along and so
he became its spokesman actually.... You didn't have to be a member of
the union to be its president or one of its officers. For instance, you'd go
to a town and you'd meet a mayor and the mayor would turn out to be
the local union president although he never worked in the fields or the
grinding mill, but he'd be the president.[9]

Helstein described the trip to Puerto Rico. With his team, he went by
train from Chicago to Miami. He arranged to have a room on the train next
to Lyle Cooper. He spent the time going over the material Cooper fed him.

I would keep going over it, drumming it into me, getting the feel of it, and
then when I had questions I'd talk to him for awhile, and get him to set a
perspective. I did this for two days straight.... [B]y concentrating suffi-
ciently the stuff used to stick and fall into place and I would put it together
with things that Perlov had said or Tugwell had said so I was beginning to
get a pretty rounded picture of this.

    The pilot [of the Lockheed Constellation], who I got to know after a
number of years, used to make it into a regular Cook's tour. He'd tell you
about this island where Henry Morgan's treasure had been sunk. He'd give
you little travelogues as we went along . . . I'll always remember seeing lights
all of a sudden through the plane windows and I remember approaching the
island with great excitement.... I'd get off the plane and there are just
batches of people around.[10]

Helstein said of his experience in Puerto Rico: "It's very difficult, at least
for someone with my temperament.... [I]t was terribly frustrating for
me."[11] One problem was getting the right staff. He continued:

[W]e kept sending people in from the states to work . . . and none of them
were successful.... [O]ne of them was a Scotsman. He had been in the
British Army for a number of years and I later learned that he had been a
drill sergeant in India and I sent him in . . . and they're colonials anyway.
This was the last place for him but he meant well.... At any rate, they didn't

hit it off. . . . [H]e was out of sugar. That's why we sent him, he had been the director of our sugar operations on the mainland so it wasn't pure accident. We got rid of him.[12]

Once they arrived at a hotel in Puerto Rico, which he describes in detail, he comments:

Of course these hotels all had casinos in them because gambling was legal on the island. So for the first time in my life I watched the roulette wheels. I never played, I'm not that interested, plus the fact I played blackjack, and roulette. I simply had no comprehension of it at all. It doesn't mean anything to me. Yet you'd see people just sit there for night after night. . . .[13]

Helstein, once there, wanted to meet union people in different places on the island. A series of meetings were set up ending at Guanica at the southwest corner of the island where the biggest grinding mill was found.

Guanica was important to me on this occasion because that's where we were going to eat. [He was warned] that "they will serve you what they regard as a great delicacy." So I said, "Yes, what's that?" . . . I used to think I had a pretty queasy stomach and he said goat's meat. Well for days you know I was scared stiff. . . . I got there and I finally ate it and really it turned out to be very tasty. . . .

In driving to their destination to meet some union people, they started out with a Puerto Rican driver.

[T]hey're hooting their horns all the time. It's just driving me crazy. . . . I finally couldn't stand it. I asked them to let me drive and then they all wanted to get out and walk because it scared them. They said I drove too fast. . . .

Helstein recounts other instances in adapting to Puerto Rico culture. He found their beer "excellent" and the fish they had was "just out of this world."

I can't begin to convey the excitement I felt. Everything was so new, so challenging and so important. These people were such lovely people and they were being pushed around. . . . They weren't enslaved in our sense but the conditions under which they lived were really incredible. Running water was an unknown thing. . . . And we'd meet some of the guys who had been working with their machetes in the field and what it meant to work on the sugar cane in that blinding hot sun. Jesus!

He talks about driving through streets with "relatively big houses, very well kept . . . with magnificent trees . . . foliage of all kinds . . . and we finally got into town . . . to find the workers' houses. These were all little shacks upon stilts because of water problems. This . . . was a company town."[14]

He wanted to learn Spanish but never did succeed. Instead, he worked on a two-paragraph speech. He had told the union people that he intended to learn Spanish and when he could not, he confessed that "he had let them down" because he failed to keep his "assurances." That made a "great impression," apparently because they had never had a man of Helstein's stature apologize for letting them down. "I was shown the sugar refinery from the outside. Then we had a big fiesta that night in the town, and they took everything to the square of the town. They danced and played music. Oh, everything was fun and everyone was young and gay. Life was really exciting."[15]

Helstein and Rachel were invited to the union leader's house for Christmas dinner. There was a record player playing a rumba and 20 or 25 relatives dancing in a small house, and Helstein just sat there getting hungrier and hungrier. They served "traditional roast pig."[16] Helstein noted that Armando's wife never sat down or ate while he was there. After the meal, they went into town, and to Helstein's consternation, they never did do any business. Helstein noted that "everything moved very slowly."[17]

When he went there for the District Conference, Helstein then gave another example of the "kinds of problems" he faced in organizing unions in Puerto Rico:

I had the earphones and a translator so I could know what was going on. And somehow that meeting simply became impossible. People wouldn't sit in their seats, they came running up, screaming. . . . It was veritable chaos, we couldn't do anything. They're yelling and screaming and it seemed to me that the issue, whatever it was, wasn't one to cause that kind of excitement. Finally I couldn't stand it any longer and I got up and took the gavel and pounded that thing and said, "Sit down! There won't be a thing happening here until everyone is in their seats." Pretty soon a few people began sitting down and I'm still standing there pounding and pounding. One guy got up and started talking. I said, "I won't listen to anything. Sit down. After everyone is sitting down, anyone who wants to can talk." Finally, I pounded the gavel so hard the table broke. Everybody started to laugh. It was the best thing that could have happened. They sat down and everybody got quiet and I said, "Now you just can't do business this way." Somehow or other we put it together so that Armando could go on and conduct the rest of the meeting. I'll always remember that experience—breaking that table. . . .

I think that the last time I was back there must have been in '58 or '59, so I really can't say what that situation is now. It's an island of great beauty.

I don't happen to like the climate, I don't care for tropical climates, but there's something breathtaking about the mountains.[18]

. . . I can say that in broad long range terms the union did some things. It made them much more aware of what working together could accomplish. I'm not sure in long term perspective that one could make the same claim about unions in Puerto Rico that one could make in the United States.[19]

Helstein described the work of Eva Sandberg as interpreter as follows:[20]

I was having trouble finding a good translator when Eva Sandberg turned up. Her family had left Germany when Hitler came into power and moved to Argentina where she had lived from the age of four to twenty or twenty-two. Then she moved here so that she had three mother tongues practically, German, English, Spanish. . . . She was an invaluable asset. . . . So I turned to Eva and I asked her what was the mayor saying [a woman mayor of San Juan speaking to a crowd] that had them all excited and cheering. And she said she was just talking about how beautiful San Juan is; the climate in Puerto Pico is better than any other place in the world. Well, it took me quite a while before I really was able to appreciate this.

Eva Sandberg[21] described how she saw her work with Helstein:

I went with Ralph to Puerto Rico maybe three times . . . trying to organize the telephone workers . . . because I think they had already organized the sugar cane workers before I appeared on the scene. . . . I went as the interpreter. . . . We would stay there three, four, five days. This was in the late 50s, early 60s. And so we would meet with the district director there whose name was Armando. . . . and we would go around with him to meet with company representatives and to meet with union representatives and so on. And Ralph had a very hard time in Puerto Rico aside from the fact that he didn't know a word of Spanish because it's a very different culture. And he would ask a question and say this is what I would want to know, translate that. So I would translate the question and the answer would not be a direct answer. It would be something slightly beside the point or circuitous. That was a cultural thing. That's just how they operate. And so I would be caught between translating the answer and his saying, but that's not what I asked. He would get frustrated. Or he would start arguing with them and say that's not what he asked and then he would get frustrated saying you're not translating. He did understand it but he got frustrated nevertheless. And the other cultural thing that came up. . . . We would go with the district director from one place to the other. As he would go from place to place, he would take those people with him to the next meeting so that at the end of the day, there was a retinue of about twenty people with him. The idea was that when you meet with people you just don't leave them there, you say, OK you come along to the next meeting. And along the way, they always needed to stop at a bar for a little bit of Puerto Rican rum. We'd have to stop for Opre quito, a little bit. So Ralph after a while began to call for poquito a poquito because everywhere we stopped we stopped for poquito a poquito. It was a cultural thing. You have to be friendly to those people so as the day went on the meetings were running later and later because of all these little side excursions. So we started very early in the morning with a breakfast meeting and ended very late at night which doesn't bother the Puerto Ricans because they eat very late at night.

Both Helstein and his wife were astonished and delighted with the tropical beauty of Puerto Rico. At the same time, Helstein was motivated to end the poverty he witnessed and the terrible working conditions. At the time, the late 1950s and early 1960s, the country was run, like a colony, for the benefit of the plantation owners. He made repeated visits, toured the country, stayed in the remote villages, eating with union members, and observing their lives. When his initial appointment of someone to help with these problems did not work out, that person was replaced and more competent people were appointed to carry out programs of improvement, and to organize unions and educate workers so they could themselves better their conditions. One was Olivarez, who at the time was the Research Director of the planning Board. Each time he arrived Helstein would spend several hours with Olivarez, catching up on what had occurred since Helstein's last visit.

Helstein's visits to Puerto Rico give a bird's eye view of his character and personality—as intellectually alert and curious, ready to change methods if one did not work out, someone intensely human, a sense of humor, with likes and dislikes, human frailties, and his relationship with his wife, his lifelong companion, who accompanied him.

Chapter 7

Automation, the Women's Movement, and Helstein's Extra-Union Activities

Beginning in 1949, the United Packinghouse Workers of America (UPWA) became concerned with plant closings and the resulting loss of jobs. This concern and the contract changes demanded were reacted to much earlier by Helstein and the UPWA than by any other union.

The union responded to these employer moves by bargaining for severance pay based on length of service, providing 7.5 weeks credit for the first 10 years of work and 1.5 weeks of credit for each additional year. This principle was extended to job loss from technological changes and was further extended to lengthy layoffs by which workers would lose seniority under contract provisions. Technological changes also resulted in reduced employment. According to Bureau of Labor Statistics data, from 1956 to 1959, employment in the industry dropped from 191,000 to 161,000 from the closing of plants, introduction of new methods and processes, and mechanization.[1]

A guaranteed annual wage, already attained 20 years earlier with the George A. Hormel Company, provided workers greater security during this period. No one had a solution to the automation problem, including Helstein. He could only suggest that such changes could be best confronted "through collective bargaining by bringing together at the bargaining table all the interested parties—the packers, the farmers, the unions, and perhaps even the chain stores."[2]

Effects of Automation on the UPWA

Beginning in the late 1950s, the Big Four packers embarked "upon a comprehensive program of modernization and technological improvement, closing down their older, low-profit urban facilities and replacing them with a decentralized network of new, highly mechanized rural plants."[3] Membership in the UPWA increased incrementally from 39,000 in 1939 to 138,000 in 1953, but by 1962, because of plant closings, membership tumbled to 84,000.[4]

These plant closings decimated the UPWA. Packinghouses in Chicago, Omaha, Sioux City, Kansas City, Fort Worth, and Oklahoma City closed. Operations in the East were likewise gradually phased out. Between 1956 and 1964, over thirty-eight thousand packinghouse workers lost their jobs as employment dropped by 22.3 percent. Restructuring hit black workers especially hard, as African Americans were concentrated in the urban centers slated for closure. The Chicago plant closings exacted a disproportionately heavy toll, depriving the union of its most dynamic black activist base and effectively undermining the most durable source of left-wing support.[5]

Eugene Cotton discusses Helstein's thinking on the problem.[6]

Clearly Helstein thought the changes in the industry was something important, something big. I don't think he would have foreseen what eventually happened—the total decimation of the packinghouse industry, the breakup of the companies, which was not the result necessarily of technological advance, although it was a factor. It was a result of a whole new atmosphere in labor relations and I don't think there was evidence of his foreseeing that, or of anybody foreseeing that.

Maybe we're talking about two different phenomena. . . . In the 1950s, what started was the movement from the large centralized packing plants to the plants that were closer to the source of the supply. And that was a product very largely of the development of refrigerated cars. You could slaughter them close to the source and then ship the product. He did foresee the breakup of plants, and it all happened on his watch in the 1950s. What I was referring to was the breakup of the big companies. That, I don't think he foresaw, and I don't know anybody did so at that time. . . .

Technological change is not something that comes today and you're suddenly unaware of it. It sneaks up on you gradually. It has a number of different elements. For example, there may be no job loss initially, but you substitute a mechanical saw for a hand saw and there is an effort then to decrease the size of a gang working on a chain to do the same amount of work, or an effort to increase the volume of work that's expected, and so you get into an argument over rates or over job loads, because the technological improvement is used by the company as a means of trying to affect the job load. You get into arguments over whether to give a fixed rate for a particular job, and then they introduce a mechanical saw in place of a hand saw and they call this, instead of the job of merely of sawer, it's called the job of mechanical sawer, and they give it a lower rate or a higher rate, a different rate anyway, and you claim a higher rate, so the technological improvement initially really makes itself felt in job loads and rates. Then comes the point at which it starts to affect jobs so that we were very much aware of this in the job load and in the rate category, and there were constant arguments in negotiations over rates and job loads. We were aware of it then in terms of the severance pay in negotiations, manifestation of our awareness of the technological improvement as a source, more as a cause of loss of jobs. And then it became so widespread with the movement of whole plants, whole departments, or the reduction of whole departments, that that's when we got into the negotiation of some sort of compensation, some sort of negotiation about what do you do about automation internally? And we set up the automation committee. I would have to say that I don't think the committee really solved the problem of technological unemployment, but it was widely hailed as evidence of joint industry-manager, industry-labor recognition of a problem and desire to approach it.

[Helstein] was a guy who was, part of it was thoughtfulness, did very frequently try to step back [asking] where are we going, what are we doing, what's the answer or the solution, and it was a good provocative instinct, when he would sit down and think in terms of future contract demands. He would be thinking in terms of what we do with this problem and should we look ahead. So he was conscious of the need to try to visualize trends. He was a member of various special committees that were set up among elite or intellectual circles to visualize the future.[7]

"The UPWA was forced to grapple with the problems of deindustrialization twenty years before it became a widespread phenomenon, and it did so in an innovative manner.... In 1959 the union succeeded in convincing Armour ... to establish" a union-management committee, the Armour Automation Committee, to oversee these programs.

Helstein participated in a seminar "sponsored by Graduate School of Business—University of Chicago" in which he set forth the UPWA's process of collective bargaining,[8] pointing out that in the 1950s, there had been important changes "in the character" and in "competitive relationships" in the food industry, such as the development of frozen foods and TV dinners. These changes have been "reflected in the problems presented in the collective bargaining conferences." Responding to these challenges the UPWA "has expanded its ... membership [to include] sugar production and refining, canning, poultry, agriculture (factories in the field), and miscellaneous operations involving fish and dairy products among others."[9]

Helstein commented on how the union faced up to automation:[10]

Other unions weren't prepared for it. We, at least did all that was possible. We set up a retraining program, company financed moving around; we provided for system rights and minorities; we provided for a six months notice of close down; we had alternatives to separation pay; they could retire at 55 with 1 and ½ his total pension benefits as if he were 65, and so we set up many protective provisions. . . . This whole problem of plant closedown is something the country should have been wrestling with way back in the 60s. It was already clear. We issued a pamphlet called the "Triple Revolution," around 1964, and sent it to Johnson, and got no response from him, of course. It was circulated among many people. The Civil Rights movement created a situation where you had more people entering the labor market and therefore you needed more jobs, and automation changed the notion of how many jobs you could possibly make available; and the impact of these things coming at roughly the same time, and in addition the fact that these companies didn't want to make the capital investment.

We were aware that General Motors had blueprints for a plant where not a human hand touched the equipment but it would involve capital investment in the millions. It was a time during the 1960s and 70s when people were blindly going ahead, a time of highest growth, and a time when I was arguing with some of my colleagues on the Executive Council about the importance of freezing that growth at a certain level and taking that surplus to redistribute wealth so we could begin to attack the inequality.

Irv King, Cotton's partner in the Chicago law firm that represented the UPWA, spoke of Helstein:

[H]e had a vision, he had a vision which was extremely broad, a world vision. And he understood economics, he understood the meaning of what we were doing there, and the implications of it far beyond cutting meat. I think he contributed vision, and a mission, and I think that if Ralph had not been in that position I don't think that the same degree of work or attention and focus on civil rights would have been there, and I don't think that the union would have developed the progressive kinds of collective bargaining program that they did. I posed certain questions to King about how Helstein handled the automation issue:

C: How far ahead did he see the problems that came up?

I: There're two things. One is the automation. The other's the whole movement of the plant. He saw that coming. He understood the significance of it, and negotiated provisions for financing that, and that committee came up with various, contract provisions, intraplant transfer for example which nobody in the basic industries had at that time: intraplant transfer, technological adjustment pay, training programs, things of this sort.

We saw it with the development of the so-called new-breed of packers, Iowa Beef and Missouri Beef, and those that sprang up in Iowa from Maryland.

I: Well, at first it was developing new strategies and implementing strategies that had been developed right around 1961, to deal with this, but one thing that was never done, and as far as I know, it was never seriously debated, was that the union never attempted to meet the threat by reducing, what they had gained by collective bargaining. Never a wage cut, never a benefit reduction. Never any kind of concessions, so that was one strategy that I never heard debated, and I don't know if it was even considered, talk about things like that.

C: You mean it wasn't even, wasn't good or bad. It wasn't even discussed.

I: Right. And these companies grew up, Iowa Beef and the others, grew so quickly in large part because they had low-wage breaks. They had no pension plan. They had very few benefits of any kind, and one way of possibly combating that might have been to slow down at least on the growth of contract benefits and wages.

The "Automation Committee" was composed of four company representatives, two each from the UPWA and the Amalgamated, an "impartial" chairman, aided by an executive director, with a fund of $500,000 accumulated by company payments of one cent for each hundredweight of tonnage shipped. The committee was to study problems of automation and report its findings and recommendations to the company and union "for their further consideration in connection with bargaining over a new contract in August of 1961."[11]

Since the early 1940s, the UPWA had relied upon the strategy of using its solid base in the plants of the major packing companies to secure contracts which established wage patterns for the entire industry, organized or not. The plant closings destroyed this base. In the Armour chain, for instance, union membership fell from 21,410 to 9,149 seven years later. Moreover, the company sabotaged the newly agreed security measures by maintaining that many of the new packinghouses were not replacement plants but entirely new facilities with functions independent of their old operations. Management at the new plants allowed grievances to accumulate and routinely laid off active unionists who had recently exercised their transfer rights. The much-vaunted training program produced disappointing results. Skills perfected during a career in meatpacking did not readily lend themselves to other vocations; new skills in refrigeration or small appliance repair rarely parlayed into steady jobs. . . . In 1963 the UPWA withdrew from the Automation Committee, declaring that it had degenerated into a "façade of humaneness and decency" concealing "a ruthless program of mass termination of employees of long service and cynical manipulation." . . . In 1968, despite considerable internal opposition, the union—a shell of its former self—merged with its archrival, the Amalgamated Meat Cutters and Butcher Workmen in an attempt to sustain industrial unionism in the packing industry. Although a number of UPWA officials assumed positions in the AMC's newly created Packinghouse Division, the style of the Meat Cutters remained unchanged. This was a bitter pill for many former UPWA members to swallow. . . . In 1979, the Amalgamated merged with the Retail Clerks to form the United Food and Commercial Workers (UFCW). . . . However, the UFCW's retail membership dominated the organization. At the time of the merger with the Meat Cutters, packinghouse workers accounted for less than 10 percent of the union. . . . In Chicago, Wilson and Company led the exodus from the stockyards, phasing out its killing operations beginning in 1955 and shutting its facility entirely two years later. Armour followed in 1959, and Swift exited in the early 1960s.[12]

As one writer on automation wrote:

> . . . leadership recommended that its local lodges make collective bargaining demands "including advance notice, transfer rights, moving allowances, retraining at full pay, severance pay, early retirement" and equitable distribution of production gains through wage increases.[13]

In 1969, the United Electrical Workers (UE) issued the *UE Guide to Automation*, arguing that "the new technology had been paid for by the taxpayers and was being employed at the expense of citizens and workers, to increase the power and profits of private corporations . . . and that technological change was being used as a pretext for speed-up."[14]

A more detailed statement of the changes in the packing industry is found in Wilson J. Warren's 2007 book:[15]

This new Big Three [Iowa Beef Packers, part of Tyson Foods, ConAgra, and Excel (Cargill)] revolutionized meatpacking in the 1960s in three main ways: refinement of the direct-buying strategies of earlier packers, applications of advanced technology, and consolidation of cutting and packaging operations. First, like the early direct-buying packing companies, they procured animals directly independent producers.... Second, the new Big Three eliminated through advanced technology much of the skilled knife work that used to accompany the killing and cutting process, reducing labor costs tremendously. After World War II, many packers had introduced mechanical stunners, stainless-steel conveyers, power-driven overhead chains, fork-lift tractors, skinless pork sausage-making machines, vacuum packages of luncheon meats and automated packages of various processed meats and lard. Many had also introduced motor-driven knives and handsaws for making large cuts in carcasses. IBP and its followers systematized and integrated all these technologies into its operations.... Third ... the new Big Three consolidated cutting and packaging operations of fresh meat in the same plants that killed animals, resulting in the marketing of boxed beef and later, boxed pork, which dispensed with the need for branch houses.... Retailers no longer needed to lure skilled butchers to transform dressed carcasses into the precise cuts that customers wanted. By 1989, boxed beef made up 80 percent of the beef sales in the United States.

Women's Movement: Women's Advancement in the Union

Several factors reduced women's influence in the union: Women represented no more than 20% of the workforce at its height. As a result of layoffs and as technological changes proceeded in the 1960s, that percentage descended to 10 percent in the largest locals. In addition, there were divisions among women.

Black women, and most younger white women, generally favored eliminating separate male-female jobs and seniority. Older women, especially older white women, were more likely to oppose merging the seniority lists because they were afraid that high seniority men would take well-paid female jobs in departments like sliced bacon and force the older women into work that would be too physically taxing.[16]

Helstein, perhaps reacting as a lawyer, recommended that there was no hurry to implement Title VII's ban on sex discrimination. A July 1965 memo from Helstein to UPWA officers stated: "WE SUGGEST THAT ALL LOCALS MOVE VERY CAUTIOUSLY. There is absolutely no reason for wild haste. The law has no criminal provision."[17]

Perhaps, more than any other area in his union career, in regard to women workers' rights, Helstein showed his limitations. Similar to other men of his time, he believed that the man should be the prime family wage earner and therefore that a woman working was merely supplementing that wage. This belief led to a series of policy decisions, including little push on women's compared with racial issues, and the failure to develop a cohesive policy to pursue defined goals to achieve gender equality.

In 1954, commenting on a resolution ordering locals to device plans to include women in leadership roles, Helstein stated:

> [I]t seems to me that what is being sought by this resolution is an attempt to establish a policy that every local will do everything it possible [sic] do to see to it that there is participation at all levels of the local union of workers in the activities and interests of the local.[18]

Helstein, in April 1966, while assuring women that sex discrimination would not be tolerated, entered into an agreement in Waterloo that, according to Helstein, "would . . . make as few changes . . . so that the practices which you have been able to pursue in the past will be continued with a minimum of disruption." The inability of Helstein to answer criticism of the ABC job system, in one of the few times in his career as president led to growing factionalism, not only between men and women but between genders of different age groups.[19] More than problems of job classifications, women were regularly harassed for not dating men or were physically threatened and attacked. Attempts to bring their complaints to the union were rebuffed.[20]

The contest over job classifications continued and was unresolved at the time of the 1968 merger with the Amalgamated and continued in the union's successor organizations until the Ottumwa plant closed in 1973. Women unionists formed the Coalition of Labor Union Women (CLUW) in which Addie Wyatt played an important role.[21]

A large portion of the decrease in female employment and wages resulted from the changes in the industry in the 1970 and 1980s. Firms such as Illinois Beef Packers (IBP), Con Agra, and Cargill completely transformed meatpacking from largely family-owned businesses to corporate giants interested only in the bottom line.[22] These corporations "sought rural locations. . . . The traditional antipathy of rural communities to unions helped the IBP to curb the power of unions and to lower wages and benefit costs."

> In 1963, 95 percent of Midwestern packing workers were working under union contracts; by 1984, this figure had dropped to 72 percent. In 1963, 72 percent of Midwestern production workers lived in urban areas; in 1985, only 33 percent lived in urban areas. . . . Simply by moving from large

cities to the countryside and by substituting women for men as workers, packing companies could anticipate wage savings of 50 percent, with added savings in the reduction of benefits negotiated by unions.[23]

Lawsuits filed by some women showed how Helstein had miscalculated. Frustrated by union inaction on women's issues, women in Waterloo and Ottumwa, Iowa, brought a complaint before the Equal Employment Opportunities Commission (EEOC) against the UPWA and its companies under the 1964 Civil Rights Act.

The UPWA then established a national commission of female leaders that proposed a compromise accepted by all factions: the ABC system. Thus, UPWA female members "anticipated many of the demands of women workers in the 1970s and 1980s."[24]

Unionization of Women Workers

As with male workers, women organizers in Chicago recognized that packing companies used unorganized black women to replace other workers. In 1902, the Amalgamated's Chicago local welcomed them. Numbers of black women entered packing during World War I when fewer white men were available. But organization of all blacks stalled as race riots swept the nation in 1917 and 1919. After the defeat of the Amalgamated in the 1921 strike, "more black women than ever before were employed in the packinghouses."[25]

By, 1920, women represented almost 13 percent of the work force, the vast majority in unskilled work, at pay scales lower than men, even for the same work; the shortage of labor during World War I drew large numbers of married women into packing. As early as the 1930s, the Packinghouse Workers Organizing Committee (PWOC) called for equal pay for equal work, finally attained in 1956.[26]

James Weinstein divides the Women's Liberation Movement into two time periods, the first from the pre–Civil War period until the adoption of female suffrage just after the World War I and thereafter. After women obtained the right to vote, there was a quiescent period until the 1960s. The Communist Party did little with women's issues until World War II, when millions of women entered the workplace. The movement took off among women in the 1960s of the New Left whose political consciousness had been raised to the point that they revolted against male dominance in the movement. "It rapidly grew into an autonomous movement to end the systematic oppression of women in all areas of social life...."[27]

In 1940, before a certification election at Armour, the union realized that if it were to win, it would need the support of women. Resistance came from the older women, mostly Polish "who were highly paid by piece-work; the company often made racist appeals that blacks would take their jobs." But even when women began to join, there were obstacles to their becoming active. The union was a "traditionally male world." Many, especially white women, believed that men properly should and would look after their interests. Activist women faced obstacles such as men spreading rumors of their involvement with men, especially blacks. The union, to encourage women's participation, demanded equal pay for equal work, established a women's division, and held separate meetings for women. Women who did become active were usually those without family obligations, came from union backgrounds, were leftists, or had boyfriends or husbands active in the union.[28]

The PWOC's family orientation reinforced traditional female roles. The equal-pay demand won the support of many men less for what it offered women than as a protection against employers replacing male with female workers, which had become a prevalent practice during the Depression. Working-class women in Chicago had frequently taken part in union activities before the mid-1930s. Their militancy in the 1921 packing strike, when they threw rocks, bottles, and red pepper at mounted policemen while shouting "Cossacks! Cossacks!" had become lore in Back of the Yards. But the Congress of Industrial Organizations' (CIO's) conviction that recruiting the family's breadwinner was not enough, "that women needed to guide a family union culture, institutionalized the family unit in the union in a new way that both encouraged women's participation and restricted their turf."[29]

The PWOC was more successful than other unions in appealing to women because of the large representation of black women who saw the union not only as a means of economic advancement but also unique means of obtaining racial equality. Nevertheless, the CIO, and even the PWOC "expected that the male breadwinner would represent the family's interests in policy making, that in its power structure the union would replicate the social relations of the traditional family." The union was more sensitive to ethnic and racial issues than to gender.[30]

Beginning in 1953, a continuing series of national conferences called for the discussion of special problems of women. A practical policy was finally arrived at in which certain types of jobs were defined as more appropriate to men, others more appropriate to women, and a third group suitable for either gender. It was agreed that men would voluntarily refrain from exercising their superior seniority rights that might drive women out of less physically demanding jobs. On the other hand, women would not ask to attempt the more physically taxing jobs.[31]

From 1953 on, the UPWA had antidiscrimination and women's conferences together with contract meetings. But women's advancement was hamstrung by male attitudes. Even among the leadership, it was believed that women's employment was temporary. Helstein, for example, spoke in terms of a family wage. "We believe firmly in the rights of a worker to have assurances of an annual income adequate for men workers to meet his needs and that of his family."

Change of Name

In 1960, the UPWA changed its name to the "United Packinghouse, Food and Allied Workers" to reflect the "actual scope of its membership" to include "food canneries of all types, employees in edible oil manufacturing plants, employees in vegetable and fruit packing and processing plants, employees in candy manufacturing plants, employees in gelatin manufacturing, employees in frozen food plants, etc."[32]

In 1979, the Retail Clerks International Union (RCIU) merged with the Amalgamated, with a membership at the time of 1.2 million members, forming the United Food and Commercial Workers (UFCW), which includes packinghouse workers. "Its members work as grocery clerks, department store sales people, meat cutters, meat packers, registered nurses, nursing home workers, beauticians, pharmacists ... to name a few." Packinghouse workers were in the packinghouse division, which made up less than 10 percent of union membership.[33]

Helstein's Extra-Union Activities

Helstein[34] was a member of various special committees that were set up among intellectual circles to visualize the future of unions. This was partly because of his interest in basic things to start with; it was partly because whenever somebody set up one of these organizations to look at the future, they figured we ought to have a representative of labor on here, and that couldn't always be Reuther. If you looked beyond Reuther to try to find some labor leader who evidenced the intellectual capacity to be able to participate in this kind of discussion, the range was rather limited, so Helstein had a lot of groups that came to him and said, would you be on that committee?[35] He was also affiliated with a number of Jewish organizations.[36]

In May 1972, Helstein joined 21 other labor leaders to call a conference to set up an organization, "Labor for Peace," aimed to bringing the Vietnam War to an immediate end. The group recognized that the war in Vietnam lay at the "root of all of our current economic problems. Only an immediate end to the war . . . could end inflation, put the unemployed back to work, utilize resources 'now being squandered' in Vietnam to meet the needs of the cities, repair the division in the nation, and end the alienation of youth' and stop the killings in Vietnam." Labor leaders opposing the Vietnam War were opposing the stand taken by George Meany, president of the American Federation of Labor and CIO (AFL-CIO) supporting the war.[37] Other labor leaders included Patrick E. Gorman, secretary-treasurer of the Meatcutters, and Victor Reuther, former international affairs director of the United Automobile Workers (UAW).[38]

In September 1973, when Helstein was president emeritus of the "Meatcutters," he participated in a . . .

> call for a founding convention next month "for a new American socialist organization" by Michael Harrington and 45 labor leaders, university professors, writers and others. . . . The call was made by the Democratic Socialist Organizing Committee. . . . An eight page program called for educational and political efforts toward a socialist system that would "substitute the democratic rule of the people for the domination of the corporations or the commissars."[39] One aim was to set up a sort of "socialist caucus" within the Democratic Party, according to Mr. Harrington . . . the author whose 1962 book, *The Other America*, stirred President John F. Kennedy in a drive against poverty.

The Democratic Socialist Organizing Committee's (DSOC)

> 1973 organizing convention did not exactly rival the 1917 Congress of Soviets of Workers' and Soldiers' Deputies in historical significance. . . . The delegates included some highly prized luminaries from the labor movement, including . . . Ralph Helstein, emeritus president of the Amalgamated Meatcutters and Butcher Workmen and Victor Reuther, the retired former international affairs director for the UAW, Helstein and Reuther were elected as vice-chairmen of DSOC. . . .[40]

Helstein was also a member of the Citizen's Committee to Elect Abner J. Mikva as State Representative,[41] and a member of Sheriff Lohman's

Citizens Committee for Lohman for Sheriff in 1954, and in that capacity was invited to an "Anniversary Luncheon" during which a "Report to the People," was made.[42] Helstein was selected by the Clarence Darrow Commemorative Committee and the Clarence Darrow Community Center as the recipient of a Clarence Darrow Humanitarian Award "for [his] contribution to the community in the tradition of Clarence Darrow," which was presented on Friday June 29, 1962, at the Sheraton Chicago Hotel.[43]

At the time of Helstein's continued liberal stance, numbers of former liberals, many of whom were New York Jews, were beginning a turn to the political right, later to be known as neo-conservatives, including Irving Kristol, Nathan Glazer, Norman Podhoretz, and Daniel Bell.[44] But this was also a time of increased politicization in the labor movement fueled by the Vietnam War and the growing black power and women's liberation movements. In 1972, the Coalition of Black Trade Unionists (CBTU), and in 1974, the CLUW were activated.[45]

Helstein was an avid reader. His correspondence files that he ordered for the UPWA account included *Labor Disputes and Their Settlement and The Political.* For himself, he ordered *Science and the Course of History*[46] and *Economy of Monopoly.* He was a subscriber to *The New York Times.*[47]

As a well-known labor and intellectual leader, Helstein was invited to socialize with other leaders. Thus, he was invited by Marshall Fields, editor and publisher of the *Chicago Sun-Times,* to an "informal dinner in honor of Mr. and Mrs. David Riesman," author of *The Lonely Crowd* and a Columbia University professor.[48]

Helstein was also on demand as a speaker and conference participant, particularly at Jewish events, including the Institute on Judaism, Management and Labor, sponsored by the Central Conference of Rabbis (April 25, 1947); Chicago B'nai B'rith Women's Council (Cost of Living Symposium, October 11, 1947); The Jewish Center, Milwaukee (March 2, 1947); Back of the Yards Council (emergency community meeting, November 1, 1947).

Helstein was a member of various boards, including K.A.M. Temple (August 22, 1947).[49] Apparently, these meetings became burdensome; in a letter dated January 10, 1948, he wrote:

> It has been so long since I have had an opportunity to attend a meeting of the 5th Ward, IVI [Independent Voters of Illinois] Executive Board, that . . .
> I do not believe I can continue to function as a member of the Board with any sense of responsibility.[50]

He was also a member of the National Lawyers guild, a left-wing lawyer organization (the attorney general made repeated unsuccessful attempts to list the Guild as a subversive organization).[51]

The union made contributions to numerous civil and human rights organizations and politically left causes in the post-war period, including the Georgia Workers Education Service; Emergency Committee of Atomic Scientists ("This appears to be a worthwhile cause"); National Committee to Abolish the Poll Tax; Southern Conference for Human Welfare; National Consumer's League; American Federation of the Physically Handicapped; Greek War Relief; Citizens Committee on Displaced Persons; National Child Labor Commission; The "Committee of 100"; California Labor School; National Service Fund of the Disabled American Veterans; Food, Tobacco, Agricultural & Allied Workers of America; Architects, Engineers, Chemists & Technicians; United College Fund; andLabor Education Services.

Helstein was invited by the executive editor of the Knight Newspapers to meet Cecil King, Proprietor of *The London Mirror*, and was invited by Marshall Field, publisher of the *Sun-Times* to a dinner with Mr. and Mrs. Milton Friedman, an economist at the University of Chicago.[52]

Helstein was also on the board of the Rath Packing Company as that company first went into bankruptcy and then through a series of failed attempts at employee ownership.[53]

Helstein "addressed the President on behalf of the United Packinghouse Workers of America expressing grave concern over the transporting from Palestine to Hamburg, Germany of 4,400 Jewish refugees from the *S. S. Exodus 1947* by the British authorities."[54]

A letter to Professor W. Willard Wirtz of Northwestern School of Law (Cyril's law school teacher), replying to one by Wirtz, states in part:

> It is nice to feel that you have been responsible for stimulating thinking on any level, and I take particular pleasure in participating in courses of this type. As a matter of fact, I have often wondered if I wouldn't be happier teaching one of them; however, I think at the same time that, although I enjoy them at the moment, I am not sure how I would make out as a regular diet.[55]

As a member of the 1934 Minnesota Law School graduating class, Helstein was asked on January 26, 1959, to the 25th anniversary class reunion, to which he responded in part as follows: "I would be very much interested in attending . . . [and] I would do everything possible to be there."[56]

Helstein also participated in the "YE OLD FISHERMAN'S CLUB," consisting of Russell Bull, Eugene Cotton, Seymour Flanagan, Charles Fischer,

Charles Hayes, Milton Siegel, Bud Simonson, and A. T. Stephens. A memo, dated August 10, 1951, states: "The time has now arrived for all you good men to take your fishing equipment out of mothballs, and to try your luck at catching the 'one that got away' last year. 1. Reservations have been made for September 8 through 16 at Gold Pines, Ontario, Canada." The memo was signed by E. R. Fitzpatrick on District 4, Kansas City, Kansas stationery.[57]

A letter to Mrs. Ralph Helstein, dated June 14, 1956, is an acknowledgement from Murray Boat Shop, Traverse City, MI, of a week rental of a Grumman Metal canoe with paddles with delivery to Elk Rapids.[58]

Helstein also had a liking for football, as shown by an exchange of letters in November 1959 between Helstein and Bob Lewin of the *Chicago Daily News*, which illustrates the joking banter he often used:

November 27, 1959—Dear Ralph: I can't accept the four bucks because you didn't go to the game. You missed a humdinger . . . as I said, the best game I've seen. It was a thriller until the last play. Not a fumble of any consequence in the whole game. Sorry you had to miss it. Best. Sincerely, Bob Lewin.

Helstein replied November 30, 1959, writing in part:

Needless to say I cannot go along with your way of looking at the situation. It was very nice of you to send me the ticket. . . . I wish I could have used it and it was my loss that I couldn't—as well as my responsibility, which I cannot allow you to assume for me. So I am herewith returning the check and I hope that you will understand my position and use it. Kindest regards.[59]

In September 1958, Helstein, accompanied by Rachel, attended a "conference" in Vienna, Austria. Their itinerary shows them flying to London and then the same day to Vienna, where they stayed from September 19 to 25. Then they traveled to Rome, Athens, Israel (October 2 to 9), Geneva, Paris, and London, and they returned to Chicago on October 19.[60]

Hunger March in the Chicago Stockyards, 1932.
(Courtesy of the Illinois Labor History Society)

John A. Bittner announces formation of PWOC October 1938 at Engineering Building Auditorium, 205 W. Wacker, Chicago.
(Courtesy of the Illinois Labor History Society)

First national conference of the Packinghouse Workers Organizing Committee held in summer of 1939.
(Courtesy of the Illinois Labor History Society)

Ralph Helstein and Chicago's Bishop Bernard J. Sheil shake hands at 1948 Convention.
(Courtesy of the Illinois Labor History Society)

UPWA negotiating team with Armour & Co., August 1954. Jesse Prosten sits to left of Helstein.
(Courtesy of the Illinois Labor History Society)

AMCBW & UPWA negotiate with Armour Co., 1959.
(Courtesy of the Illinois Labor History Society)

Press interview Ralph Helstein in front of Wilson & Co. general office located in the Prudential Building, Chicago, during the 1959–60 strike.
(Courtesy of the Illinois Labor History Society)

Ralph Helstein and UPWA delegtes to national convention in Washington D.C. bring a tribute wreath from the UPWA Puerto Rico District to the grave of Medgar Evers in Arlington Cemetery, September 1963.
(Courtesy of the Illinois Labor History Society)

Ralph Helstein joins well-known civil rights leaders on the speakers platform during the 1964 Civil Rights Rally in Chicago's Soldiers Field to kick off Martin Luther King's Chicago Campaign. Coretta Scott King is at the microphone.
(Courtesy of the Illinois Labor History Society)

1967 Swift negotiations.
(Courtesy of the Illinois Labor History Society)

Ralph Helstein on the phone in his office, 1972.
(Courtesy of the Illinois Labor History Society)

Chapter 8

Merger with the Amalgamated, Highlander, Economic Benefits of Unionization, and the Revolt Against Helstein

Amalgamated–UPWA Merger

Helstein was always in favor of the merger of the Amalgamated with the United Packinghouse Workers of America (UPWA). Speaking to the 1956 Amalgamated convention, he observed: "In recent years, we have been able to overcome many of the disadvantages that grew out of the divisions, but what we have been able to do is nothing compared to what the future holds for us when in a united organization we move forward and together." A merger was coming to be thought to be in "the best interests of both organizations."[1] Helstein predicted that "in the not-too-distant future the many trade unions presently active in various sections of the food industry will find it essential . . . to consider the kinds of mergers that will eventually result in the establishment of a single union in the food industry as a whole."[2]

But before that merger came about the two organizations (the American Federation of Labor [AFL] and Congress of Industrial Organizations [CIO]) engaged in tortuous and frustrating negotiations. The merger of the Amalgamated and the UPWA was preceded by the merger of their parent organizations—the AFL and CIO in 1955.[3] Although the Amalgamated and the UPWA had for years been "natural" enemies, they were like two animals in the same cage, one the tiger (UPWA) and the other (AFL-CIO) seen as the domesticated cat. But those antipathies hid affinities. They both organized packinghouse workers; their disputes hindered their organizing efforts; and over the years, it became obvious to leaders of both organizations that more could be gained by cooperating against their common antagonists, the packers, than by continued mutual combat. David Brody's chapter heading, "Rival Unionism: From Warfare to Interdependence"[4] well sums up the two union's dynamic relationship during the 1950s.

At the time, merger negotiations were unthinkable because of the Amalgamated's "sell-out" in the 1948 strike, the time it took for the UPWA to recover from that disastrous strike, and unsuccessful attempts by the Amalgamated to take advantage of the weakened UPWA by raiding their locals. Nevertheless, for Herb March, always a proponent of unity, the lesson of the failed strike was that "we have got to learn a lesson." His district passed a no-raiding agreement and called for a joint national wage conference.[5] The Amalgamated also concluded that a defeat for the UPWA in the 1948 strike had deleterious effects on them. The result was that in 1949, the two unions engaged in joint negotiations, and the two union presidents issued a joint statement pledging no raiding and further cooperation.[6]

After renewed charges and counter charges in 1952 and early 1953, in June 1953, the two unions entered into a pact that they would conduct joint negotiations, would no longer enter into an agreement without the other's approval, would recognize each other's picket lines, and would end raiding.[7] In that same year, the unions signed a no raiding and mutual assistance agreement, agreed to bargain jointly when they represented different plants of the same company, and agreed not to enter into a bargaining agreement without the other's approval. In addition, they pledged to respect each other's picket lines and to exchange collective bargaining information.[8]

By 1960, technological changes in factory design, which no longer required the packers to be in river towns, allowed plants to be moved closer to the source of cattle in the southwest. Plant closings thereafter reduced slaughterhouse employment by 30,000 workers.

Changes in the political climate with Republican administrations less friendly to labor and recessions in 1949 and 1954 pushed the AFL and the CIO to merge in 1955. Moreover, while the Amalgamated was growing, in large part because of its retail acquisitions, the UPWA was in decline with 110,000 members, 5,000 fewer than in 1957.[9] In 1960, the UPWA changed its name to the United Packinghouse, Food and Allied Workers while retaining its designation, UPWA. The union extended its jurisdiction to sugar locals in the South in 1947 and thereafter to sugar locals in Puerto Rico.[10]

There had been "exploratory talks" in 1947 and 1950, and in April 1953, there was a joint meeting of their executive boards to discuss unity. A committee was appointed to further discuss the matter. But because of difficulties involved in each being part of larger rival organizations, talks did not progress. This problem was resolved by the 1955 AFL-CIO merger.[11]

What initially appeared to be agreement was snuffed out by a telegram received by the UPWA from the AFL-CIO: that in view of the "new and impossible interpretations" that the UPWA has applied to the merger agreement, "in the interests of both organizations our Executive Board and Unity Committee has [sic] postponed the special and merger conventions until some later date." On October 20, 1955, the Amalgamated Executive Board decided to withdraw from the merger negotiations.[12]

This was a clash of cultures. The concern of the UPWA was that it would be "absorbed" and that its spirit, if not its structure, would disappear into the Amalgamated colossus. Helstein later told the "special convention" called on October 24 that:

> We had said to you [the members], time and again and again and again that no matter what else happened in this merger, you could rest assured that the way we conducted negotiations . . . grievances . . . wage rate problems would continue, that our program activities would continue. . . . We expected to have an industrial department . . . that would provide our membership with the same kind of services that they have been accustomed to. We expected to have a program department . . . that would provide functions such as education, our farm-labor program, our political action program . . . discrimination . . . women's activities.

To the Amalgamated, to give in to the UPWA demands would have meant that "the entire internal structure of the Amalgamated would have been wrecked. . . ."[13] Helstein speculated as to the reason for the merger's collapse:

> I had long since discovered already that dealing with [Patrick E.] Gorman [Amalgamated's secretary-treasurer and leader] it was very difficult for me to get anywhere because he was afraid of me. He wouldn't get in any serious discussion [for] fear that he might get outmaneuvered in some way or another. . . . I have always felt that what was going on essentially was that Gorman at the last minute got to looking around that office of his, saw us coming in. He knew he'd gone through those negotiations and really worked out a deal but he'd seen the way we operated. I think he just plain got scared. . . . And it is a fact that if that merger had taken place at that time in 1956

with all of us being much younger, with our having many more ambitions, being physically healthier and with our union the size that it was, as organized and progressive, with their structure and with our know-how, if we had gone in at that time I think that within a relatively short period of time we would have taken over the union.[14]

Helstein noted that AFL officials didn't make a distinction between their "personal" well being and that of the union. These are interrelated entirely.[15] "[Gorman] talks about how we wanted to get control of their assets. They have ten million in assets. Relatively speaking for the period of time we had both been in existence, for the nature of our two operations—our assets in relation to our membership, we had a better relationship in relation to our membership than they had to theirs."[16]

But the fact that the merger had failed did not mean that the two unions did not have a continued comity of interests. The leaders of both unions assured the other that they did not intend to return to the old ways of raiding or competitive collective bargaining.

As time went on it became clear that the black members of our committee and many of the black unionists—first of all they started with real suspicions of the Amalgamated to begin with. . . . But in those days the Amalgamated may have had one Negro member of the board of nineteen and he was completely inadequate, an inarticulate guy who our union people looked at with contempt. . . .[17]

Detailed negotiations between the two unions resumed in December 1955. In hammering out a constitution, the "division of powers and functions tended to follow the Amalgamated pattern of locally autonomous operation with strong powers of supervision invested in the international executive officers."[18] The Amalgamated's president, Earl W. Jimerson, worried about the financial costs in the merger (pensions and the UPWA's costly centralized servicing of local unions), the central part played by Communists in the UPWA, and control of the organization. Although at the time, Helstein was only 47 years old, Gorman was 63 and Jimerson 67 years old.[19]

After a number of meetings and dinners participated in by the executive boards of the two organizations, the two boards sent a telegram, dated December 7, 1955, to the convention that was meeting in the armory in New York. It was signed by Earl W. Jimerson President and Patrick E. Gorman, Secretary-Treasurer for the Amalgamated Meatcutters and by Helstein and G.R. Hathaway as Secretary-Treasurer for the UPWA. The telegram read:

The unity Committee of the Amalgamated Meatcutters and Butcher Work-men and the United Packinghouse Workers of America in meeting during this historic convention unifying the American labor movement and stimu-lated by the interests of the working men and women of the nation, are happy to advise you that we have reached an accord which we are certain represents the basis for an early merger of our two organizations.

The Unity Committee agreed on a thirty-three member executive board, twelve positions going to the UPWA, and twenty-one to the Amalgamated. The numbers had no relationship to the membership but had been arrived at by making sure that it got the support of major leaders in both groups. There was a third office created that was known as the general vice president, that had been a tradition among many AFL unions. The three officers, the president, the secretary-treasurer, and the general vice president, would con-stitute the executive committee. We set up a retail, industrial, program, poultry and fur and leather division and the program division. The latter was really a carry over from the old UPWA program department that had played such an important part in connection with our anti-discrimination program. We were very concerned about keeping it alive.[20]

Helstein estimated that the UPWA had about 150,000 members, and the Amalgamated had about twice as many.[21]

At the Amalgamated convention in June 1956, the merger passed with-out a dissenting vote. A September 1956 strike against Swift by the unions acting jointly was a signal success.[22] A constitution had been drafted but one issue remained for the Joint Unity Committee, an agreed salary sched-ule so that retirement pensions could be calculated. This issue raised others more fundamental: the UPWA Unity Committee demanded that:

... the Amalgamated's education department be made part of the program department; that the Amalgamated's industrial engineering department be placed under the industrial department; that all departments be headed by vice-presidents (four in the Amalgamated were not) and that the executive officers should not direct the work of the department heads.[23]

It was apparent that the Amalgamated was the "dominant party in the merger," obtaining 21 of the 26 seats on the merged union's executive board. In the merger, Helstein became special counsel and vice president.[24]

Thus, two things were apparent from the time of the merger: (1) the Amalgamated would determine the structure and personality of the com-bined union and (2) Helstein would have a diminished role in affecting the policy of the new organization.

After the two unions united, Helstein, as "special counsel and vice president," moved into a small office where he was ignored by AFL officials, and over time, the aggressive tiger was tamed by the domesticated cat. Helstein expected this result, so although he was unhappy in his diminished role, he was consoled by his belief that the merger of the two unions was inevitable and would ultimately benefit UPWA members.

The Highlander Educational Experience

In 1949, Myles Horton, an organizer with the Highlander Folk School, was made education director of the UPWA.[25] From the beginning, problems of limited resources and lack of commitment dogged the program. Much of the time, Horton was assigned to other duties, for one period, to the Wilson boycott. From 1948 on, Highlander had been involved in various capacities in UPWA educational efforts.[26] During this period, Horton and Helstein became fast friends, and as we consider Horton's personality, formation, and interests, it is easy to see why.

Myles Horton was born in 1905 in Savannah, Tennessee. He was raised in a Presbyterian family that believed in aiding both poor blacks and whites "less fortunate than themselves" by providing food and clothing. So Horton grew up with a "concept of social service . . . to people of different social, economic, and racial backgrounds."[27]

In 1930, Horton entered graduate school in the University of Chicago's sociology department, where he learned that the educator's task was to use conflict (a la Saul Alinsky) to move people in the direction they wanted to go.[28]

Horton's "most important discovery in Chicago" was the Danish folk school movement.[29] To learn more of the movement, he spent fall 1931 traveling around Denmark. Returning to Tennessee on November 1, 1932, with some friends, he started the Highlander Folk School in Grundy County, an area of "poverty, disease and illiteracy." Industry, based on lumber and coal, had long ago disappeared. "[B]y early 1933 the three major features of Highlander's adult education program—residential courses, community programs, and extension work—had begun to emerge."[30] Horton "proposed to educate industrial and agricultural laborers to exert greater control over their jobs and to build a new society embodying the ideals of democracy, brotherhood, and justice" that "reflected his own commitments to Southern Appalachia and to fundamental social change."[31]

As early as 1933, the school involved itself in union organizing and strike activity, and in 1934, it brought in a black professor to lecture on the benefits of interracial unity in union activity, an action that resulted in threats to dynamite the school.[32] The school's faculty saw as one of its primary purposes to train "potential labor leaders; to discuss their problems, discover new ideas, and act upon what they learned."[33]

The contradiction between rank-and-file education encouraging steward initiative and the union bureaucracy was well-stated by Helstein in a 1981 interview:

> Myles' notion was if you've got an educational program, its function is to make people aware of what their problems are and to make them want to do something about them. Well, of course, that sometimes shook the vote politically for these [UPWA district] directors and they began complaining like hell. And he said, "Look it's going to get you into trouble." And I said, "That kind of trouble I can take care of. . . ." Well, what happened was, they made it harder and harder for him to work. He really wasn't able to do the things that he said he wanted to do in the union.[34]

According to Norman Dolnick[35] even before Myles Horton, Ralph had another education director, Lou Krainock, who also came out of Highlander Folk School.

> Lou was a very good education director, a brilliant speaker, very enthusiastic, brilliant storyteller, but he wouldn't stand up to Ralph. He said okay, everything's okay. That could ruin a guy, just going okay with Ralph. Once you start that thing with Ralph, he has contempt for you. Lou had good programs going, good ideas, good speaker, and it just charmed the locals he worked with. But he didn't have that quality to be strong with Ralph. . . . So Myles took over the education program, which I thought was a terrible mistake, cause you shouldn't have somebody tied down to some place in Tennessee. Somebody should travel all over the country and go where the locals are. So that was a disastrous mistake. Myles Horton had dual interests. His major interest was the Highlander Folk School and the Packinghouse Workers would just be tangential.

Highlander, during the period 1951 to 1953, was charged by Helstein with proposing a plan and implementing it. The plan was an agreement between Helstein and Horton and called for Highlander to provide five educational directors to be placed in districts that had weak educational programs. Because of the low pay and the traveling required, Horton was unable to find packinghouse workers who wanted the job, and for the most part, he had to settle on people without union experience.[36]

Les Orear, in a December 1950 memo to staff going to Monteagle, Tennessee, instructed the staff as follows:

> Highlander is a very informal place, so bring your sport or outdoor clothes and shoes. . . . Bring a flashlight and a raincoat. There are hikes to be taken on mountain trails. . . . At Highlander, staff and instructors have cooperative work each day. There will be regular crews on housekeeping. The Highlander staff is very limited and receive no salaries. Cooperative work helps keep costs down.[37]

With the limited resources at his disposal, Horton pushed stewards to train other stewards to increase shop-floor militancy. At the 1952 constitutional convention, education was promoted as a means to activate and nurture a more militant rank and file. The union's leadership seemed to strongly accept this vision of how education could be used to develop new leaders.[38]

Nevertheless, the Highlander educational program lasted only 18 months. Several factors led to Horton's resignation in March 1953: (1) The arrangement under which Horton had the joint responsibility as director of Highland and director of the UPWA education department left the program without clear direction and supervision, leading to a lack of constant communication with and among his staff. (2) Horton began the program at a time when the CIO was growing more bureaucratic and less responsive to its membership. (3) Horton was unfamiliar with the union structure and bureaucracy, yet the success of the program depended on working with that bureaucracy. In particular, there was friction with Vice President A. T. Stephens, who saw the educational program as one that would "push the programs and policies" of the union through its representatives rather than a bottoms-up approach of rank-and-file members so they could solve their own problems and run the union themselves, a course that set Horton on a collision course with the union bureaucracy represented by Stephens. (4) Horton showed an inability to effectively communicate the goals, merits, and successes of his program so as to build a broad enough base of support to withstand Stephens's attack on the program.

There came a time, therefore, when Helstein had to choose between Stephens, a respected and well-thought-of collaborator, and Horton, a temporary employee. Moreover, because union resources were limited, money given to Horton was taken away from Stephens' organizing efforts.[39] Stephens was legitimately concerned with how Horton's efforts would affect his organizing. Stephens saw the educational program as one that would push the programs and policies of the union through its representatives rather than the bottoms-up approach of Horton. The developing split between Stephens and Helstein may also have affected the decision to drop Horton.

In December, 1952, without Horton's knowledge, the executive council reorganized the Education Department so that Horton was to work with a staff member under Stephens and Vice President Lasley. When Horton realized that he would now be carrying out a "top-down" program in which the local leadership would merely be carrying out designated union policies, on March 14, 1953, he sent a letter of resignation to Helstein.

Horton and his staff's efforts to promote bottom-up activity had some significant successes. Undoubtedly, it was these successes as much as communication failures that led to problems he had with the union hierarchy.[40]

The UPWA educational program after Horton's departure "de-emphasized member participation" and reflected "the changing nature of the Industrial Labor Movement during the CIO years."[41] Summing up the evolution of the UPWA program, one author stated:

> Education in the UPWA only succeeded in achieving democratic goals when the rank and file actively participated. This occurred during the PWOC [Packinghouse Workers Organizing Committee] years up through the UPWA's turbulent years in the late 1940s and early 1950s. The militant rank and file, spurred by the radical left, accounted for many of the UPWA's early successes. Yet, as the union became more institutionalized and bureaucratized, education as a force for greater democracy was co-opted.

Helstein was personally and spiritually very close to Horton. In an interview with Eliot Wiggerton of Highlander, Helstein had occasion to set forth his philosophy of organizing workers:

> ... the crucial problem is to make people feel that they're human beings and that they've got rights. And that's really what got me involved in this—is the sense of how do you make people feel that they got a right—I just went nuts in law school many times. And by the way, this is the thing that Myles [and I] have so much in common. It's a comprehension of the fact that people not only have rights, but they've got to understand that they have rights, and you've got to educate them to understand. ... [T]he great thing about Myles ... was ... that Myles never saw people as they were, he saw people as they could be. ... Myles made them as they could be in many cases. ...

And it was not that he saw what they could be, but it was that he produced what they could be. . . . He got people to do things that they didn't think they could ever do. Like nothing further than to sit down and eat dinner with a black. . . . And by not saying nothing, just doing it. Now that was something.[42]

Helstein's choosing Horton over Lou Krainock illustrated a chink in Helstein's armor. He chose someone who appealed to him personally (Horton) over someone (Krainock) who could not stand up to him even though Krainock was more effective at his job. This choice eventually led not only to a less effective worker but also to the conflict between Horton, who eventually left that job anyway, and Stephens. Moreover, that unfortunate choice set the stage for Stephens to organize a "plot" against Helstein.

Revolt Against Helstein

Revolt came from a most unlikely source, Tony Stephens, vice president for organization.

During the early 1950s, long before "black power" appeared on the American scene, it took form in the UPWA. This development involved a mix of a Machiavellian figure, Dick Durham, hired as an aid to Tony Stephens, the influence of Communist Party members, and the creation of a "'black caucus' whose object was to place a number of black leaders in leadership roles as part of a plan either to control or to replace Helstein." When Helstein became conscious of this "plot," he quickly moved to suppress it. Stephens and others involved were forced out. An attempt by Stephens to counterattack by filing charges with the CIO claiming that the UPWA was "communist-dominated" was repulsed. Alongside these bizarre events, there was an inter-office romantic entanglement that partially fueled these maneuvers.[43]

Helstein, over the years, had developed a very close relationship with Stephens. He describes how Stephens entered the scene:

When I first came to the union in '42 one of the first assignments I had as a lawyer was to handle a representation case before the Labor Board involving Rath Packing Company in Waterloo, Iowa. . . . Well I went to Waterloo and I met Stephens there. This was still in the days of the Packinghouse Workers Organizing Committee. And Stephens then was appointed . . . as director of the district which included Iowa [Nebraska and Colorado one of the largest districts in the union].[44] He was a young big husky guy, with a real warm personality.[45] He had worked for Swift and Co. in Sioux City, Iowa back in the late '30s ... There'd been an abortive strike at that plant as a result of which he'd gotten fired. The CIO was starting this organizing drive and he was picked up ... as an organizer for PWOC. ... [46]

Again, according to Helstein, Stephens:

... had been one of the important voices in the union during the strike and immediately afterwards. He had stood for progressive causes all the way through and was a very very close ally of mine. I thought of him in many ways as a sort of protégé, able, competent, and he worked hard at the job. After the '48 strike Tony had taken over the responsibility from Frank Ellis [an old Wobblie], who at that time had been the vice president of the union, in handling the organizing campaign we were involved in when we had all those elections that we had to go through with as a result of the raiding attempts. ... And he had really given leadership to that and had been responsible in an important way for many of the results. So it was a perfectly natural thing that he at some stage had to move into the upper echelons of leadership of the union.[47]

Tony and I [Helstein] established a very close relationship which increased over the years.There was ... a difference [in age] close to ten years between us. ... And he had been exposed to a totally different life than I had. He was very temperamental as well as he had a lot of dynamism, a good deal of charisma about him. ... He had many habits that I didn't approve of and that I would have liked to have him change but then I wasn't his father, although I think in many ways I was. That may have been part of the problem. ... Well you couldn't rely completely on his stability. In a fight he was a great guy to have on your side but you couldn't always be sure how he would respond to different sorts of stimuli. ... On top of that he was very much a lady's man.[48] He got himself involved in all sorts of problems that way at home. He was married and had a daughter and two sons. ...

Richard Durham entered the picture[49] when the union tried unsuccessfully to organize a Swift Company plant in Kansas City.

Stephens asked for Durham to go down with him to write pamphlets. ... And Stephens came back talking about Durham as though he was an absolute genius.[50] ... Durham ... clearly was a student of black history and really understood the problem. He was saying things in those days [1953] that people started saying in the '60s. This was way ahead of his time and I think in many ways he gave us an early education which contributed substantially to our being open. . . . which was not true of most unions.

Les Orear suggested the organizational motivation behind some of these events: "After the 1948 strike, the racial policy called for local unions to shape up. They've got to run all this chauvinism out of there, and make sure that black people are elected as officers."[51] Part of that program was an educational staff seminar in Monteagle, Tennessee, set up by Stephens.[52]

During one of the Monteagle sessions Russ Bull [District 3 Director][53] got into a big battle over his use of the term, "boy."

Miles [Horton, director of Monteagle][54] took me [Helstein] aside and said, "Ralph, this thing is going over the brink. This is no longer a matter of integration or black rights. This has become something a lot more. Whites are being intimidated. Bull got an awful beating about the boy story. He objected that he couldn't call somebody a boy who was a friend of his. He said, if I want to go fishing with somebody, I can't say, 'Hey, boy, I'm goin' fishing'. Oh, no, you can't do that. Hell, I'm going to do it."[55] The same thing happened with Frank Brown from Kansas City when he spoke about some of his "boys." Frank is black and an older man. He referred to some of the "boys" down at the plant and they proceeded to take poor Frank apart and just gave him this whole big lecture.[56]

[A]ll of a sudden we found ourselves off on many of these civil rights issues in ways that just were wrong. We were alienating many people in the way we were doing it. There was never any question about not making issues out of any question of discrimination—that was clear. But to find it impossible to give a speech on any subject without beating people over the head about how discriminatory the whites were just became a little bit too much and that was what was going on. . . .

I [Helstein] finally said to him [Durham] at one point, "Look, let's understand one thing. We are a trade union and we operate on the principle that as a trade union we cannot survive unless all our membership are treated equally and so we are opposed to discrimination in any form. But we are not the NAACP. Our primary job is to advance the interests of our membership which we think we can do only in a community that is open, in an open society. . . ." At any rate, Durham exercised a tremendous amount of influence within the union and on many people, not just on Stephens . . . and we were constantly pushed in that direction. I was sort of dragging my feet. I had become the most conservative force in the union, insisting that our main function was trade unionism.

Well, now this background becomes important because in the context of the merger discussions . . . in '56, Tony began to go out a lot with AFL people. They all had kinds of different standards. To them it was all right to go to the most expensive restaurant in town, and use credit cards. And all of a sudden we noticed that Tony was sort of liking to live that way too. . . .

. . . We had a formal merger committee and Stephens was coming back to our committee which met regularly. A number of them began to get a little restive about this. . . . And then I can see from the correspondence, Tony ran into problems with Charlie [Hayes]. For instance, when Charlie was supposed to be appointed international representative, there was a memo sent to Tony Stephens asking for his approval, and he said forget it. That's his words, and of course Ralph apparently made the decision that Charlie should be a representative. But apparently there was some friction, and Charlie says it's because he didn't support Tony more for vice president.[57]

Out of [the] merger negotiations . . . a lot of things came. Internal friction was set off within our union. . . . [W]e were in one of these sessions and he started to talk about how he [Stephens] did this and he did that. All of a sudden Charlie Hayes just exploded. He said, "Who in the Hell ever gave you the authority to do all those things?"[58] . . . It wasn't that important an issue. It was really the fact that he was running this thing, you know. Hayes said, "You're not chairman of this committee. If anybody should be meeting with these people, Ralph ought to." Well, that breach was never healed. Not only they remained enemies but it went much further. . . . It leads up to the '58 convention where there was a brief effort to take over the union—our union . . . by Stephens, yes. . . . I discovered that the source of it had really been Stephens.[59]

In 1957, during one of the union's merger discussions, Stephens raised an objection to Lasley as vice president. Helstein did not at first oppose the person proposed by Stephens[60] because he saw Lasley as:

. . . not very adequate. He was not a very strong or aggressive person. Absolutely reliable, he'd do anything he was asked to do. [But] he had little initiative on his own. . . . Stephens indicated there was a guy by the name of Walker out of Indianapolis he thought would be a good substitute. Well I confess that I didn't find much to argue with on that score. . . .

[The union] had a practice of having a broader caucus meeting before the convention and discussing potential candidates. In this meeting the question was raised about replacing Lasley. Lasley had been spoken to and agreed to step aside for Walker. Then Stern, who was the director out of New York, said he could just sense something funny. . . . [I]t must have escaped everybody else. But Stern all of a sudden said: "Well, now that that's out of the way I move that we agree that all the other incumbents will be supported by this caucus." And at this point Stephens began to object and it developed into a first class row. I [Helstein] said, " . . . What are you objecting to?" And finally he said, "Well how do I know who else may want to run? I may want to support somebody else." I said . . . "Is there somebody else that we're talking about?"[61]

It developed that Stephens wanted to replace Charlie Hayes with a UPWA employee out of Indiana, Clayton Sayles. When I heard that I couldn't believe what I was hearing. . . . Sayles was a guy out of the Hy-Grade plant in Indianapolis. . . . He was a competent young guy, black, and he did a good job. . . . But you know he was not in Charlie Hayes's class. Few people are, as a matter of fact. Charlie was a remarkable guy, still is. . . . Well you know I began to look at this situation and began to take count and people began talking to me and telling me what was going on.

Then Charlie began telling me what this guy Oscar Brown was doing in his [Charlie's] district. He'd been carrying on an open campaign against Charlie. [Hestein said], "Tony don't overstep the boundaries. You're going awful close, now stop it. . . . You can't support Sayles to Hayes. . . ." Well he kept it up and it got worse. They went all over the country at this point and finally I'd just had it.

People had felt that he [Stephens] himself either was using the communists as his wedge or was one himself. What occurred really was that he was the communist hatchet man and was red in that sense. One of the reasons they always tied me in was because he used to go around telling people he was speaking for me and I never knew that. . . . I didn't even realize what was going on until about two weeks before the convention. I don't understand how I could have been so blind but I was.[62] And the way it came out—finally the whole thing was exposed, blown up and killed off because he was just too greedy. He didn't know when he ought to let something lie and give it time to jell. If he had he might have gotten away with it but he didn't.[63]

I called him up and I said, "Tony I want to meet with you."[64] This was just a few days before we were scheduled to go to New York [where the union had its convention]. I said, "I've had it and I want to sit down and talk to you." Well okay he said, where. He'd been trying to get me. . . . I'd been avoiding him because I didn't want to get into any more arguments with him. So I arranged to meet with him at the Quadrangle Club [at the University of Chicago] because I wanted to be away from the office. . . . Now he already had an inkling of what was up because he had a letter which he gave me in which he set forth his undying and unswerving loyalty, that he had heard that I felt that this was now a fight between him and me and that he was really trying to take over the union and that was just not true. . . . So I read the letter very carefully . . . and I put it in my pocket.[65] I said, "Tony

I want to tell you that I'm going to have a slate in New York to run for office and you're not going to be on it." He said, "What! Didn't you read the letter?" I said. "Yeah, I read your letter. It's too late, I've made the decision and that's the way it's going to be. . . ."

I don't think that meeting lasted ten minutes. It involved a lot of tension. I was so tense I was just on the edge because we'd been so close for so many years it was not an easy thing to do but I was bound and determined it was just impossible to work in that kind of setting any more. It was just awful! . . . I made the decision a few days before I actually called him. First I had to get somebody for that job and it was not easy to find someone to fill it. So he ended up on the outside looking in . . . he was not slated and withdrew and was done. . . .[66]

Thereafter, Stephens filed an undated "affidavit" with the CIO in which he recounted his work experience with the UPWA, described "the Communist Party apparatus in UPWA" [*sic*], where and how often the Communist Party meetings took place, elections of Communist Party officers, and that Party policies "were announced in connection with various pending union programs and activities." Named as Communist Party members or officials who attended these meetings were Jesse Prosten, Herb March, Sam Parks, Les O'Rear [misspelled in the text], Charles Hayes, Donald H. Smith, and others who were prominent in the UPWA leadership. Stephens recounts that "[a]fter I became Organizational Director of the International Union in July, 1948, I complained to President Helstein that Herb March, as a nationally known Communist, was 'too hot.' " [Stephens does not indicate Helstein's response.]

> In the Reuther letter dated October 30, 1953, President Helstein was advised that he was expected to "take affirmative action in dealing with the Communist influence at the local and district levels." President Helstein was expected to remove all Communists and fellow travelers from the staff of the international union and the staff of all subordinate bodies of the UPWA. . . . To my knowledge, no efforts have been made to remove any Communists or fellow travelers from office or from the staff of the International Union, or the staff or any subordinate body.[67]

It is significant that Stephens does not charge that any action of Communist Party members was detrimental to or had a detrimental effect on the union.

A Helstein Memorandum dated October 24, 1958, notified Stephens that unnamed "officers" have determined that Stephens "cannot properly or adequately discharge the responsibilities as COPE [Committee on Political Education] representative," and therefore he was

> ... directed ... to immediately turn over to Secretary-Treasurer Hathaway all of your files and records.... On Monday, October 27, 1958, you will please begin your unused vacation period.... You have been requested on several occasions to present to the officers and Board, such material as you might have supporting your charge of Communist domination and penetration. You have consistently failed to be more specific than the generalized charges you have once more engaged in....

The memorandum invited Stephens to appear before the international Executive Board to present his material at the following week's meeting.[68] In a response to this letter, Stephens wrote in part:

> [O]n the assumption that you have the authority to make decisions in this connection, even though unfounded and arbitrary ones, I take this opportunity to advise you that I will accept the vacation period which you have demanded.... In doing so, I want you to know that my action is involuntary and I deeply resent your action in preventing me from fulfilling the important assignment to which I have dedicated myself [as COPE representative] in connection with the current political campaign.... In response to the invitation ... I now advise you I am willing to appear before the International Executive Board ... to present the data pertinent to the Communist problem in our International Union under the monitorial auspices of President Meany or any representative ... whom he may designate....[69]

Apparently, in response to the Stephens charges and in preparation for an impending hearing on those charges, Russell R. Lasley sent a letter to all those who had

> submitted [m]aterials to this sub-committee [indicating] that there has been testimony to the effect that you were during certain periods before 1949 a member of the Communist Party.... In order that we may determine whether any question of possible violation of this paragraph [Paragraph 4 of the AFL-CIO Ethical Practices Code], exists in your case, we ask you, on your honor as a trade unionist, to answer the questions on the attached page

He then asked them to return the completed questionnaire to the union. The three questions asked were:

1. Are you a member of the Communist Party? 2. Have you at any time since December, 1957[70] been a member of the Communist Party? 3. If your answers to either one or both of the above questions is "No," do you now support or have you been at any time since December, 1957 a consistent supporter of, or have you actively participated in any activities of the Communist Party? If the answer is "Yes," to any part of this question, supply the occasion or occasions and the nature of the support or participation.[71]

Finally, on February 18, 1959, a letter signed by Helstein and R.R. Hathaway, secretary-treasurer, notified Stephens that "By direction of the International Executive Board you are advised that your leave of absence will be terminated as of February 22, 1959, and that on that date your employment with this union will end.... Sincerely and fraternally yours."[72]

The UPWA committee promulgated "Rules Proposed by UPWA Executive Board Sub-Committee for Handling Cases Arising Under Ethical Problems Code III Paragraph 4" Which said, "The purpose of the provision is to guarantee that the union will be free of communist or fascist influences."[73]

After a series of acrimonious communications between Stephens and Helstein, Stephens complained that the UPWA was not acting on his complaints. On February 15, 1961, the UPWA Public Review Advisory Commission produced its unanimous report by the appointed members: Professor Ronald Haughton; Rev. Martin Luther King, Jr.; Rt. Rev. Msr. John O'Grady; and Nathan P. Feinsinger, chairman, whose purpose was to investigate "charges of Communist influence within the UPWA in light of the Ethical Practices Code...."

The report stated in part:

The UPWA Executive Board appointed a special Sub-Committee to investigate the charges and to report to the Board. After listing the members of the Sub-Committee, officials of the UPWA, the Sub-Committee proposed the establishment of the Public Review Advisory Committee. This proposal was approved unanimously by the AFL-CIO Executive Council, with the understanding that the Commission "*will review any and all actions by the Executive Board of the United Packinghouse Workers of America as they relate to compliance with the Ethical Practices Codes.*" The Sub-Committee submitted its report ... to the UPWA Board which approved it and in turn submitted it to the Commission for review.... Copies of the Report were submitted to Stephens and that a hearing be held in Chicago on January 21, 1961 with notice to Stephens with opportunity to be heard. Stephens appeared at the hearing. The Commission met with the UPWA Sub-Committee, and thereafter met in executive session.

Stephens asserted that "President Ralph Helstein would not support him for reelection, and influenced the Union's General Executive Board to withdraw its support, because Stephens had suggested that Meany be asked to investigate Communist activities in their Union" (p. 3).

The Report then recounted the distribution of questionnaires to those union officials accused of communist activity, "followed by face to face interrogation. . . . The Commission concludes that the procedure followed was reasonably appropriate to resolve the basic issue. . . ." And determined "that on the basis of its examination of the materials which have been submitted . . . we are satisfied that UPWA is presently in full compliance with the requirements of the Ethical Practices Code. . . ."

Nevertheless, the Report recommended that "the UPWA Executive Board and each Local and District issue a clear and unequivocal statement re-emphasizing its determination to resist Communist attempts at infiltration and warning persons holding office or appointive positions of the penalty of removal for membership in, support of or participation in the activities of the Communist Party, and calling attention to the existence and functions of the special UPWA Sub-Committee and of this Commission" (p. 45).[74]

For all intents and purposes, this report ended this affair. But beyond the facts revealed by the foregoing documents themselves, there is an uncharacteristic anger and hard feelings exhibited by Helstein. It is obvious by the language used in the correspondence on both sides that the Stephens-Helstein affair was much more than an inter-office spat. Helstein's daughter Nina reveals the depth of Helstein's reaction to his break with Stephens, who earlier had been Helstein's protégé, "like a son to him."

My dad was so hurt by Tony,[75] when he got hurt like that, he didn't like to talk about it. He wasn't one you'd think [would react like that] because he was such an effective person and he could use his anger effectively at times. You'd think that he would be articulate about those kinds of hurts, but he just pulled into himself. . . . [He felt] [j]ust betrayed. . . . This was a big disappointment with Tony. . . . I know the kind of loyalty my father had, and what he would do for people that he loved, and it was anything. And he didn't really understand when other people didn't feel the same way. . . . Most people . . . only feel it for their children . . . but once he took someone in to himself in that way, he would do anything [for them].

Did this affair have lasting effects on the union? Not according to Eugene Cotton.[76]

Those in the national office knew about it, some surrounding circles knew about it. . . . I suspect that if you went out among a large number of locals, some of them would not even recall there was somebody by the name of Dick Durham. After Dick Durham's departure, I have no recollection of their being any festering sores of any people to whom Dick Durham had been in any sort of leadership position. . . .

There always was a group of leadership blacks who were cognizant of racism in society and who were more conscious of it and more dedicated to working on the problem than others in the union, There were, at one point or another, snippets of white backlash, a racist reaction at various places within the union. I'm thinking of the southeast area and I am sure whatever difficulties surrounded Dick Durham were related to the problem of black versus white. But I guess if the difficulties with Durham, is with Dick being a very very militant black nationalist, is my recollection of him, I don't think we had a very high level of that at any point in the union. And so Dick was a sort of isolated phenomenon in high-leveled positions in that respect.

The history of the creation of the "Advisory Committee" is useful in understanding how Helstein operated when confronted by a challenge. Les Orear[77] was asked if there [was] something special about him [Helstein] that allowed him to stand out? Things that other people couldn't do? Well, I would say that he had the ability—he had the wits; he had the understanding of when to—what to yield on and what not to. There was one episode when the UPWA . . . had [fired the District 8 director—Texas]. . . . It was over [an incident in the early 60s] where the district director was involved in organizing a picnic of some kind. . . . It was made clear that black people were not invited. And the black leadership in the district rose up in horror. . . . [T]he officers removed this director for failing to abide by UPWA constitutional principles so then that guy appeals to the CIO in Washington that this is communist domination that threw him out of the union. . . . [A]t this point Reuther was president of the CIO and Reuther called a meeting with Helstein to come and explain himself and face the possibility of expulsion from the CIO on the grounds he engaged in some arbitrary action to strip an elected officer etc. And Helstein's response there was, All right, if you think [says Helstein to Reuther] we're acting like dictators here, I'll tell you what, we'll set up a citizen's committee, a permanent commission, a tribunal so anybody can appeal for a review of our policy to determine whether it is the result of a communist conspiracy or contrary to . . . our union's policy. We agreed to that and proceeded to set up such a national committee on which among others Martin Luther King [Jr.] was a member.

What does that tell you about Helstein? It tells you he can negotiate, that he wasn't some kind of a stiff-necked ramrod; he wanted to put his policies before a board, wily that he is. It was innovative; it wasn't following somebody else's policies. . . . That was the end of it. A new director. Helstein got what he wanted.

The people he appointed were supper-competent people—at the highest level of competence. He was happy to depend on competent people.

How do we get behind these facts and explain this singular episode? For one thing, it tells you that one technique of Helstein was to raise the stakes. You want an inquiry. I'll not only examine this situation but set up a board consisting of high-profile irreproachable members who will take care of not only this problem but all such problems in the future.

Examining other lesser actors, Richard Durham and his secretary and lover, Cathy Brosnan will be helpful to dig into the background of these bizarre events.

Catherine Brosman Carey [her married name], as Catherine Brosnan, worked at the UPWA Chicago office as a secretary, 1951 to 1953, and as assistant to Tony Stephens from 1953 to 1958. She was a graduate of Rosary College [now Dominican University, River Forest, Illinois], a Catholic passionately interested in improving race relations. She was one of the few people who had a close relationship with both Stephens and Durham.[78] Because there appears to have been no interviews with either Stephens or Durham, her views of the period are useful in explaining Stephen's motivations for engaging with Durham and acting against Helstein.

Brosnan described Durham as articulate, intellectual, brainy, brilliant, compassionate but pretty hard and hot-headed. Stephens was "a man of action. . . . I don't know of any friends he had; he was sort of a man's man kind of a guy, maybe if you were in the locker room, he'd tell jokes, slap you on the back kind of thing."

Comparing Stephens' relationship with Helstein and Durham, the difference was that Durham and Stephens came together more or less as peers, but with Helstein, it was father–son or teacher–pupil.

The same sort of appeal that Tony had for Helstein in the beginning, he had for Durham in the later part of my tenure there. I think Stephens really was the kind of person who had to have some other kind of liaison and so when it diminished with Helstein, he made it with Dick. I think Stephens began to resent the sort of patronizing approach to him by Helstein. He kind of grew up and had enough of that and wanted to sort of get on with things. He'd matured. Durham took Helstein's place.

People in the union like Stephens mostly came from working class backgrounds. Stephens had a lot of rough edges still showing, whether it was language or behavior or need to display. While he was losing the relationship with Helstein, I think a lot of other things were probably falling apart for him. He basically lost his constituency over the years—his hands-on connection with ordinary rank-and-file members. . . . I think Stephens caught on to the so-called black power question because for him it was . . . something around which he could . . . get back into the middle of things.

The end product of the black power thing was to get more blacks on the joint executive board that was going to come out of the merger [with the Amalgamated]. Tony isn't black so it was a question whether it was really in Tony's interest. Tony probably wouldn't have been on that board. I think he may have overplayed his hand. I think he thought that by supporting and encouraging this black power development, that this would be possibly his new constituency, and that somebody else would have to go and not Tony. He thought Durham might support him. He could no longer rely on Helstein to do this.

Oscar Brown, Jr., who was employed at the time as program chairman of District 1 under Charlie Hayes, explains the composition and history of the Black Caucus and its relationship to the Communist Party:[79]

The whole idea was to try and unite, and increase the power base of the black workers [in the UPWA]. In 1955 . . . the union was in serious negotiations with the Meatcutters union to merge. Then the question began about the role black leadership will play in this new merged union. The butcher workers' union was right-wing. They had one or two black guys. So now, on this new merged board, there's going to be "X" number of spots. How many are black leaders going to get? . . . [T]here were more executive board members than there were jobs. So that meant that slating of the people who were entrenched would have to go in order to accommodate this integrated new board. Among those who were slated to go then, and the person who was determining a lot of these positions that the black leadership was taking, was Dick Durham. This naturally caused hostility towards him, especially when Tony Stephens who had hired him looked around and found out . . . that he was not going to be an official in the merged union. This was even making Helstein nervous, to think that this guy who was coming into the union to write leaflets, could exert that kind of influence.

Tony Stephens had a mistress, Cathie. Dick was also sleeping with Cathie. Dick was something else. She was crazy about Dick. She was hired because she was Tony's mistress, and then she started with Dick. Tony obviously didn't know this was going on. Dick was a fascinating dude.

Tony and Durham were pretty close during this thing. They were sort of political allies. Well that was largely why Tony wanted Durham. He needed a power base, and Dick was able to organize his black power base. Dick was in the program department that reached into everywhere, and whatever influence it would have, would accrue to Tony. So this was part of an empire-building thing in order to give him added power in the union. And from Durham's standpoint it was an opportunity to get into this union and to bring black leadership up out of the ranks into positions of power. So it was something that at least temporarily benefited both of them. I don't think that Stephens was just gung-ho on black advancement. No, he was gung-ho on Tony Stephen's advancement. . . .

There was a large black leadership in Chicago, in District 1. . . . There wasn't a large black membership in the union as a whole. The black faction developed after Dick Durham got in there. Before, there was no particular black faction. . . .

After Dick Durham organized the Black Caucus, he was successful in getting Charlie Hayes, for example, elected as the first black director. . . . He had the insight, to begin pulling people together. For the black membership to sit down and talk about black issues was not done until Dick came along, and that was what the Black Caucus was about. He'd say, now wait a minute. We've got all these members here and we only have this membership. And when it comes to delegations to this and a determination of what the policy is going to be in the union, even as to our employment there was no organized movement before Dick.

Dick and I were both Communists, but it was not the Communist Party that was driving this. It was Dick Durham that was more or less driving the Communist Party. . . . [A]nd after a while, we were on the outs with the Party. We got so far ahead of the Party that they concluded that I was a Negro Nationalist.

And is Tony Stephens ever fucking mad about this. This whole set-up was engineered by the Black Caucus that resulted from his hiring Dick Durham who was his man. You're captured by your own creation. Here you've created a Black Caucus, now there's going to be a merged union, now [in the UPWA] where there are 30 jobs, there's only going to be 20 jobs [in the merged union]. Which ten guys are going?

The interests of Tony Stephens and Dick Durham at that point diverged to the point that where in the new merged union Tony was not going to be on the board. Just as the bride was about to kiss the groom, the whole thing fell apart.

Once the merger fell apart, then all of those officials of the CIO union who would have lost their jobs in the merger, particularly due to the machinations of the Black Caucus, all of them are now zeroed in on Dick. We're back, we're not dead. We survived it, well? What caused our problem? This guy is the one who's been calling all over the country and organizing all this stuff and got all these black people up in arms and ready to fight for positions in the union. And oust us, if need be.

Stephens and Helstein perceived that there is a black threat that is coming from the left, then that's double jeopardy. I mean you, you know, you're not only are you, putting an influence on our union that keeps us in hot water with the CIO, but you're not trying to actually take our jobs in the spirit of progress and Negro rights, and we're not going to have any of that shit, and who's going to have the Negroes who need help join forces with us and make sure that this shit does not take place again.

Tony Stephens wanted to see black people rise in the union, but not to his job [laughter]. When Durham came into the union, there was Lasley and hardly anything else. When he left the union, Charlie Hayes was the district director here, somebody else was the district director there, and if they ever merged there was going to be black representation in it and the workers, the black workers, and the union overall, as far as from a democratic standpoint of concern, benefited as a result of Dick Durham being in there. I thought the union was the beneficiary of Dick Durham's services, including Charlie Hayes, and I don't think he was appreciated for that.

Benefits from Unionization

Union building in these [Midwest] cities accounted for much of the improvement in workers' material lives between 1930 and 1950. Before the 1930s, unionism had played only a minor role in any of these communities' histories.... By the 1950s, meatpacking workers' average hourly earnings had started to outpace those of all manufacturing workers.... [T]he improvements in workers' standards of living since the 1930s reflected the widespread unionization of the industry, particularly the UPWA and AMCBW's [Amalgamated] aggressive efforts to improve workers' economic benefits.[80]

This same study found that in later years as the industry changed and as unionization was turned back, wages in meatpacking went from leading other industries to lagging behind.[81]

In the nation as a whole the percentage of employees represented by unions in the meat packing industry has declined from 83 percent in 1963 to 71 percent in 1984.... Both meat industry segments are following the national trend which shows union membership in manufacturing dropping from 45.8 percent in 1966 to 23.2 percent in 1987. Total employment in meat packing has been decreasing steadily since the 1960s . . . as older plants have closed and newer, more efficient plants have replaced them. At the same time, the number of unions represented workers dropped from approximately 110,000 to 59,000 from 1953 to 1984. . . .The largest decrease occurred between 1979 and 1984, a reflection of the turbulent years the industry endured in the early 1980s as many of the older, unionized plants closed or were moved because they were considered to be noncompetitive.[82]

After decades of disappointing wage growth for many American workers, a new report from the Center for Economic and Policy Research (CEPR)[83] shows that unionization significantly boosts the wages of service-sector workers. The report, "Unions and Upward Mobility for Service-Sector Employees," finds that unionization raises the wages of the average service-sector worker by 10.1 percent, which translates to about $2.00 per hour. (See http://www.cepr.net/index.php/publications/reports/unions-and-upward-mobility-for-service-sector-workers.)

On average, unionization increases the likelihood that the average service-sector worker will have provided health insurance by 19 percentage points. Unionized vice sector workers were also 25 percentage points more likely to have a pension than their non-union peers. "The vast majority of jobs in this country are now in the service sector," said John Schmitt, a Senior Economist at CEPR and the author of the study. He continues:

The data show that workers in service jobs benefit as much from unionization as workers in manufacturing do. . . . The impact of unions on service-sector employees in low-wage occupations was even more substantial. For workers in the 15 lowest-paying occupations, unionization raised wages by 15.5 percent. The likelihood of having health insurance increased by about 26 percentage points and the likelihood of having an employer-sponsored pension increased by about 23 percentage points. . . . Unions give the biggest boost to workers in low-paying occupations because these are the workers that have the least bargaining power in the labor market. . . . Unionization can turn what would otherwise be low-paying jobs with no benefits into middle-class jobs.

Over the period covered in the report, 13.3 percent of service-sector workers were either members of a union or covered by a union contract at their workplace. The report analyzed data on workers from the Census Bureau's Current Population Survey (CPS) for the year 2004 through 2007.

Chapter 9

Retirement, Summing Up, Helstein's Death and Memorial, and Post-UPWA History

A letter of November 30, 1972, signed by Joseph Belsky and Patrick E. Gorman, secretary-treasurer of the Amalgamated Meatcutters, notified the membership that "Ralph Helstein, Special Counsel for our International Union, is retiring from his official duties with the organization." They then went on to add certain complimentary remarks about Helstein's contribution to the two unions, including "being one of the architects of molding two great unions in the meat packing industry into one." The letter also mentioned the creation of the Helstein Fund.[1]

The announcement from the Illinois Labor History Society stated in part:

> In consideration of the distinguished career of Mr. Ralph Helstein as President of the United Packinghouse, Food and Allied Workers of America from 1946 to 1968,[2] and as Vice-President and Special Counsel of the Amalgamated Meat Cutters and Butcher Workmen of North America from 1968 to 1972, and now President emeritus of the Amalgamated Meat Cutters, the Illinois Labor History Society announces the formation of the Ralph Helstein Fund for Education in Labor History.[3] ... The Illinois Labor History Society believes that the establishment of a Fund with these purposes in the name of Ralph Helstein is most appropriate in view of his long and active career as a practitioner of labor leadership, as a student of labor philosophy, and as a maker of labor history.

Summing Up

Only one other labor leader of the time can be compared to Helstein, Walter Reuther of the United Auto Workers (UAW). But by the late 1950s, Walter Reuther's options as a unionist and politician had been dramatically reduced within both the collective bargaining system and his domestic policies. Reuther, throughout his career, remained a whirlwind of activity and a fount of proposals, ideas, and initiatives. Yet as time wore on, Reuther no longer commanded a political instrument that could make its full weight felt or feared at either the bargaining table or the ballot box. Manipulation of his own constituency had for so long taken the place of mobilization that a kind of institutionalized hypocrisy became second nature. As his friend Joe Rauh put it, "Walter was lost in some fantasy that life depended on his being more virtuous than anyone else." Indeed, there was a larger hypocrisy at work, one that reflected the crisis of American liberalism itself. Harvey Swados reflected at the time: "One cannot complain, as one might with almost any other union, of an absence of intellect, or of a lack of application of that intellect to the problems of our age. What one can say, I think with justification, is that the UAW leadership no longer takes its own demands seriously."[4]

Such a diagnosis could never be said either of Helstein or of the union he led. During his entire tenure as president of the United Packinghouse Workers of America (UPWA), Helstein continued to apply his "intellect to the problems of our age," and both Helstein and the union's leadership always took "its own demands seriously."

Les Orear, who knew Helstein as a long-time unionist and a fellow worker and who was a talented observer, journalist, and historian, observed:[5]

How does he compare—intellectually, educated, subtle. He would see the big picture. I would say that . . . he could see consequences; he could see all the connections, all the possibilities what could play out. . . .

His personality—accessible, easy, he was not a person who would tell you to get all kinds of permissions to speak to him; he was the kind of person who would answer a telephone call from some guy in Dubuque, Iowa who would want him to settle a bet. . . . He might have said, for Christ's sake, afterwards. I think he liked to talk to these folks. I really can't overstate things because I really don't know but he did talk to them in an engaging way. He did not make any enemies by snubbing anybody. He could phrase things in a way that was accurate, might be unpleasant but did not have barbs, rough sandpaper over it—to make it easy and understood rather than by command—to make you agree with him.

During conventions, you'd find him, not standing up at the [cocktail] bar, seated someplace. [A]nybody could come by and say, Hi, Ralph. He told me that the answer to the objection that they shouldn't elect as international president somebody who didn't come out of the industry [was that] everybody knew I planned to visit, visit, visit, see, see, see with my own eyes processes so that I would know and they appreciated that. And he did; he went around on the ground to Omaha and all these places and went through the visitor's route—he got to know people by their names.

I think the heritage of the UPWA is still an unknown quantity, unremembered. It's the union that was not a part of national CIO [Congress of Industrial Organizations] policy, politics, I should say. It was not a union that the eastern newspaper correspondents—they wrote about the UAW and these other big manufacturing unions—why pay attention to this outfit in Chicago? We were overlooked, unknown; we're just doing these things on our own pretty much. . . . Helstein, as a lawyer, could have done other things and made money. Why do you think he gave his life to the UPWA? Well, it's an instrument that he could mold. He could affect the lives of 100,000 people.[6] That's more than you can do in a place where you can make a lot of money. I never asked him, what is your motivation, Ralph? All I can say is . . . so did [Eugene] Cotton could have been in a bigger field. This was a certain period. . . . This was a certain period when situations were in flux. You can make moves that move thousands. This influence that we had on civil rights was fantastic, enormous. . . . We were in a spot where we could help, shape the direction. It was exciting, indeed yes. Always, there was conflict. . . .

The district directors, the people in charge in the field, were members of the board of directors of the international union, delegates of their district. Helstein would exercise his leadership over local leadership absolutely by power of persuasion convincing people that this was a useful policy. What do you think is a useful policy here? Here's the pros, the cons, here are the forces working in this equation shall we come down. This is democratic not only in spirit. We would all go to the restaurant for lunch and we'd be sitting around the same table as Helstein. . . .[7] Helstein was a telephone operator. He did a great deal of his work by telephone. He did a lot of dictating letters and reading mail.[8]

In a *Chicago Tribune* obituary of Helstein, Orear was quoted as follows:

He was an innovator in collective bargaining. . . . He set elimination of male-female and geographical wage differentials as one of the union's first priorities.

During the 1950's he was one of the first—with the union members facing wide-spread plant closures—to encourage inter-plant transfers, job retraining at company expense and comprehensive severance pay schedules.

The obituary also noted that "Helstein's union was the first to give financial support to the efforts of Dr. Martin Luther King, Jr. He was one of the few vocal critics of the demotion in 1954 of Chicago Housing

Authority Executive Secretary Elizabeth Wood because she pushed for integration of public housing in Chicago."[9]

Helstein's Death

An article in *The New York Times* dated February 14, 1985,[10] wrote that "Ralph Helstein, former president of the United Packinghouse Workers of America who was a longtime labor union leader, died today after suffering a heart attack at his home here [Chicago]. He was 76 years old." After recounting his career and the various mergers of the American Federation of Labor (AFL) and Congress of Industrial Organizations (CIO) and the union with the Meatcutters and the Packinghouse Union's organizational changes, the newspaper noted that "[t]he union's choice of a lawyer as its chief executive was regarded by *Business Week* at the time as 'precedent-making.' " Robert Gibson, president of the Illinois AFL-CIO, remarked that "Ralph was a great intellectual in the labor movement. He spent his whole lifetime working on behalf of the poor and underprivileged in our society."

Mr. Helstein's support for the civil rights views espoused by the Rev. Dr. Martin Luther King, Jr. was recalled by Representative Charles A. Hayes, Democrat of Illinois. "Helstein was one of the few trade union leaders who participated in marches with King in the South and in Chicago," Mr. Hayes said.

In summing up Michael Harrington's [Mr. Socialism's] life, his biographer said something that is equally applicable to Helstein:[11]

> In the years since Michael's death, no claimant has emerged to pick up the mantle of Debs and Thomas and Harrington. Michael seems to represent the end of the line. Like his predecessors, he believed that to awaken the conscience or change the consciousness of a nation, one had to be prepared to build an organization, start a publication, speak in a thousand halls to crowds of hundreds, or scores, or tens, if necessary, recruiting one's followers from those converted by the sound of one's voice and the strength of one's arguments. An honorable, even heroic, vision, it was also, as Michael reluctantly conceded in the last years of his life, one for which there remained precious little room in American political culture.

Memorial Service

The memorial service for Helstein was held on March 24, 1985, at the KAM Isaiah Israel Temple, a reform temple in the Hyde Park section of Chicago where Helstein and his family lived and occasionally worshipped. A large number of people came to pay their respects; among them were his daughters, Nina and Toni; Eugene Cotton, the UPWA's attorney and a personal friend; Msgr. John J. Egan, Office of Human Relations & Ecumenism, Archdiocese of Chicago; Myles Horton, director of the Highlander Center, New Market, Tennessee; Michael Harrington, author; Charles Hayes, Studs Terkel, and Mayor Harold Washington.

A statement prepared for the occasion gave a short statement of Helstein's professional life and accomplishments. It stated in part:

Since September, 1972, Helstein had been President of the Industrial Areas Foundation; a member of the following boards: Citizens Board of the University of Chicago; the Chicago Institute of Psychoanalysis; Illinois Family Planning Council; and the Board of Trustees of the Martin Luther King, Jr. Center for Social Change. He is author of the chapter on collective bargaining in the meat packing industry in "The Structure of Collective Bargaining" (University of Chicago Graduate School of Business Administration) [cited elsewhere]; he is also one of the initiators of the concept of the "Triple Revolution."

Nina Helstein, Ralph Helstein's daughter, in her presentation, recounted an anecdote involving her sister, Toni. At the time, in the mid-1960s, Toni was a student at Sarah Lawrence College in Bronxville, New York, populated by "some very proper and very well-to-do people." Toni and some other students organized in support of a local of hospital workers out on strike. As a leader of the march, Toni was approached by "a well-dressed and very proper woman" who angrily said to her, "Young woman, your father would be ashamed to see you now." Toni replied, "Madam, you don't know my father."[12]

Nina continued:

We're here today because we did know my father. . . . Dad's wisdom and his strength were fueled by his unrelenting hold on the reasons of his heart. As he paid attention to our hearts and to our minds, so did we. In a very real sense for my sister and me, for people of our generation . . . Dad was a great teacher. But perhaps most important of all was his enthusiasm, for life and for us. Not only did we know him but he knew us.

Eugene Cotton, UPWA general counsel and personal friend, provided his personal experiences with Helstein:

I am going to talk about the facts and the details of twenty-five years of achievement by Ralph Helstein. . . . His greatness lay in his attention, his willingness to pay attention to the nitty-gritty of daily life in the packinghouses at the same time as he was able to relate facts to the vision and the foresight which characterized his social outlook. . . . Sam Sponseller, chairman of the Packinghouse Organizing Committee . . . brought Ralph down as his general counsel during that year in 1942 . . . and that began a remarkable . . . career of contributions to labor history and to the status of working people in the packing industry, that I think is probably unmatched in any other industry.

Ralph came into an industry when he started as general counsel, an industry which many of you may remember was the then current product of the conditions which Upton Sinclair described some decades earlier in his novel, *The Jungle.* He came into an industry which the organization that existed in the major packers . . . had gone through devastating strikes which had left a shattered industry as far as organized collective bargaining was concerned; he came into an industry in which the base labor rates were roughly 70 cents per hour, no pensions, no medical or any other kind of insurance, no paid holidays, a six day work week without any overtime, without any premium pay for Saturdays, vacations in which only after 10 years did one achieve a two week vacation level. He left that industry in 1968 when his union merged into the Amalgamated Meatcutters as an industry which had a pension program equal to that of any major industry in the country, it had a medical and surgical program the equal of any industry in the country and better in many respects than most; it had paid holidays; it had a five-day work week; it had vacations that ran up to four and five and even six weeks of entitlement after certain numbers of years of service. He left the industry with a major turnover in the direct working conditions of the people working in the industry.

The best kinds of achievements, which is one basic measure of what a labor leader has achieved for the people he represents, is only the beginning point of Ralph's impact on the industry and the contribution to those same working people. You've heard the song, "Bread and Roses," and Ralph understood the importance of roses as well as bread. He understood something else; it was not merely the rhetoric of roses; it was not merely the symbolism of the rose, it was not merely words although he came into the industry and remained a man who had never wielded a knife on the chain; he was part of the people he worked with; he was not an intellectual who was in on a do-good basis trying to help others; he was a fellow worker who embedded himself into the heart and fiber of what the life of the people in the plant meant. He familiarized himself to the point of feeling of job load, the meaning of the number of people assigned to a gang to a moving chain; he understood the importance of rest in the work schedule; he understood the importance of mealtime.[13] These are the things that constitute the detailed work, the hard negotiating work, the grievance work that mark a leader who identifies himself with the lives of those with whom he is working in the union. That was a second measure of true leadership because he was a man who could bring to his job the intellect and the background and the training of the lawyer, the intellect and the training of a college degree, but at the same time could merge them into an understanding of the details of life, could sweat the details, sweat the specific items that require things in order to achieve things and not just rely on making speeches about things.

He combined that with yet another quality, a broader measure of greatness in labor union leadership, the capacity to analyze and understand and foresee the trends of the industry and the needs of the future as well as the needs of the present. We've been going in recent years through an era of plant closings, plant removals, technological advances, moving people out of jobs. Those were matters of conjecture, matters of uncertainty, matters with which labor leaders didn't fully comprehend, with which they didn't deal knowledgably and understandably until the impact of them was already upon them. This is way back in the late 40s that Ralph started to address the attention of his fellow members and of the leaders in his own industry of transposing and while other industries have done what he did, namely to negotiate substantial separation allowances to take care of the impact of those effects when they occurred, Ralph was among the first to put into labor contracts in the industry requirement of advanced notice of intention to close a plant to the point that when he left the industry no plant covered by any of the master agreements in the industry could be closed without six months advanced notice to the union and the workers to the fact that closing was imminent, something very few unions have even to the present day and something which a legislative suggestion, not even acted upon in most instances throughout the industry today. It is not just separation allowances and notices of closing that marks his vision; he brought into his negotiations a concept of job preservation; he formulated and negotiated in the industry the concept of interplant transfers, that is, an obligation on the part of the major packing companies, to offer employment in other plants in other parts of the country when plants close and to preserve seniority rights and to preserve pension rights in the making of that transfer. The packinghouse contracts introduced these contracts very early on, we're talking about the early 1950s, and middle 1950s, a contract that was coming to deal with the older workers faced with a plant closing, and with a phrase that has become very common in the labor movement, too young to die and yet too old to find employment anywhere else. And so in the packing industry the union developed the concept of an extra and enlarged pension for the older worker payable immediately upon the plant closing and payable at higher rates until social security came available so that it is an industry until this day the extra pay payable to the 50-year old worker with twenty years of service and payable until he reaches 62, something not common in the industry today and something that was negotiated fifteen years ago by a leadership with vision and with an effort to foresee trends and to deal with these trends before the catastrophe struck.

Again, the measure of what he did in those respects for the workers in the packing industry is a measure of leadership in terms of accomplishment for those he represented. But his leadership went beyond that. He instilled into the Packinghouse Workers Union a depth of intellectual understanding of their plight that I think is unique in the labor movement in the history of as far as I have been aware of. He came into an industry which was characterized by geographic differentials in wage rates, higher rates in the North, lower in the South, higher in certain cities, lower in others. In step by step negotiations, the contracts in the packing industry moved toward the elimination of geographical differentials by insisting on higher increases for the southern plants than for the northern plants, an extra nickel, an extra 2 cents, an extra dime to gradually bring them up to the level of the entire industry and achieve uniformity in the industry.

He came into an industry characterized by sex differentials. There was a male rate and a female rate. There were male jobs and female jobs and the female jobs started at a lower rate of pay. Step by step the male-female differentials and starting long before the Civil Rights Act of 1964, starting back in the 50s and finished by the time he concluded his career in the packing industry with equality of male and female rights. And if you stop to realize what that meant that the total wage package had to be divided in which the northern workers had to be willing to accept a somewhat lesser share of the increase in order to bring up their fellow workers in the South. The male workers in the industry had to be willing to accept a lesser rate of increase in order to bring the female rate up to the male rates. It required an understanding and acceptance of the basic concept of trade unionism of brotherhood and sisterhood and the realization of their self-interest as well as their ... [interest] in achievement of equality. And the most important aspect of that same understanding in the field of race relations.

From the very start, by the time I arrived on the scene as general counsel, in 1948, it was a conscious policy of the union, a requirement of the union that no contract be signed without the inclusion of a clause that stated that they'll be no discrimination by reason of race, sex, nationality, religion, both as to current employees and as to applicants for employment, And no contract was ever signed by Ralph unless it had that clause and this was in 1948 and this was something that existed before the strength of the civil rights movement developed, before it became fashionable to stand for this. For Ralph, this was not merely words. There were confrontations that he had to confront, local unions in the South, in Texas where the unions were insisting that segregated locker rooms be abolished as a violation of that clause of that contract. And there were local unions that rebelled and locals that withdrew from the union in protest, and the union was prepared to take that too, and to insist that any local union which would not recognize that that was a basic precept of this organization just didn't belong in the Packinghouse Workers and they could depart.

This dedication to the equality of unity, regardless of race was so deeply embedded in this union that it too became unique in that respect in a whole variety of ways where dedication to equality and to elimination of discrimination was merely a token phrase or the occasion for a token . . . in leadership. This was a union [where] on the executive board of some 12 or 13 there was a vice-president Russ Lasley, the director of the Chicago district, was a black that has gone on to greater and greater things, Charlie Hayes, our congressman. The district director for the California district, Tony Morrison was a black; the district director of the New England region, Don Smith, was black, and perhaps the most amazing of all, the district director of the southwest, embodying Texas, Arizona, Arkansas, Louisiana, George Thomas was black. And these were blacks elevated to leadership by an atmosphere in a union that recognized merit and fought actively against the impact of race discrimination in its own ranks.

It was a union which required every local union to have an anti-discrimination committee, to seek out problems within the local and to remedy them and to enlarge its activities into the community. And this was an organization which contributed to Martin Luther King's activities and campaigns far before he became a national figure when he first appeared on the scene and when he was first becoming recognized as a militant leader of the fight against racial discrimination in this country. So that this is a union that became imbued with far more than the need for self-advancement, the need for amelioration of their own conditions, but which would look to the community and look to the needs of the country at large.

I had occasion in preparation for my comments tonight to reread a number of Ralph's state of the union speeches, at the Packinghouse Conventions. He took those speeches very very seriously. He prepared for days and weeks in advance.[14] It was a measure of the respect that he accorded to his membership that he felt he owed it to them to give of the best of himself in his presentation of the state of the organization and state of the world. And they are models of detailed analysis; they are models of precision of thought and they are models of appeals to the best in his membership to bring out the same kind of morals, integrity and vision that he embodied in his own thinking. And it was in those speeches that he articulated one other aspect of his dedication to the principles of this country and the principles of the trade union movement which he managed to weave into the very fiber of the organization; his dedication to the principle of civil liberties, freedom of speech. This was one the few if not the only major union in the establishment organizations, those who remained in the respectable order of the labor movement, that never adopted loyalty tests, never adopted oaths of a political character as a condition of continued membership or as a condition of leadership, and Ralph's speeches are imbued with his reiteration of the values inherent in the First Amendment; his reiteration of the strengths and integrity of the founding fathers who used democracy as a forum for open discussion in which the values of democracy can stand up to and win victory over other ideologies by the force of their own intellectual strength and didn't have to rely on repression. In speech after speech in the 1950, 1952 convention, 1954 convention, 1956 convention it took on McCarthyism head on at a time when this was not a fashionable or safe thing to do. And he bemoaned the fact that it became a test of your patriotism that your own dedication to the principles of the founding fathers and to the principles of the constitution became in and of itself something that had to be defended against charges of lack of patriotism. He proclaimed himself a conservative in that respect and stated it in those terms to his membership, a conservative who wanted to conserve the traditions of this country, conserve the principles of the founding fathers, and conserve all of the values for which this nation stood. And the union held fast to that and he held fast to that. And in those same speeches he directed their vision not merely beyond their union and not only beyond their own individual well-being and to these higher principles but to the world at large. In one of his speeches he devoted the better part of the speech to reminding his audience, an audience of rank and file working people delegates of the various local unions that they lived in a nation in which he emphasized six facts—I couldn't simply take excerpts and read them here because they hold together as a whole with such adhesion that taking it apart is impossible because it holds together as a whole but he reminds us that most of the world lives not in the so-called Western World but in Asia and Africa. He reminded his audience that most of the world was non-white; the reminded his audience that most of the world was poor; most of the world was ill-fed, most of the world was sick and most of the world was illiterate, and he reminded them that whatever affluence they might achieve in this country, this nation could not continue to exist surrounded by a world of poor, ill-fed, illiterate people in safety.

And he brought the union up to that at a time when he was pointing to the problems that were then developing at the 1954 convention; he reminded them of the problems in Vietnam, and he was pointing then to a problem which it took this nation unfortunately a long, long time to realize and to come around to his point of view and to his level of understanding.

He had his union, his membership with him because he brought them with him. He didn't talk down to them. He was part of them and they appreciated it. Finally, because it was only logical that he would carry this kind of vision and understanding, and of dedication into his own relationships outside the organization—others will deal with that, to his personal relationship to the activities of Martin Luther King in its earlier stage, long before it was fashionable for people to claim a relationship to an already acknowledged leader, his personal relationship with Saul Alinsky, the social activist of the Industrial Areas Foundation. He was a much sought after speaker in the academic and in the social service world because he could unlike any other labor leader that I'm aware of articulate the needs and aspirations of the working people because he lived and worked amidst them and because he had the capacity born of special training. I tried to give some sort to what his place may be in history had he been in the leadership of a much larger union, a union with more direct impact on the labor movement by sheer numbers, there would be no doubt that he would be among the very best. He was a leader of a smaller union in the time period—four years of Reagan, very much of the tangible accomplishments of his period of leadership, has been gutted. The industry is characterized by corporate manipulations, plant closings, which have wiped out contracts in many plants, which have reduced benefits in many plants back to those of years ago, which have created plants in which there are no pensions back to the 40s, in which there are very meager if any insurance programs, plants that are brought back to where he started. But there are many plants still today, which the union developed in negotiations, still remain effective. They are there as an inspiration to the ones who are suffering under the deprivations of being back where they were. Ralph would have been among the first, I'm sure, to say that if we have to do it all over again we'll do it. He would have been among the very first to say that we start from a slightly higher understanding now because we have the seeds planted out there. There are packinghouse workers out there who will not forget that they once had an excellent pension plan, that they once had all these benefits from these negotiations; they will not forget the seeds that he planted of dedication to the basic principles of the labor movement, dedication to the basic principles of our country; from that point of view, I guess it's something like the old labor song about Joe Hill that he may be gone in person but the part that cannot be killed is the will to organize. And one thing, my own understanding of what Ralph stood for, is a certainty that if and when the labor movement and the nation regain an appreciation of the kind of moral integrity, the kind of social values that Ralph stood for, the nation will again be better for it and the labor movement will be better for it. And those of us who worked with him, had a rare privilege that comes to few people and for that I can only say thanks.

Congressman Hayes said at the memorial service:

To Rachel, to Nina and to Tonie, Ralph's contribution is to the whole collective bargaining arena throughout the years. Ralph was a man, a total man, one who made contributions to the lives of workers. I met Ralph in 1943. . . . We elected him president in Canada to run our national union. . . . He blazed many trails as president of the United Packinghouse Workers. Of course, leaders are only as strong as their followers. You have to be in a position where you can convince your membership of the direction you're going and that the direction is right and it's a benefit to them. Ralph was a master in doing that. . . . I can recall having set up a convention where members of the Klan were delegates to the Convention; they displayed the Confederate flag at the Convention. I remember going into the hither lands of Louisiana into the sugar industry where the director of the union was a member of the Klan; where the staff representative who we road with to explain to the leadership what our program was with respect to the end of discrimination. The blacks who were members of our union had to stand in the rain out from under the canopy if it was raining in order to collect their paycheck. This we had to end because of the policies of our union under Ralph's leadership . . . . I can recall that Ralph was one of the few white labor leaders who marched between Selma, Alabama and Montgomery, Alabama, I recall Ralph having marched here in Chicago at a time when they were spitting on you on the Southwest side of Chicago. . . . I don't want to paint a picture that Ralph did all these things by himself. There were others on the Executive Council who felt like he did. I can remember that I worked closely with Walter Reuther and other people on these kind of programs. God only knows some of the things we had to do to trail blaze by people like Ralph and others. We need more Ralphs. He was a legend in his time.

Studs Turkel's remarks included:

I sense in all the eulogies one common denominator and that was that Ralph obviously had a vision and that's a rare attribute these days especially now with the labor landscape being so bleak. He had vision of a society in which it would be easier for people to behave decently to one another. And he knew that that couldn't be unless people all had the basic necessities of life. But something else he recognized, and very few in labor today recognize, and it is such contrast to say to someone who would be a cold war cookie for the joint executive committee on Central America. Ralph would never dream of something like that because the vision he had was beyond that; it was beyond wages and hours; it was beyond sweat shops; it was beyond pork chops; I know that pork chops is not the most appropriate word in the temple this afternoon. But nonetheless his was not the usual labor state's approach.

So when it came to preparing for the book, *Working*, I called on the obvious labor leader, the only one I could think of calling upon, Ralph, of course, there was no contest. And of course, he came though and wrote the introduction and I read verbatim; I'm quoting Ralph, and I asked about work, what it's all about down through the history of the human race. Of course, Ralph also carried on his hip poetry and literature, and music, as well as basic economics, and this is a quote of Ralph in the book, "Learning is work, caring for children is work; community action is work." Once we accept the concept of work as something meaningful, not just as a source of a buck, not to worry about finding enough jobs; there's no excuse for mules anymore; society doesn't need them; there's no question about our ability to feed and clothe and house everybody; the problem is going to come in finding enough ways for man to keep occupied so that he can keep in touch with reality. I think that was Ralph's idea, that his ideal was also the only way to achieve the reality, that is, if we're all to be full human beings. Our imagination, and here's the part, our imagination has obviously not yet been fully challenged. He's aware then of the possibility in human beings, all human beings, of course, and so at this very moment, when finality seem to be in the saddle, when a kind of incredible shallowness is in the saddle, Ralph was speaking of those possibilities not yet tapped, and that's why he was so interested in perhaps the most exciting educational institution in this country, the Highlander School in Tennessee. He was one of the founding members of that a nonpareil among educators, and Myles Horton. And Myles knew Ralph very well; they worked together, and so Myles sent Rachel a message, and I'll just read a portion of it. It [the Highlander School] was originally burned out by the Klan and then reformed. Incidentally, Highlander has had several Klan members attend the school and they graduated; indeed they were transformed by the school, and I remember Ralph told this story once of this Klansman playing cards one day and he was playing cards with a black guy, and the black guy blew him at poker; he bluffed and he beat him; the Klan consists of pretty stupid people, doesn't it? And he switched.

Ralph has a passionate moral like Myles Horton. Ralph had a passionate moral and intellectual commitment to justice and the democratic ideal and tested the truth of his beliefs in practice. He not only simply championed the packinghouse workers struggle for decent wages and working conditions and non-discriminatory practices but also their right to self-government and again came that Helstein idea calling upon the capacity not yet tapped of people, self-government. He resisted the threats of the national CIO officials during those witch hunt days to dismember the Packinghouse Workers

Union—the communists were not constitutionally prohibited from holding office. He was the most principled labor leader I know and then, of course, he led his union into the alliance with the emerging civil rights movement much earlier than most union officials. . . . He marched with Martin Luther King and supported Highlander when we were under fire. I think that's the key. He was never a la mode. He was always there when it really counted, when the allies were few. And perhaps the best way to end this tribute to Ralph is to quote a poem. Here's a labor leader carrying a poem on his hip and it's Pablo Neruda. I'm thinking of whether or not labor leaders I can think of know Pablo Neruda that Ralph liked.

I must speak to the dead now; as if they were here brothers;

It will go on; our fight will go on in the land, in the factories, on the farms,

In the streets, the fight will go on;

And then out of the silence, your voices will rise and the mighty shout of freedom

When the hopes of the people flames and the hymns of joy!

Myles Horton, director of the Highlander Center and formerly education director of the union said in part: Helstein "was the most principled labor leader I know. He led his union into an alliance with the emerging Civil Rights Movement. Much earlier than most union officials he marched with Martin Luther King. He supported Highlander when we were under fire. Those of us who loved Ralph will miss his provocative arguments and intellectual clarity, and sense of honor. He was a joy to be with."

The service concluded with the kaddish, the Jewish prayer for the dead.

Post-UPWA History

When after 1975, when Helstein disappeared from the scene, dramatic changes in industrial and labor relations had already taken place and would continue in the same direction. By the 1980s, these reactionary forces were such that even had Helstein been on the scene he and his union could have done little to stem the tide. The bottom line became the dominating value wherein workers were the base of that bottom line, and their welfare of little consequence. A penny saved in paying workers a minimum became a penny saved to profit the shareholders. Workers' injuries were a cost of production. Unions were to be avoided at any cost. There were numerous law firms whose very existence depended on their ability to snuff out any hint of union activity.

The turmoil in the industry's labor relations in the 1980s contrasts sharply with the relative tranquility that characterized those relations for the preceding two decades when little was heard of from the industry in terms of collective bargaining or employee safety. The changes in the character of the industry's relations coincided with the same types of more basic changes in industrial relations systems as were taking place elsewhere in the unionized sector of the economy. [Until the end of the 1970s] unionism dominated and was accepted in the heartland of the industry which was and continues to be geographically somewhat west of the heartland of the economy. The industry had not embraced the concept of an annual improvement factor (AIF) but had accepted cost-of-living adjustments (COLA), and its average hourly earnings had consistently tracked and generally exceeded that in not only all manufacturing but also durable goods manufacturing. Finally, the United Food and Commercial Workers (UFCW) through its Packinghouse Division as heir to the meatpacking segments of the former United Packinghouse Workers (UPWA) and the Amalgamated Meat Cutters and Butcher Workmen of North America (AFL-Amalgamated) was the custodian and in the words of one industrial representative interviewed for this study, ruthless enforcer of pattern bargaining within the industry. By 1985, all that had changed: unionism was no longer 'accepted' particularly by the two largest corporate presences in the industry; hourly earnings which fell in absolute amount between 1980 and 1985, were below those in both durable goods and all manufacturing; and even the union was talking openly about its "long road back to wage stability and pattern bargaining."[15]

Employment in the meat packing industry declined steadily between 1958 and 1965 from 215,000 to 140,000, a drop of 75.000 or almost 35 percent.... Average hourly earnings in the red meat segments of the industry... paralleled in the level and trend (those in the durable goods manufacturing between 1950 and 1980, making them high wage industries. Its status in that respect was altered by an absolute decline in average hourly earnings in meat racking and meat processing between 1982 and 1985.[16,17]

In 1985 [the meat packing industry] had the highest injury and sickness rate among all industries—30.4 injuries or illnesses per 100 full-time employees, compared with a rate of 10.4 for all manufacturing industries.... A Bureau of Labor Statistics (BLS) survey in January through April 1981, found that the occupation "meat cutters and butchers in manufacturing" suffered thirty-five hand injuries in a survey population of 944. Only two occupations, machinists and carpenters, experienced a larger number of hand injuries.[18]

Eugene Cotton, the union's chief counsel and a close personal friend of Helstein throughout his career, said, in part during the Memorial Service,

Ralph came into an industry which Upton Sinclair described in his novel, aptly called, *The Jungle*. He came into an industry in which the base labor rates were roughly 70 cents per hour, no pensions, no medical or any other kind of insurance, no paid holidays, a six-day work week without any overtime, without any premium pay for Saturdays, vacations in which only after 10 years did one achieve a two week vacation level. He left that industry in 1968 as an industry which had a pension program and a medical and surgical program the equal of any in the country and better than most; it had paid holidays; it had a five-day work week; it had vacations that ran up to even six weeks of entitlement after certain numbers of years of service. He left the industry with a major improvement in the working conditions of the people working in the industry.

No other leader then or since can boast of such achievements for the workers they led. What other measure of greatness can there be for a labor leader than the benefits he obtains for his workers? He was able to lead his workers not only because he got them economic benefits but unlike officers of the Amalgamated, he was one of them. In fact, of course, he was not. He was not a worker; he was white while most of them were black. He was an intellectual; he was a Jew, he lived far from where they lived. He had almost nothing in common with them. But by his desire to know everything about their work, to do everything in his power to improve their lives, to gather around him like individuals who lived for the union, he conveyed to the workers a love and respect that they eagerly returned. Ironically, one of the sad aspects of the union's uniqueness is that it remains unique and has not been reproduced since.

Notes

Preface

1. Halpern, Rick, *Down on the Killing Floor, Black and White Workers in Chicago's Packinghouses, 1904–54* (Urbana, IL: University of Illinois Press, 1989); Horowitz, Roger, *"Negro and White, Unite and Fight!" A Social History of Industrial Unionism in Meatpacking, 1930–90* (Urbana, IL: University of Illinois Press, 1989); Halpern, Roger, and Horowitz, Roger, *An Oral History of Black Packinghouse Workers and Their Struggle for Racial and Economic Equality* (New York: Twayne Publishers, Prentice Hall International, 1989).

2. Stanley Rosen.

Introduction

1. E-mail from Toni Helstein, Helstein's daughter, October 24, 2008, in which she writes: "Helstein's 'middle name' was Leslie, which, for some reason he intensely disliked. He was named after a grandfather (great grandfather? I'm not sure) whose name was Olazer (sp?) and his family translated that from the Yiddish into Leslie. Dad's maternal grandfather was named Ralph Leslie Littman. Dad didn't use it, but he did sign his name as Ralph L. Helstein. His handwriting was so bad that it was hard to make out, but that was his typical signature."

2. Letter from November 30, 1972, from Joseph Belsky, president, and Patrick E. Gorman, secretary-treasurer, announcing Helstein's retirement. In the accompanying document, "The Ralph Helstein Fund for Education in Labor History," the Illinois Labor History Society states that Helstein was president of the United Packinghouse, Food and Allied Workers of America from 1946 to 1972, and vice president and special counsel of the Amalgamated Meat Cutters and Butcher Workmen of North America from 1968 to 1972, and now is President Emeritus of the Amalgamated Meat Cutters. For a short history of the successor organizations to the UPWA, see the Epilogue in Halpern, Rick, *Down on the Killing Floor, Black and White Workers in Chicago's Packinghouses, 1904–54* (Urbana: University of Illinois Press, 1997), pp. 247–250.

3. Edward Fruchtman died of a heart attack in 1957.

4. Interview with Eva Sandberg, secretary to Helstein, October 7, 2006. She stated, "The UPWA had its office in an extremely old building so there were high ceilings, bare floors; no carpeting; probably asphalt tile, which was common in those days. From the elevator, as you came into the space that we occupied, there were the four secretaries, his other secretary, Louise Cooley, and the woman who made the airplane arrangements. . . . Where I sat, you looked out on Dearborn, and going along Dearborn was the door leading to [Helstein's] office. It was a large office; there was a desk and a couple of chairs facing the desk; there must have been . . . a couch or a couple of couches, so that's where he sat, at that desk. Then going back out, there was a corridor, a long hallway leading to [other offices], and then beyond that a place where all the mimeographing and all the mailing were done, and there was a teletype machine and a copier that kind of burns the copy and an old-fashioned spaghetti-type switchboard. . . . There was the publications department that had all these files in the same office with the Research Department."

5. Ibid. At the time she was hired in 1967 as his secretary, Sandberg described Helstein as "a little roly-poly Jewish man. . . . You know, this little guy. I was taller than he was. He was bald at that time. . . . And a very round face like a little troll."

6. Kann, Kenneth, *Joe Rapoport, The Life of a Jewish Radical* (Philadelphia: Temple University Press, 1981).

7. Ibid., p. 236.

8. Helstein stated at various times that he was an adherent of "prophetic Judaism," which for him meant a life dedicated to the pursuit of social justice.

9. Sorin, Gerald, *The Phrophetic Minority: American Jewish Immigrant Radicals, 1880–1920* (Bloomington: Indiana University Press, 1985), p. 3.

10. Ibid., pp. 167–168.

11. Kann, p. 72.

12. Ibid., pp. 85–86.

13. Sorin, pp. 42–43.

14. Glazer, Nathan, *American Judaism* (Chicago: University of Chicago Press, 1972), pp. 133, 135, 136. A frequent complaint of party leaders was that the party was "too Jewish." See also Schneier, Rabbi Marc, *Shared Dreams, Martin Luther King, Jr. and the Jewish Community* (Woodstock, VT: Jewish Lights Publishing, 1999), pp. 157–158.

15. Ibid., p. 138.

16. Ibid., pp. 139–140.

17. Ibid., pp. 142–146.

18. Kushner, Tony, Forward, Sholem Aleichem, *Wandering Stars* (New York: Viking Press, 2009), p. xiii.

19. Howe, Irving, *World of Our Fathers*, Chapter 1 (New York: Harcourt Brace Jovanovich, 1976). With the assassination of Czar Alexander II on March 1, 1881, the reign of a moderate monarch ended and that of a tyrant, Alexander III began,

and with it repressive legislation, rampant poverty, famine, and a wave of pogroms that spread through Russia. Howe estimates that between the assassination of Alexander II and World War I, one-third of East European Jews from Russia, Poland, the Austro-Hungarian Empire, and Romania immigrated, principally to the United States. In their own countries, many immigrants had been active in political or revolutionary action in organizations such as the Bund. These aspirations, impossible for Jews to attain by political organization in Eastern Europe, could be, many believed, asserted in the United States. Of course, Jews were only a miniscule proportion of immigrants to the United States before World War I, by which time "35,000,000 Europeans had reached these shores, 4,500,000 from Ireland, 4,000,000 from Great Britain, 6,000,000 from Central Europe, 2,000,000 from the Scandinavian lands, 5,000,000 from Italy, 8,000,000 from Eastern Europe, and 3,000,000 from the Balkans. This was America." Herberg, Will Protestant, *Catholic, Jew* (New York: Doubleday & Co., Anchor Books, new edition, 1960), p. 8.

20. Konner, Melvin, *Unsettled, An Anthropology of the Jews* (New York: Viking Compass, 2003), p. 335. Livesay, Harold C., *Samuel Gompers and Organized Labor in America* (Boston: Little, Brown & Co., 1978). For other Jewish labor leaders, see Gould, Jean, and Hillman, Sidney, *Great American* (Boston: Houghton Mifflin Co, 1952); Dubinsky, David and Raskin, A.H., *David Dubinsky, A Life of Labor* (New York: Simon & Schuster, 1977); Danish, Max D., *The World of David Dubinsky* (Cleveland: The World Publishing Co., 1957); and Jacobson, Matthew, *Sidney Hillman, Statesman of American Labor* (New York: Doubleday & Co., 1952).

21. Palmer, Bryan D., *James P. Cannon and the Origins of the American Left, 1890–1928* (Urbana: University of Illinois Press, 2007), pp. 137–138.

22. Greene, Melissa Fay, *The Temple Bombing* (Reading, MA: Addison-Wesley Publishing Co., 1970), pp. 181–182. I was one of those lawyers, one in Jackson, Mississippi, and then in Selma, Alabama, the first time between semesters when I was a teaching assistant at the University of Michigan Law School.

23. A history of the Jewish labor movement, 1892 to 1924, with its numerous splits, conflicts, early leaders, and strikes can be found in Epstein, Melech, *Jewish Labor in the United States, An Industrial, Political and Cultural History of the Jewish Labor Movement* (New York: Trade Union Sponsoring Committee, 1950).

24. Sorin, Gerald, *The Prophetic Minority, American Jewish Immigrant Radicals, 1880–1920* (Bloomington, IN: Indiana University Press, 1985), p. 120.

25. The A F of L was so unpopular that when it was mentioned at union meetings workers would boo and hiss.

26. Howe, pp. 349, 356. Fraser, Steven, *Labor Will Rule* (New York: Free Press, 1991), p. 1. Sorin, Gerard, *The Prophetic Majority, American Jewish Immigrant Radicals, 1880–1920* (Bloomington, IN: Indiana University Press, 1985), p. 40.

27. Fraser, p. 14; Sorin, pp. 37–38, 94–95.

28. Sorin, p. 221.

29. Epstein, pp. 282–287.

30. "Jewish unions" refers to "those in the needle trades . . . which have either a majority or a crucial plurality of Jewish members and in which the leadership has been heavily Jewish. . . .[T]his would include the unions in the women's clothing, men's clothing, fur, and hat industries. Over the years . . . locals of the bakers' and painters' unions, could also be called Jewish," Howe, pp. 295, 308. For the personal history of a Jewish knitting worker, see Kann, p. 7.

31. Social benefit and burial societies that Eastern European Jews brought with them. Sorin, p. 67.

Chapter 1

1. Eastern European Jews first came to Minneapolis from Russia in the 1880s after the outbreak of pogroms in 1881. For the most part, they earned their living by peddling, although Helstein's father, a boat captain, likely started at a higher level. Gordon, Albert I., *Jews in Transition* (Minneapolis: University of Minnesota Press, 1949), p. 18.

2. Interview with Eliot Wigginton at Highlander Folk School, May 4, 1981.

3. Gordon, pp. 39–41.

4. Weiner, H. A. "Whistling 'Dixie' While Humming 'Ha-Tikvah,'" *American Jewish History*, Vol. 93, No. 2, pp. 211–237, 218. For a novelist's story of this progression, see Singer, I. J. *The Family Carnovsky* (New York: The Vanguard Press, 1969), pp. 274–277.

5. Schloff, Linda Mack, *And the Prairie Dogs Weren't Kosher. Jewish Women in the Upper Midwest since 1855* (St. Paul, MN: Minnesota Historical Society Press, 1996), pp. 29–31; Gordon, p. 36.

6. Schloff, p. 44.

7. Schloff, Linda Mack, *"And Prairie Dogs Weren't Kosher": Jewish Women in the Upper Mid-West States, 1868* (St. Paul, MN: Minnesota Historical Society, 1984).

8. Gordon, pp. 83, 87.

9. Gordon (p. 37) notes: ". . . . Arthur Brin, born of Lithuanian parents in Chicago . . . has . . . attracted the attention of B'nai B'rith and in 1905 he was invited to join the lodge."

10. Mt. Sinai Hospital was founded in 1950 by a group of Minneapolis businessmen. An important motivation was to open up hospital privileges for Jewish physicians who were otherwise barred from admission to area hospitals (Schloss, pp. 194–195).

11. Although I have no specific information on the immigration patterns of the Fligelman family, unlike many other immigrant groups in which male immigrants preceded and outnumbered women, almost half of all Jewish immigrants

were women. Jewish women came either as part of the family or shortly thereafter to join relatives (Ibid., p. 19).

12. "Members of the Council attended study classes each Saturday afternoon. . . . [T]he council established a sewing school for young girls . . . and provided a corps of teachers from among its members. . . . [It] also started a day nursery on the North Side, and later a Sunday School . . . ." (Gordon, pp. 8, 16–17).

13. Schloff, p. 206.

14. Material on Arthur and Fanny Brin prepared by their son, Howard Brin, date not indicated. See also Schloff, p. 57.

15. Sara Newman, "Helstein Family Reunion" (1978), from an oral history told to cousin Gretchen Tselos.

16. Ibid.

17. E-mail from Nina Helstein, Ralph Helstein's daughter, to the author, January 29, 2008.

18. Cornelia T. Williams, *This We Teach, A Study of General College Students* (Minneapolis, MN: University of Minnesota Press, 1943), pp. 174–176. A survey in Minneapolis showed that in 1946, there were Jews in the following professional categories: 92 lawyers, 59 physicians and surgeons, 32 dentists, 173 pharmacists, 32 accountants, 13 teachers in public schools, and five journalists (Gordon, p. 8).

19. Gabriel Schoenfeld, *The Return of Anti-Semitism* (Varda Books, 2006), pp. 207–208.

20. Ralph Helstein, interviewed by Stan Rosen, Side "A," undated, transcribed by the author and by Elizabeth Balanoff, May 3, 1972, pp. 1–2, in the possession of the Roosevelt University Library. The text above includes excerpts from these interviews, which I have slightly shortened and modified (Wigginton interview, pp. 3–5).

21. "Proportionally, three times as many Jewish young people were going to college in 1950 as young people of their age generally." Herberg, Will, *Protestant, Catholic, Jew* (New York: Doubleday & Co., 1960), p. 188. In the 1930s, this statement was true but less likely for young women.

22. Traditionally, it was "boys far more often than girls [that] were encouraged to stay in school and do well there. Women in the Jewish world, as in many traditional societies, were seen as future wives and mothers; and formal learning, until the middle of the twentieth century, remained the monopoly of Jewish males." Sorin, Gerard, *Irving Howe, A Life of Passionate Dissent* (New York: New York University Press, 2002), p. 29.

23. Ralph Helstein, interview by Stan Rosen, Side "A," undated, transcribed by the author.

24. In Minneapolis, Gordon (p. 178), noted: "There appears to be an emotional bias against the Yiddish language among the children of the immigrants. Often one hears such persons hush up anyone who begins to speak Yiddish . . . in a public place. They speak of not liking the language because it is so 'gutteral.'

On the other hand the children of these self-conscious parents look upon Yiddish as they look upon any other foreign language, utterly without emotional bias."

25. Helstein's mother was part of a distinct minority of Jewish women in Minneapolis, no more than 20 percent, who purchased kosher meats, there being only one kosher meat market with about 300 regular customers on the West Side (Ibid., p. 84).

26. Wigginton, pp. 9–10.

27. Keeping a kosher house, of course, meant following the rules of Kashrut, two rules of which are separating *milchig* (milk) and *fleishig* (meat) dishes and not eating pork or pork products. In modern times, where kosher stores are available, this duty is relatively easy, but not in the time of Helstein's ancestors, some of whom lived in St. Paul. Amelia Ullman in the 1850s, where kosher products were available only when the Mississippi River was navigable, "learned to eat whatever was available." The woman in the family usually was the repository of religious values, and it was often the father who, occupied with his business affairs, strayed from religious observances except for the High Holidays; Helstein was not far from this model. Diner, Hasia R. and Beryl Lieff Benderly, *Her Works Praise Her, A History of Jewish Women in America from Colonial Times to the Present* (New York: Basic Books, 2002), pp. 123–128.

28. As Helstein's family's financial circumstances improved, they moved to the Jewish section of Minneapolis, where the Talmud Torah was located (Balanoff, p. 2). "Ida Levitan Sanders worked at the Talmud Torah of Minneapolis in the 1920s. The school was then located in a densely Jewish neighborhood in the city's North Side, which encompassed Orthodox and Conservative synagogues and well-to-do and struggling Jews alike." And she remembers walking "up and down streets, [so that] we could literally smell the Sabbath, the fish and the chicken. . . ." (Schloff, p. 102). The Minneapolis Talmud Torah was founded in 1894 (Gordon, p. 24).

29. Ralph Helstein, January 14, 1981, interview by Les Orear, transcribed by the author, Tape No. 5.

30. Ibid.

31. "The Jews on the North Side used to be afraid to walk anywhere above Fifth Street North. It was actually dangerous to go there, because the Germans and the Irish lived there. There was a lot of beard pulling and name calling. The children of these Germans and Irish people would very often tip over the apple carts or wagons of Jewish peddlers and in general they made life miserable for them (Gordon, p. 21). Gordon (pp. 43–68) reviews the anti-Semitism in Minneapolis in housing, employment and exclusion of Jews from organizations and political office. Gordon traces its history from its early German and Irish settlers. No anti-Semitism was found at the University of Minnesota. Anti-Semitism was often associated with Communism just as later racial justice advocacy was associated with Communism. Gordon contrasted the lack of anti-Semitism in St. Paul, pointing out that Minneapolis has large Fundamentalist and Lutheran

populations. For a review of anti-Semitism in Minnesota, especially Minneapolis, see Gordon (pp. 43–68).

32. Note that Helstein says that the lesson was not that he must not discriminate against "black" people; it was that he must not discriminate against "people." Helstein did not see the black passenger as a "black" person but as a "person" discriminated against. Irving Howe "believed in *menshlikhkhayt*—decency, compassion, that root sense of obligation which the mere fact of being human imposes on us." Being a *mensch*, that is, doing the right thing, without any thought of personal advantage, I think, became an unconscious component of Helstein's life actions" (Sorin, p. 232).

33. Balanoff, p. 9.

34. Wiggerton, pp. 40–41.

35. Balanoff, pp. 12–13.

36. Balanoff, p. 5.

37. Wigginton, p. 1.

38. It may be that anti-Semitism was not a defining theme in Helstein's life, but it is a constant that cannot fail to be part of any Jew's background noise. Sam Zell, who became a billionaire investor and whose parents escaped from the Holocaust in Poland, confessed that his "family's history has had a great effect on him.... I'm an immigrant kid. I have a different perspective on the world than someone who grew up in Chicago and led what I would call a normal life. I think that being Jewish means you're vulnerable forever. Was there a stronger Jewish community anywhere in the world—more intellectual, more successful Jews—than Germany in the late twenties and early thirties, before Hitler? And seven years later they're building concentration camps! So, do I expect something like that to happen in the United States? Of course not. Do I think it could? Absolutely." Bruck, Connie, "Rough Rider," *The New Yorker*, November 12, 2007, p. 52, 58. Recall the story of Isaac Bashivas Singer who reputedly always kept a suitcase ready and packed just in case.

39. Harper, Steven J., *Straddling Two Worlds, The Jewish-American Journey of Professor Richard W. Leopold* (Evanston, IL: Northwestern University Press, 2007), p. 53. Earlier pages tell of anti-Semitism of other Ivy League institutions. Lowell reputedly told a "Jewish alumnus" that Jewish and Christian students "just don't mix." That to become "real Americans," Jews would have to become Christians because "to be an American is to be nothing else." A further, perhaps more practical reason, was that if Jews were admitted based on their often superior academic record, wealthy non-Jews would not get in (Diner & Benderley, p. 281).

40. Harper, pp. 61, 69

41. Ibid., p. 27. ".... Harvard, Yale, Princeton, and many other elite private men's and women's colleges established quotas, often 10–15 percent of the student body, on Jewish enrollment." But those Jews actually admitted fell far below this number. For example, although in the mid-1930s, half the applicants to medical schools were Jewish, fewer than a fifth were admitted (Diner & Benderly, p. 281).

42. The period from the 1920s to the 1940s has been called the "peak years of American anti-Semitism" (Ibid., pp. 207 ff.). Diner and Benderley describe the factors that led to wide anti-Semitism in employment and educational institutions. See also Gartner, Lloyd P., "The Midpassage of American Jewry," in Dawidowicz, pp. 228–229. The worst period of anti-Semitism was in the late 1930s. Carey Williams, in a 1946 article in the magazine, *Common Ground*, called Minneapolis the nation's "capitol [*sic*] of anti-Semitism." The new Minneapolis mayor, Hubert Humphrey, created the Mayor's Council on Human Relations to study discrimination against, Jews, blacks and Asians. Their 1948 report resulted in passage of anti-discriminatory legislation (Schloff, p. 56). Lucy S.A. Davidowicz, "The Jewishness of the Jewish Labor Movement in the United States," in Bertram Wallace Korn (ed.), *A Bicentennial Festschrift for Jacob Rader Marcus* (New York: American Jewish Historical Society/KTAV1976, reprinted in Jonathan D. Sarna (ed.), *American Jewish Experience* [New York: Holmes & Meier, 1986]).

43. Wigginton, p. 2.

44. According to his obituary in the *Chicago Tribune*, February 15, 1985, p. C10, the notice that Helstein failed the exam "was in error on the school's part but, by then, he was studying law."

45. Balanoff, p. 12.

46. Helstein attended the University of Minnesota Law School (1931–1934). His law school records for 1931 to 1932 show that his object of study was "practice" as opposed to "business"; he was "partially" self-supporting, and in from 1933 to 1934, he was "wholly" self-supporting. His birth date is listed as December 11, 1908; his father was Henry and mother was Lena. He attended Central High School (graduated 1926) and received a B.A. at the University of Minnesota. In his first year at law school, he was ranked 44th and had a grade average of 75.2 in a class of 84; second year, a grade average of 75.1 and 42nd in a class of 71; and third year, a grade average of 74.8 and 45th in a class of 65. His best subjects (Bs), were Criminal Law and Procedure, Property II and Wills, and Conflict of Laws. His worst subjects (Ds) were Agency, Trusts, and Evidence. He received his L.L.B. on June 18, 1934 (University of Minnesota Law School files, available pursuant of Minn. Statute 13.10, subd.2, which in pertinent part states that "[p]rivate data on decedents and confidential data on decedents shall become public when ten years have elapsed from the actual presumed death of the individual. . . .").

47. Wellstone, Paul, the late Minnesota senator, "Reflecting on his childhood. . . . said that his parents' commitment to social justice was rooted in their Jewish faith. . . . Wellstone's parents taught their son that his faith was necessarily connected to the struggle for justice. "I think the prophetic tradition of our faith is that to love God is to love justice. . . ." Lofy, Bill, *Paul Wellstone, The Life of a Passionate Progressive* (Ann Arbor, MI: University of Michigan Press, 2005), pp. 19–20. The concept of "prophetic Judaism" is extensively treated in Auerbach, Jerold S., *Rabbis and Lawyers, The Journey from Torah to Constitution* (Bloomington, IN: Indiana

University Press,1990), pp. 49–50. The prophets are called the "moral conscience of ancient Israel" (p. 49).

48. Balanoff, p. 18.

49. "Most Jews . . . enthusiastically embraced Franklin D. Roosevelt and his New Deal. . . . More Jews served in the Roosevelt Administration than in any other previous administration. . . . [H]undreds of young Jewish women and men flocked to Washington, D.C. to work in the new government programs and regulatory agencies, which they believed would recover prosperity, relieve suffering, reform the economy, and give them a chance to carve out meaningful careers in public service" (Diner & Benderley, pp. 237–238).

50. Balanoff, pp.18–19. Helstein was 24 years of age at the time. He had failed the bar exam "and I wasn't admitted to the bar but I couldn't have cared less."

51. Diner & Benderley, p. 89.

52. Who later became a United States Supreme Court Justice.

53. *Schechter Poultry Corp. v. United States*, 295 U.S. 495 (1935) (the sick chicken case). Schechter processed chickens locally and sold them to kosher markets in New York City. He was convicted of federal laws concerning slaughtering and selling of poultry. He challenged on the grounds that the federal laws were an unconstitutional delegation of congressional authority, that Congress was in effect regulating intrastate commerce, and that the laws violated his Fifth Amendment due process rights. The Supreme Court agreed and reversed the conviction.

54. Balanoff, pp. 21–22. According to the records of the Minneapolis Federation for Jewish Services in 1946, there were 92 Jewish lawyers in Minneapolis (Gordon, p. 8).

55. "His partner Doug. . . .was a big, tall young man." Telephone interview with Mrs. Rivan Morris, Helstein's secretary, February 19, 2008.

56. This means of advising unions had a more radical alternative. One day, as a young lawyer in the 1950s, I was in the office of one of my mentors, David Rothstein, in Chicago, who represented the United Electrical Workers, a left-wing union subsequently ousted from the CIO. Rothstein was on the telephone instructing the union official calling him about a problem, telling him not to ask his advice before he took action. He told the official to take what action he felt was best for the union. If the union got into trouble, Rothstein, in his capacity as the union's lawyer, would try to get them out of it.

57. Gall, Gilbert J., *Pursuing Justice, Lee Pressman, the New Deal, and the CIO* (Albany, NY: State University of New York Press, 1999), p. 81.

58. Ibid., pp. 85, 102.

59. Ibid., pp. 134–140.

60. Ibid., pp. 139–140.

61. Ibid., supra n., p. 184.

62. Ibid., supra n., p. 212.

Chapter 2

1. Cohen, Lizabeth, *Making a New Deal, Industrial Workers in Chicago, 1919–1939* (Cambridge, UK: Cambridge University Press, 1990), p. 301.

2. Zacharakis-Jutz, Jeffrey T., *Straight to the Heart of a Union, Straight to the Heart of a Movement: Worker's Education in the United Packinghouse Workers of America Between 1951 and 1953* (DeKalb, IL: Northern Illinois University, 1991), pp. 45–48.

3. Zacharakis-Jutz, pp. 48–50.

4. Halpern, Rick, *Down on the Killing Floor, Black and White Workers in Chicago's Packinghouses, 1904–54* (Urbana: University of Illinois Press, 1997), pp. 185.

5. Horowitz, Roger, *"Negro and White, Unite and Fight!," A Social History of Industrial Unionism in Meatpacking, 1930–1990* (Urbana: University of Illinois Press, 1997), pp. I–92; Halpern, pp. 365–367.

6. Cohen, pp. 340–341.

7. Unemployed Councils in the early 1930s, largely sponsored by the Communist Party, engaged in anti-eviction activity, often interracial, that radicalized many blacks. On the South Side, home of a large percentage of blacks, 85% of blacks older than 10 years of age were unemployed compared with 28% elsewhere in Chicago. Communist activists led groups to evicted families and carried their furniture back in; turning back on the gas, electric, and water; and leaving signs reading "Restored by the Unemployment Councils." Although most blacks would not have approved of Marxist rhetoric, the concrete actions of party members endeared them to the Communist Party.

8. Halpern, pp. 274–288.

9. Brody, David, *The Butcher Workmen, A Study of Unionization* (Cambridge, MA: Harvard University Press, 1964), pp. 162, 164–168.

10. Horowitz, pp. I–242; Halpern, pp. 311–318.

11. Zacharakis-Jutz, pp. 82–83.

12. Cohen, p. 297.

13. Brody, pp. 158, 198.

14. Halpern, pp. 397–403.

15. Cohen, p. 298.

16. Horowitz, pp. 248–265. The Catholic church-sponsored organization Association of Catholic Trade Unionists (ACTU) was extremely important in mostly anti-Communist activities. See Levenstein, *Communism, Anticommunism and the CIO* (Westport, CT: Greenwood Press, 1981), pp. 110–120.

17. Horowitz, pp. 521–525.

18. The PWOC office was in the Engineering Building at 205 W. Wacker Drive across the river from the Merchandise Mart. The Steelworkers regional office was in the same building, and it was an obvious move for Van Bittner to establish the PWOC on the same premises. E-mail from Les Orear, February 28, 2008.

19. Brody, p. 183.

20. Ibid., p. 217. Clark had been business agent of a Wilson plant at Cedar Rapids. He was appointed to the PWOC staff in 1940 and shortly afterward was promoted to director of District 3. Clark was first "vice-chairman, then secretary-treasurer of the PWOC... Clark ... had led his union out of the Amalgamated and had helped found the PWOC. He was the object of that special hatred reserved in the labor movement for disruptionists and successionists."

21. Ibid., pp. 184–186.

22. Ibid., p. 222.

23. Balanoff, p. 58.

24. Rachel Helstein, interview by the author, November 23, 1994, at her home.

25. Eva Sandberg described the interior of the house as follows: "The spaces were small. The kitchen was small; the staircase was cramped. He took me upstairs to the loft which was where his study was, and that was very light and bright, and the furniture was modern" (Balanoff, p. 61).

26. Ibid., pp. 57–59.

27. MSS 118, Box 3, folder 4, UPWA chairman, Constitutional Convention, Wisconsin Historical Society.

28. See Chapter 1 for a detailed description of the union history preceding Helstein's election.

29. Ralph Helstein, September 15, 1980, Tape 1, interview by Les Orear and transcribed by the author, "Helstein's first presidential election."

30. Herbert March, Tape 293, side 1, transcribed by the author. M3818. Tape series 1106A. The interview was conducted on October 21, 1986, by Rick Halpern and Roger Horowitz for the State Historical Society of Wisconsin UPWA Oral History Project; Herb March, Tape 3, March 21, 1995, interview with Herbert March transcribed by the author.

31. Providing information and cooperating with the FBI and other government agencies investigating "red" activities of trade unions was not so rare, particularly during congressional committee witch hunting. See Stepan-Norris, Judith and Maurice Zeitlin, *Left Out: Reds and America's Industrial Unions* (Cambridge, UK: Cambridge University Press, 2003), pp. 272–273, and Schrecker, Ellen, *Many Are the Crimes: McCarthyism in America* (Boston, MA: Little Brown & Co., 1998), p. 209. The FBI had thousands of informants spread among "vital facilities."

32. Halpern (p. 222) describes how union members saw Clark at the time of the election: "During the [1946] strike, Clark had alienated the members of the strategy committee. Behaving erratically, he disappeared suddenly for hours at a time, showed himself unable to follow discussions, and provided a minimum of leadership. Clark was a nonentity.... He didn't know what was going on. He ... didn't know how to negotiate; he didn't want to negotiate. He just wanted all the honors and all the perks that go with being president. Apparently, during the showdown with the government, Clark suffered some kind of breakdown in front

of the entire strategy committee. In contrast, Helstein emerged as an unparalleled strategist during the strike. He handled all negotiations with the packers and after Clark's collapse, he served as the union's spokesman. His dynamic performance convinced those present of his talents."

33. Some unions have constitutional provisions that only members who have spent time working in the trade should be eligible for staff positions Wilensky, Harold L., *Intellectuals in Labor Unions: Organizational Pressures on Professional Roles* (Glencoe, IL: The Free Press Publishers, 1956), p. 266. Pat Gorman, in 1942, was elected as secretary-treasurer of the Amalgamated (the equivalent of President), was also a lawyer.

34. Apparently, this idea about lawyers was held by others. In a survey of union officials, one "top officer" was quoted as saying, "I'll tell you my experiences with lawyers. They're always telling you what you can't do. That's the trouble with lawyers. . . . Tell me truthfully now. You're up around Chicago. Don't you think that having a lawyer as President of the Packinghouse Workers has slowed 'em up?" (Wilensky, p. 55). The survey found that "hostility to lawyers is widespread among union leaders," but this refers to lawyers in general, not to their own house counsel (Wilensky, p. 75).

35. Wigginton, pp. 57–58.

36. Oscar Brown, Jr., September, 23, 1995, side 2, interviewed and transcribed by the author.

37. Interview by the author, March 31, 1995.

38. Haywood was Philip Murray's anti-Communist point man to stem Communist gains. For example, in May 1946, there was a left–right split in the Cleveland CIO council "that led to a walkout by Amalgamated delegates and a plea for Murray's intervention. Murray sent Haywood who placed the council" in receivership and restructured its rules to block the left (Levenstein, p. 211).

39. Interview by the author, March 31, 1995.

40. A similar incident occurred when a union official, William Sentner, a member of the Communist Party, recently elected to be president of the United Electrical Workers (UE) local in St. Louis was quoted in a *Fortune* article as stating to the Communist Party head who criticized him for not following the party line, "You run your organization and I'll run mine" (Stepan-Norris Judith and Zeitlin, p. 12).

41. Interview, March 21, 1995, by the author at March's home.

42. Levenstein, p. 16.

43. "St. Paul unionist Milt Siegel nominated Helstein as a union president able to lead the UPWA in the toughest battles ahead 'not only as negotiator and administrator, but I know he will be able to cope with any situation.' Other supporters described him as 'above reproach' and 'a man above 'isms'" (Horowitz, p. 172).

44. Balanoff, pp. 183–184.

45. Interview by the author with Eugene Cotton, September 21, 1995.

46. Interview of Jesse Prosten by Halpern and Horowitz, M3431; 25:05 Tape 48, side 1, UPWA O.H.P. December 18, 1985, summary and transcription by the author. "Helstein was also internally a compromise. Who the hell would ever have thought of a lawyer, but he was trusted and he was an honest guy and a liberal guy, and he was put in with a combination of people out of Chicago, Boston, St. Paul, Omaha and they tried to run a slate against him, but it was completely ineffective because we did have a kind of rank-and-file basis that they couldn't get at. Our conventions did not consist of business agents and all that stuff; they consisted of guys out of the floor of the plant."

47. Wiggerton, pp. 49–50.

48. How is it that Anderson seemingly could make such an important decision on his own? Schoenebaum, Eleanor W., editor. *Political Profiles, The Truman Years* (New York: Facts on File, 1978), pp. vi–vii, writes that Truman "was one of the few Presidents in the postwar period who administered the federal government through a strong cabinet. He regularly held cabinet meetings and rarely interfered with a Secretary's administration of his department."

49. Ralph Helstein, September15, 1980, Tape 1, interview by Les Orear and transcribed by the author; Wiggerton, pp. 50–53.

50. Wiggerton, pp. 47–48.

51. Halpern, p. 222.

52. Levenstein, p. 53.

53. Balanoff, p. 233.

54. Ibid., pp. 233–234.

55. Ibid., pp. 234–235.

56. Ibid., p. 235.

57. Ibid., p. 235.

58. Ibid., p. 236.

59. Lichtenstein, Nelso, *Walter Reuther, The Most Dangerous Man in Detroit* (Urbana, IL: University of Illinois Press, 1995), pp. 147–148.

60. Foner, Philip S., Ronald L. Lewis, and Ronald Cvornyek, "The Black worker since the AFL-CIO Merger, 1955–1980," Vol. III. *The Black Worker, A Documentary History from Colonial Times to the Present* (Philadelphia: Temple University Press, 1984), pp. 241, 246, 254.

61. Wilinsky, supra n., pp. 215–216.

62. Storch, Randi, *Red Chicago, American Communism at its Grassroots, 1928–35* (Urbana: University of Illinois Press, 2007), p. 35.

63. Les Orear interview, November 21, 2006, interviewed by and transcribed by the author.

64. Interview of Charlie Hayes, a black UPWA official and early a member of the Communist Party, Halpern and Horowitz, 1106A, l52 side 1, Wisconsin Historical Society. Madison, WI; transcribed and summarized by the author.

65. Irv King, September 25, 1995, interviewed by the author and transcribed by Deb Morrow.

66. Helstein, p. 162.

67. Ibid., p. 164.

68. Balanoff, supra n. 26, p. 237.

69. Ibid., pp. 237–238.

70. Ibid., p. 240.

71. Murray hired McDonald, who had been with the Mine Workers, as his secretary.

72. Balanoff, pp. 242–243.

73. In a letter to Cooper, dated August 16, 1944, he is informed he will be employed as research director assigned to the technical division at an annual salary of $6,000; four years later, his salary had been increased to $6,600. WHS MSS 867 Helstein Correspondence January to September 1944, Box 1, folder 3.

74. WHS MSS 118 General Correspondence & Subject file, Convention, 1948, folder 1. In the employee list dated March 16, 1950, salaries are no longer included. WHS MSS 118 General Correspondence & Subject File, Convention, 1950.

75. Interview October, 16, 2005, with Toni Jane Helstein, daughter of Ralph Helstein, by telephone. "The union was pretty much the focus of family life. . . . [H]e was gone on trips a lot of the time as I was growing up, and when he was home, there was a lot of catching up that he liked to do."

Chapter 3

1. Both with the Communist and Socialist Parties, Jews provided "a dispro-portionate" number "of its political backing and internal leadership. . . . [I]n the 1920s, up to 15% of the Communists were Jews. . . . In 1929, [when] the party had no more than 10,000 members. Jews were [the] largest ethnic group, and increased in the 1930s and 40s, perhaps as much as 50%, a large part from NYC. . . . Until 1929, the headquarters of the party was in Chicago. . . . The Jewish leadership, who tended to be long-term, became even more important because of the quick turnover of most members." Liebman, Arthur, *Jews and the Left* (New York: John Wiley & Sons, 1979), pp. 55–61. A survey of unions officials, in this case, "professional service types," found about one-third to be "of Jewish origin" and as of 1951 "about half of . . . the present Professional Service are Jews" (Wilensky, p. 137, n. 20).

2. Although these Jews were officers of a labor union, their jobs were white collar rather than working class. "During the 1930s, roughly 11 percent of employed Jewish males could be classified as professionals. Shortly after World War II, approximately 15 percent could be so classified" (Liebman, p. 359).

3. Eugene Cotton, March 14, 17, 1995, interviewed and summarized by the author. Cotton died at the age of 95 years, *The New York Times*, November 19, 2009, p. B12.

4. Interview by the author at Cotton's home, March 24, 1995, transcribed by the author.

5. "On March 25, 1931, nine young African American men were accused of raping two white women aboard a freight train near the northern Alabama town of Scottsboro as they all rode the rails in search of work. . . . [The] 'Scottsboro boys' (as they became known) were tried, convicted, and sentenced in three days time. . . . [W]hat set the Scottsboro case apart from others like it was the initiative of the Communist Party (CP) in bringing the episode to the world's attention. . . . The CP dispatched a legal team to take over the young men's legal defense, demanding new trials. Fosl, Catherine, *Subversive Southerner, Anne Braden and the Struggle for Racial Justice in the Cold War South* (New York: Palgrave McMillan, 2002), pp. 16–17.

6. See Ginger, Ann Fagan, *Carol Weiss King, Human Rights Lawyer, 1895–1952* (Boulder, CO: University of Colorado Press, 1992).

7. Lee Pressman's Jewish and professional life and social views paralleled Cotton's. Pressman's father emigrated from Minsk, Russia, in 1893 to avoid military conscription and to "seek his fortune." He entered the garment industry in New York City and later became an employer himself. In 1906, their first child, Leon (Lee), was born, and they lived on the better-off edge of the Lower East Side Jewish "ghetto." His mother was a "very forceful woman" who constantly pushed her children to excel in education. Lee, at an early age, contracted infantile paralysis, which withered his legs. His mother was able to find a doctor who performed an operation that allowed him to walk unaided. He was briefly religious, but thereafter his interest was pursuing a professional career. He entered New York University at 16 years, and after a year, on the recommendation of his English literature professor, he finished his college career at Cornell University. There he met his future wife, an extremely intelligent and educated woman, whose moniker was Sunny. While she finished at Cornell, he entered Harvard Law School in 1926. He made law review, where one of his fellow editors was Alger Hiss. Pressman doubtless knew Helstein because similar to Helstein, he was close to Carol Weiss King, editor of the International Juridical Association bulletin. Pressman also became close to Jerome Frank, a professor at Harvard. When Frank became general counsel for the Agricultural Adjustment Administration (AAA), Pressman was called to Washington, D.C., to be assistant general counsel. In February 1935, Pressman, Frank, and a number of other left wingers were fired over their insistence that the AAA aid small farmers. In June 1934, Pressman joined the "Ware Group," organized by Harold Ware, a Communist Party organizer. Although the exact reason Pressman joined the party is unknown, one author suggested that "Jewish culture in New York City provided fertile soil for communism's appeals."

First, social revolution was a "dominating strand" in Jewish life. Plus, there was a need to "become," and that "could be socialist, anarchists, Zionists or Communists." In recruiting government workers, the purpose of the Ware Group was to influence the policies of the federal government. Having become disillusioned that the Roosevelt administration would be able to fundamental change, Pressman turned toward the turbulent labor movement, which just then was undergoing momentous organizational change under the leadership of John L. Lewis. After pursuing Lewis for a job as union counsel, Lewis named Pressman as general counsel of the newly formed Steel Workers Organizing Committee. Gall, Gilbert J. *Pursuing Justice, Lee Pressman, the New Deal, and the CIO* (Albany, NY: State University of New York Press, 1999), pp. 5–16, 35–40, 48–57.

8. "[Cotton] moved into the CIO building. . . . He found himself soon caught up in what he considered the most exciting job of his life; he believed in what he was doing and seemed to be on the right side of all of the issues" (Gall, supra n., pp. 150–160).

9. Interview of Irving King, September 25, 1995, by the author, transcribed by Deb Morrow.

10. E-mail from Nina Helstein.

11. Herbert March, October 21, 1986, Tape 293, side 1, transcribed by the author. This interview was conducted by Rick Halpern and Roger Horowitz for the State Historical Society of Wisconsin UPWA Oral History Project.

12. March was subpoenaed to testify before the Committee on Un-American Activities, House of Representatives, 82nd Congress, Second Session, September 5, 1952, Communist Activities in the Chicago Area—Part I. March was represented by Eugene Cotton, general counsel of the UPWA. He was asked about his change of name. He testified that he changed it from Herbert Fink to March when he was 16 years old. He completed high school in 1928 and spent a year at the College of the City of New York. From 1935 to 1937, he worked at Armour & Co.," and in 1937 became an organizer for the CIO "in the packing industry." He was asked various questions as to other names he had used and whether he had been arrested. At one point, he stated: "I have devoted the whole of my adult life to building unions and fighting for workers, and that has been my life's activity . . . ," p. 3818). Various questions identified him as a "member of the national committee of the Communist Party, from which he resigned after the union voted to comply with the Taft-Hartley law, that in 1933 he was the district organizer for the Young Communist League, and that he had participated in various left-wing organizations and peace groups, and had been an instructor at the Abraham Lincoln School in 1944."

13. There is very little information about March's religious experience, but in an interview on March 24, 1995, Jane, his wife, describes her visit to his family in 1933: "A very lovely family, very much like ours, with all the aunts and uncles and everybody being friendly, with the big dinners. . . . And I was accepted even

though I was a gentile, cause they were not very Jewish. They weren't Orthodox Jews.... They were so worried that he would have for a girlfriend some kind of a wild-eyed Communist (laughing), you know, with uncombed hair and I was a nice, sedate lady..."

14. Richard March, March's son, March 20, 1995, interview by the author, transcribed by Deb Morrow, stated: "His dad blamed Herb for his mother's death because he left to do political work, and they were on bad terms after that. He wound up marrying my mother, a gentile, from this very big, very tight family, and [he] got accepted in that family. My dad really liked the fact that everybody would say that he really looked Croatian [his wife, Joan, came from a Croatian family]. I think he was very ambivalent about being Jewish. He wasn't religious, and when he was pinned down to ask about his origins, he would say well, I'm Polish and Lithuanian. Being Jewish didn't mean much to him, from all I can tell. I found out he was Jewish when my brother Bill was about 15 and I would have been 8, and my brother said, hey, you know, you're Jewish. We always had a Christmas tree and stuff, and we never had a menorah, and my dad said, well, what the hell's that? I had no idea. We I knew that a lot of friends, ones through our radical connections, were Jewish. And I knew some of them talked about going to temple, but I didn't know what that was. He used fake names when he'd get blacklisted, as an organizer in the stockyards. March is a fake name that he made up." Irving Howe, in commenting on the "contribution of left-wing immigrant Jews to the Communist movement" that it was "neither their time, nor money, nor minds... it was their children.... From the ranks of these young people came not only party leaders... but a considerable number of middle-class members and fellow-travelers—teachers, social workers, dentists, accountants, lawyers, and doctors. Those who threw themselves full time into party work would customarily drop every sign of Jewish identity. Taking 'party names,' they made certain to choose non-Jewish ones, with the rationale that this was necessary in order to approach American workers.... (345) Strangely, Howe does not mention workers or union organizers among those who wanted to "approach American workers."

15. Herberg, Will, Protestant, Catholic, Jew 55 (New York, Doubleday & Co., 1960), p. 55.

16. March never hid the fact that he was a member of the Communist Party, which was contrary to the official policy of the Party. "Secrecy was an integral part of the CP's Marxist-Leninist perspective." It never changed this policy which frequently left them open to charges of dishonesty. People like March and Prosten who openly professed their membership were immune to such charges. Rosswurm, Steve (ed.), "An Overview and Preliminary Assessment of the CIO's Expelled Unions," in The CIO's Left-Led Unions (New Brunswick, NJ: Rutgers University Press, 1992), p. 11.

17. Gangsters were often used to intimidate striking workers or, as here, to discourage militant union officials. See, for example, Kann, Kenneth, Joe

Rapoport, The Life of a Jewish Radical (Philadelphia: Temple University Press, 1981), which explores violence in the 1920s knit goods industry. See also Stepan-Norris and Zeitlin, p. 69.

18. Storch, Randi, *Red Chicago, American Communism at its Grassroots, 1928–35* (Urbana: University of Illinois Press, 2007), pp. 152–153.

19. David Cantor, interviewed by the author, May 13, 1995, transcribed by Deb Morrow. Cantor edited District 1's newspaper, managed the winning campaign for Mayor Harold Washington, and thereafter acted as his lawyer. I have slightly edited Cantor's words.

20. Interview by author of Les Orear at the Illinois Labor History Society office, Chicago, IL, April 28, 2007.

21. Hearings before the Committee on Un-American Activities, House of Representatives, 86th Congress, First Session, May 5, 1959 Communist Infiltration of Vital Industries and Current Communist techniques in the Chicago, IL, Area, pp. 654–656.

22. Ann Prosten, April 28, 1995, interview by the author, transcribed by Deb Morrow.

23. Schloff, Linda Mack, *And the Prairie Dogs Weren't Kosher. Jewish Women in the Upper Midwest Since 1855* (St. Paul, MN: Minnesota Historical Society Press, 1996), pp. 29–31.

24. According to a telephone interview, November 8, with Sylvia Fischer, wife of Charlie Fischer, deceased, assistant to Helstein, in which she said, "Charlie's reaction to all these changes [was that the] UPWA had been a very progressive organization and [with the merger with the Amalgamated Meatcutters] it became diluted somewhat. He shared Jesse's feelings because they worked very closely together."

25. Secrecy in the Communist Party both came from the experiences in its origin in Russia as a protection from the repressive Czarist police and from the domestic experience from the "red-scare of 1919–1920 when the federal government rounded up thousands of foreign-born radicals for deportation, [and] official repression forced the fledgling party underground." Schrecker, pp. 11–12; Draper, Theodore, *Roots of American Communism* (New York: The Viking Press, 1957), pp. 205–206. In view of this history and the many disadvantages, personal and financial, of being openly Communist, these actions by March and Prosten are truly remarkable. See also a similar courageous stance by a St. Louis labor leader, Sentner, William, Jr. and Rosemary Feurer, *Radical Unionism in the Midwest, 1900–1950* (Urbana: University of Illinois Press, 2006).

26. Stepan-Norris and Zeitlin, supra n., pp. 28–29.

27. March 7, 1996, interviewed by the author, transcribed by Deb Morrow.

28. Cotton was honored at the Illinois Labor History Society Union Hall of Honor dinner, November 19, 2001 (e-mail from Les Orear).

Chapter 4

1. Interview of Les Orear May 16, 2006 at the Illinois Labor History Society (ILHS) headquarters by the author and transcribed by the author. What Orear recounts here is partly hearsay because at the time of these negotiations, Orear was in Kansas City.

2. Stromquist, Sheldon, "Promise and perils of the postwar era," in *Solidarity & Survival* (Iowa University Press, 1993), p. 177.

3. Interview with David Cantor, pp. 11–12.

4. Ibid., p. 11ff.

5. Brody, n. 84, pp. 233–234.

6. Saposs, David J., *Left-Wing Unionism, a Study of Radical Policies and Tactics* (New York: International Publishers, 1926), p. 5. According to Saposs, most "factional struggles" arise out of attempts by "radicals" to seize power from "conservatives." Such a picture was true at the time of writing in 1926, but by the 1950s, at least in the UPWA, conservative forces were trying to recapture power from the "radicals."

7. In 1945, shortly before President Franklin Delano Roosevelt's death, Wallace became Secretary of Commerce. He held that position until September 1946, when he was forced to resign because of his open opposition to President Harry S. Truman's foreign policy. In 1948, he helped launch a new Progressive Party, which charged the Truman administration with primary responsibility for the Cold War. The Wallace candidacy for president under the Progressive Party auspices reawakened the left–right split in the union. The CIO backed Truman and tried to suppress Wallace sentiment.

8. Interview with Les Orear by the author; Balanoff, p. 170.

9. Interview with Les Orear; Brody, p. 235.

10. Such factions were not at all unusual within the CIO, particularly in the internal struggle between Communists and anti-Communists. In the September 1944 UAW convention, there was the "Rank and File Caucus" demanding the abandonment of the No-Strike pledge, and in May 1946, "UE insurgents" formed "UE-Members for Democratic Action" (interview of Les Orear by the author). Levenstein, Harvey A., *Revolution at the Table, The Transformation of the American Diet* (New York: Oxford University Press, 1988), pp. 174–175, 211, 212. In October 1946, CIO anti-Communists formed the "CIO Committee for Renovative Trade Unionism" to combat Communism in their union. See also Lichtenstein, Nelson, *Walter Reuther, The Most Dangerous Man in Detroit* (Urbana: University of Illinois Press, 1995) regarding the formation for numerous factions.

11. Halpern, n. 1, pp. 232–233. One of the criteria for a democratically run union was the presence of factions (see below). Was factionalism common or rare among CIO unions? One researcher found that "[i]nternationals, such as the American Newspaper Guild (ANG), the UAW, and the UE, the incumbent

leadership appears to have regularly faced internal opposition." Stepan-Norris and Zeitlin, p. 67.

12. UPWA papers, State Historical Society of Wisconsin, Mss188, Box 308, F2, Q2.

13. Ibid. Of course, it was not mentioned that it was union policy not to pay its officers during the strike.

14. Horowitz, Roger, "'This community of our union,' shopfloor power and social unionism in the postwar UPWA," in Stromquist, Shelson and Marvin Bergman (eds.), *Unionizing the Jungles, Labor and Community in the Twentieth Century Meatpacking Industry* (Iowa City: University of Iowa Press, 1997), p. 198.

15. Ibid., pp. 202–203; Halpern, n1, p. 237.

16. WHS 1948 UPWA Constitutional Proceedings, pp. 16–22, June 28, 1948.

17. WHS, proceedings of the 5th Constitutional Convention, July 29, 1948, pp. 164–165, 171.

18. Ibid., pp. 174–175.

19. Ibid., pp. 383–387.

20. Halpern, pp. 236–237.

21. Horowitz, p. 203.

22. Rachel Helstein, interview November 23, 1994, at her home.

23. Herb March, interview by the author, March 24, 1995, transcribed by the author.

24. Ibid., Tape No. 5, Side 2.

25. Interview with Herb March, Tape 4, Side 2, June 21, 1995. This interview has been shortened.

26. Halpern, p. 236.

27. Ibid., p. 232.

28. The session began with this prayer: "Help us, O God, to carry on, help us to keep on, help us to go on in the name of all that is just, in the name of all that is pure, in the name of all that is beautiful."

29. Halpern, p. 195.

30. WHS MSS118 Executive Board Meetings, December 19 to 20, 1949, Box 31, folder 4, pp. 178–193.

31. Interview by Elizabeth Balanoff, May 3, 1972, in the possession of the Roosevelt University Library, p. 170.

32. Being an attorney at such a juncture not only gave Helstein an understanding of the legal challenges and problems faced by the UPWA but also allowed him to plot a strategy on both legal and strategic grounds.

33. Balanoff, pp. 172–173. Helstein notes that "this guy got his job back..." (p. 173).

34. As a group, Jews were very supportive of civil rights for African Americans, particularly after World War II, as anxiety over their own status in American

society subsided. The Holocaust taught Jews the cost of discrimination. Jews were active in civil rights organizations pushing for civil rights bills. in legal actions to save African Americans from imprisonment or capital punishment. to oppose housing discrimination, for school integration. and to lobby for the Civil Rights Acts. The Jewish Committee hired Kenneth Clark to study the effect of segregated classrooms, a study that influenced the U.S. Supreme Court in the *Brown* decision. Various Jewish organizations honored civil rights leaders; many Jewish religious leaders participated in the March on Washington; many young Jews participated in Freedom Summer, notably Andrew Goodman and Michael Schwerner, who paid with their lives for opposing southern racism. In 1965, Rabbi Abraham Heschel declared that civil rights grew out of Jewish prophetic tradition, a view with which Helstein no doubt agreed and acted upon. Hasia R. Diner, *Irish Immigrant Women in the 19th Century* (Wiley Blackwell), pp. 265–269.

35. Interview of Eugene Cotton by the author, March 1993.

36. These arrangements were preceded by a series of letter exchanges between Helstein and John Hope II. A letter from Hope, a "specialist on Industrial Relations," a letter of June 4, 1948, said in part: "I am particularly interested in the minority problem in industrial firms and in unions and have observed with satisfaction the full participation of Negroes which seems to prevail generally in your organization. . . . I believe that the Institute . . . with the backing of the International (UPW) and the guidance of your research director such information could be obtained with a minimum of time and cost to your, I am certain, already over taxed staff" (WHS MSS 862 Helstein Correspondence 1948, Box 2, folder 2).

37. Halpern, pp. 237–238.

38. "The self-survey of the Packinghouse Union: A technique for effecting change," *Journal of Social Issues*, pp. 28–36, 1953.

39. MSS 118, Box 3, F PWOC Chairman and Conference Material, Wisconsin Historical Society.

40. According to Herbert Hill, labor director of the NAACP, the UPWA-CIO is "in fact *the only* American trade union . . . exempt from his sweeping, vituperative denunciation of racism in the past and present American labor movement" [emphasis supplied]. Street, Paul Louis,*Working in the Yards: A History of Class Relations in Chicago's Meatpacking Industry,1886–1960* (PhD dissertation, Northern Illinois University, 1993), n. 2, p. 18.

41. Balanoff, n. 26, at 178.

42. Wigginton, p. 79–80.

43. Ibid., p. 74.

44. Ibid., pp. 80–81.

45. Ibid., pp. 81–85.

46. As of 1951, only eight unions had either an "Anti-Discrimination Committee" or "Civil Rights Committee." There were "at least" 11 employees in the labor movement engaged in "minority group problems . . . one in Rubber, one

in Packing House, two in Steel, three in Auto, three in the new AFL-CIO. . . ." (Wilensky, pp. 97–98). The author concludes that much of this minority effort is largely "window dressing" (p. 99, n. 21).

47. Stepan-Norris and Zeitlin, p. 231.

48. Ibid., p. 265.

49. Ibid., pp. 257–258.

50. Levenstein, supra n., p. 316.

51. Lichtenstein, p. 324. The case brought by the Caucus was "in the matter of the United Packinghouse Workers of America, CIO, October 16, 1953."

52. Schrecker, p. 282. "These hearings became so ridiculous that an investigation that found that an employee had never joined any organization, suspect or not, itself raised suspicion. An employee who had joined only her union and a motorcycle club was advised by her employer to make up something, to say that she belonged to some organization, that she is sorry and will have nothing to do with it in the future, and have repudiated it" (Schrecker, pp. 284–285). See also Fosl, which discusses the Wade case in which the Bradens helped a black family purchase a house in a white neighborhood and the hysterical protests that resulted, including an investigation and prosecution of the Bradens for subversive activity. Such attitudes also merged with anti-Semitism. There were claims of the "Jew-led NAACP," not altogether false because its chief counsel was Jewish; claims that "Jewish Marxists Threaten Negro Revolt in America;" and claims that anti-segregationists took their orders from Jews because blacks did not have the brains or money to plan and launch such an assault themselves (Diner, p. 274). The UPWA was one of "a few unions" that "took strong stands in support of the Wades and their defenders" (Fosl, p. 183).

53. Balanoff, p. 264.

54. Ibid., MSS118 International Officers, Editorial Assistant (Richard Durham), 1952, Box 297, f14, between Hathaway and George Paulson, and Ralph Helstein, Wisconsin Historical Society. It is unclear how this problem was resolved.

55. Fehn, Bruce, "'The only hope we had: United Packinghouse Workers Local 46 and the struggle for racial equality in Waterloo, Iowa, 1948–1960," in Stromquist, Shelson and Marvin Bergman (Eds.), *Unionizing the Jungles, Labor and Community in the Twentieth Century Meatpacking Industry* (Iowa City: University of Iowa Press, 1997), pp. 172–173. This article describes the UPWA's implementation of its antidiscrimination policies in its Iowa local.

56. Balanoff, pp. 247–248.

57. Ibid., p. 262.

58. Halpern, pp. 140–144.

59. Charlie Hayes, Halpern, and Horowitz, Tape 153-l, transcribed and summarized by the author.

60. Mss 118, UPWA, General Correspondence and Subject File, District 1, Charles Hayes, Director, 1954, Box 103, Folder 5.

61. Dickerson was accused before the Illinois Senate committee of having signed "a petition for clemency for the Rosenberg atomic bomb spies, signed a request for reduction of the sentence of Claude Lightfoot, later imprisoned as a Communist leader, appealed for the release of Earl Browder, and was affiliated with a long list of organizations later labeled as communist. . . ." Helstein "was questioned about the communist connections of several union officials who took refuge in the 5th amendment when witnesses before the House committee on un-American activities in 1959." *Chicago Daily Tribune*, November 14, 1961, p. 10.

62. *The New York Times*, November 10, 1961.

63. Helstein, with his slate, had been re-elected by "delegates" to the union's convention at Chicago in May, 1960. *The New York Times*, May 27, 1960, p. 14.

64. *Chicago Daily Tribune*, November 7, 1961, p. 16.

65. Lichtenstein, p. 367.

66. Ibid., supra n., pp. 374–381.

67. "Demands first class citizen rights for all," *Chicago Tribune*, October 29, 1961, p. 14

68. "Porter union chief set to push for job rights," *The New York Times*, November 10, 1961, p. B5.

69. *The New York Times*, March 8, 1962, p. 1.

70. "Meany wins fight against Reuther," *The New York Times*, October 9, 1963, p. 74.

71. "NAACP assails rights measures," *The New York Times*, July 3, 1963, p. 10.

72. Interview, September 25, 1995, interviewed by the author, transcribed by Deb Morrow.

73. Foner, Lewis, and Cvornyek, p. 151. At this same meeting at which Helstein spoke, Leon Keyserling stated: "The Budget stems from the idea that at some time it will become apparent that the civil rights movement will have to be implemented in ridding a large part of the population from want . . . " (p. 152).

74. Interview of Les Orear by the author on April 11, 2007, at the office of the ILHS, Chicago, Illinois, transcribed by the author.

75. Horowitz, pp. 97–98.

76. Les Orear interview, November 21, 2006, by the author.

77. Interview and transcription by the author of Norman Dolnick, September 23, 1995, pp. 27–28.

78. Schneir, Rabbi Marc, *Shared Dreams, Martin Luther King, Jr., and the Jewish Community* (Woodstock, VT: Jewish Lights Publishing, 1999), p. 173.

79. Ibid., pp. 172–173.

Chapter 5

1. Balanoff, n. 26, pp. 73–74.
2. Ibid., n. 26, p. 82.
3. Ibid., n. 26, pp. 85–86.
4. Halpern, p. 224.
5. Stepan-Norris and Zeitlin, p. 1.
6. Lichtenstein, pp. 95–96.
7. As part of the union's effort at farmer-labor cooperation, in 1949 it sponsored the "Union Caravan" consisting of musicians, actors, a writer, and a director that traveled to 13 states. They performed on street corners, factories, union halls, fraternal lodges, and county fairs, creating a 45-minute performance of "comic skits, folk dances, and topical lyrics set to well-known music." A highlight of the program was the song, "Put It on the Ground," which included the verse: "If you want a raise in pay, all you have to do is go and ask the boss for it, and he will give it to you; he will give it to you, my boys, he will give it to you; a raise in pay, without a delay, he will give it to you." *Labor's Heritage* (Fall 2000/Winter 2001), pp. 20–35.
8. Lichtenstein, pp. 140–141. Lichtenstein points out that for the most part, Communist Party policy, as expressed through union members, substantially followed CIO policies.
9. The Taft-Hartley Act has been referred to as "The Lawyers' Full Employment Act." One response to a questionnaire stated: "At one time there [in a strike in 1948] they had us tied up with 30 million dollars in damage suits, 22 injunctions, 310 arrest cases, plus 375 counts on contempt.... We had to hire seven additional lawyers and keep them on about a year." Wilensky, n. 4, p. 41.
10. Lichtenstein, pp. 328–239.
11. Richter, Irving, *Labor's Struggles, 1945–1950, A Participant's View* (New York: Cambridge University Press, 1994), fn. 3, p. 69. Letter from Cotton, January 3, 1988, pp. 2–3, commenting on a draft of this book.
12. Halpern, p. 224.
13. Lichtenstein, p. 157.
14. Ellis started the union in the Hormel plant. "He used to say that if you were part of the food chain, from a producer to a consumer, you all belonged in the same union" (p. 29). Ellis' experiences spanned the 1904 meatpacking strike in St. Joseph, Missouri, the free speech fights of the IWW (International Workers of the World) in the 1921 to 1922 national meatpacking strike. Over three decades of activities, Ellis had been jailed numerous times, had become a skilled packinghouse worker, had served on the national executive board of the IWW, and had developed his own vision of union philosophy and structure. He was skeptical of electoral politics and downright hostile to craft unionism. He believed in union democracy, shopfloor organization, direct action, an industrial structure, and solidarity among all workers (p. 28). Ellis explained to an interviewer: "Most of our

strikes were sitdown, sitdown right on the job and not do a damn bit of work until we got it settled.... We had strikes every day. Hell, if a fellow farted crooked we would strike about it (p. 31).... [At Austin public speaking,] Ellis usually [got] top billing. His approach was well thought out. He would set a group of workers on edge for a few weeks, get them to do some thinking, [called] an 'agitational speaker' who managed to capture workers' restlessness. His blunt style seems to have been effective. Whenever you mentioned the AFL, he'd spit on the ground (pp. 34–35)...." In February 1935 ... Ellis told a mass meeting of Rath packinghouse workers about to go on strike in Waterloo, Iowa: "If you say so, we'll bring in militant workers from other cities who will put this thing over. We'll shut down the packinghouses in Austin and Albert Lea if necessary to get men in here to win the strike (p. 35)." This is not from an interview of Ellis, who I've never met, but a compilation by the author on Ellis from various sources. Rachleff, Peter, *Hard-Pressed in the Heartland, The Hormel Strike and the Future of the Labor Movement* (Boston: South End Press, 1993).

15. Brody, p. 227.

16. Johanningsmeier, Edward P., *Forging American Communism, The Life of William Z. Foster* (Princeton, NJ: Princeton University Press, 1994), p. 314.

17. Ibid., n. 87, p. 315.

18. These statements, known as "Communazi" resolutions became "a standard technique for distancing liberal organizations from Communism. Labor unions were especially partial" to such resolutions. Schrecker, p. 83.

19. Levenstein, supra n., p. 94.

20. Cochran, Bert, *Labor and Communism, The Conflict that Shaped American Unions* (Princeton, NJ: Princeton University Press, 1977), p. 4.

21. Jews, in general, were more liberal, more politically active, and less affected by anti-Communist sentiments than the general population. A 1952 Gallup Poll found that 56 percent of Catholics and 45 percent of Protestants considered McCarthy's tactics acceptable, but 98 percent of Jews disapproved of them. Jews had a history of involvement in unions, in the civil rights and civil liberties movements, and with separation of church and state. On the other hand, Jews had much reason to be concerned about themselves as objects of the anti-red movement, particularly as a result of the Rosenbergs' conviction and execution.*Diner*, pp. 277–278, 280. At least in southern racists'minds integrationist sentiment was seen as "part of a 'Communist-Jewish conspiracy.'" Fosl, p. 220.

22. Johanningsmeier, n. 157, p. 324.

23. Brody, p. 227. Red baiting occurred throughout society. To see how this issue played out in a small Jewish community of chicken farmers in California, see Kann, Kenneth, *Joe Rappoport, The Life of a Jewish Radical* (Philadelphia: Temple University Press, 1981), pp. 180–186.

24. Wilensky, p. 10.

25. Balanoff, p. 121–122.

26. Rabinowitz, Victor, *Unrepentent Leftist, A Lawyer's Memoir* (Urbana: University of Illinois Press, 1996), p. 48.

27. Ibid., pp. 48–49.

28. Balanoff, p. 122.

29. When Truman learned in March 1948 that Communists in the San Francisco CIO Council were circulating a denunciation of his Marshall Plan, he called Murray into his office and urged him to take strong action against these elements (Levenstein, pp. 243–244). For background on the Murray-Reuther intra-union struggle, see Cochran, pp. 262–271.

30. UAW president Walter Reuther in 1950, after defeating the center-left coalition, purged Communists and their allies in the international office and locals. Stepan-Norris and Zeitlin, p. 121.

31. Balanoff, p. 123.

32. Rosswurm, Steve, "Introduction: An overview and preliminary assessment of the CIO's expelled unions, in Steve Rosswurm (ed.), *The CIO's Left-Led Unions* (New Brunswick, NJ: Rutgers University Press, 1992), pp. 1–17. In a mid-1949 colloquy between a UE delegation and Murray asking Murray to sign a no-raiding agreement, Murray "tossed their proposed agreement on the desk" and replied, "There is only one issue, and that's Communism" (Stepan-Norris and Zeitlin, supra n., p. 270, 6).

33. Ibid., Stepan-Norris and Zeitlin, supra n., p. 270.

34. Balanoff, pp. 127–129.

35. Interview of Eugene Cotton by Dan Collins, March 1993, transcribed by the author.

36. Ibid. This incident also shows that secretaries were also included in union activities.

37. Weinstein, James, *Ambiguous Legacy, The Left in American Politics* (New York: New Viewpoints, 1975), p. 111.

38. Les Orear, March 31, 1995, interview by the author, transcribed by Deb Morrow. In 1950, the Communist Party, under constant government attack, decided to "go underground." Although several UPWA officers were Communist Party members, none went underground. Glazer, Nathan, *The Social Basis of American Communism* (New York: Harcourt, Brace & World, 1961), p. 127.

39. Schrecker, Ellen W., "McCarthyism and the labor movement: The role of the state" in Steve Rosswurm (ed.), *The CIO's Left-Led Unions* (Class and Culture Series) (New Brunswick, NJ: Rutgers University Press, 1992), pp. 140–157.

40. Ibid., pp. 142–143.

41. Stepan-Norris and Zeitlin, pp. 278–279. "Only three Communists had important posts in the federal government in the 1940s: Lauchin Currie, FDR's China advisor, Alger Hiss . . . and Harry Dexter White, an assistant secretary of the Treasury under FDR. All three had resigned by 1946." Sorin, Gerard, *Irving*

Howe, A Life of Passionate Dissent (New York: New York University Press, 2002), p. 323, n. 24.

42. Schrecker, p. 383.

43. Ibid., pp. 387–395.

44. "Investigation of Un-American Propaganda Activities in the United States," Hearings before the House of Representatives, Subcommittee of the Special Committee to Investigate Un-American Activities, 76th Congress, 3rd Session, Vol. I, September to November 1939.

45. "Communist Activities in the Chicago Area—Part I," Hearings before the Committee on Un-American Activities, House of Representatives, 82nd Congress, 2d session, September 2 and 3, 1952.

46. "Investigation of Communist Activities in the Chicago Area—Part I, II," Hearing before the Committee on Un-American Activities, House of Representatives, 83nd Congress, 2d session, March 15, 1954.

47. "Communist Infiltration of Vital Industries and Current Communist Techniques in the Chicago Area," Hearings before the Committee on Un-American Activities, House of Representatives, 86nd Congress, First session, May 5 to 7, 1959.

48. "Communist Activities in the Chicago Area—Part I," Hearings before the Committee on Un-American Activities, House of Representatives, 89th Congress, First session, May 25 to 27 and June 22, 1965.

49. "Communist Activities in the Chicago Area," pp. 3317–3318.

50. Congressional Hearings, "Communist Infiltration of Vital Industries," n. 120, pp. 516–517. Each of the union people testifying was represented by counsel, but even the selection of counsel was a strategic decision. As Eugene Cotton said: "In the first Dies hearings, I handled all the witnesses, and at the later hearings, it was decided that it would be better if it were clear that the union was not assuming any role with respect to these hearings and they were represented by a black lawyer from Washington, and another white lawyer from Washington. One, a person of independent wealth, took the first amendment; the rest took the fifth, which had already been legally tested." Interview of Eugene Cotton by Dan Collins, March 1993, transcribed by the author.

51. Congressional Hearings "Communist Infiltration of Vital Industries," n. 120, p. 584. An FBI informer testified that Prosten "was the No. 1 Communist in the packing industry," a comment Prosten no doubt would have considered a compliment.

52. The oath reads: "I am not a member of the Communist Party or affiliated with such party. I do not believe in, and I am not a member of, nor do I support, any organization that believes in or teaches the overthrow of the United States Government by force or by any illegal or unconstitutional methods."

53. Halpern, p. 226.

54. Ibid., n. 62, pp. 182–183.

55. For the various strategies adopted by left-led unions to avoid the effects to the non-Communist oath, see Schrecker, p. 150 ff. The oath was finally repealed in 1959 when it was replaced by the anti-racketeering Landrum-Griffin Act "making it illegal for a Communist or ex-Communist who had been out of the Party for less than five years to become a union official" (Rosswurm, p. 155), an act that was overturned by the *U.S. Supreme Court in U.S. v. Brown*, 381 U.S. 437 (1965).

56. Horowitz, n. 62, pp. 183–184; Halpern, n. 1, p. 232. UPWA papers, State Historical Society of Wisconsin, MSS188, Box 308, F2, Q1.

57. Interview by the author of Norman Dolnick, September 23, 1995, pp. 14–15.

58. Frank Ellis, union vice president, wrote that Joe Ollman "told me you were very disturbed about being instructed to sign the non-communist affidavits [and] that you [threatened to] resign as president." After stating that he understood how Helstein felt and that signing might "give the appearance of forfeiting certain principles. . . . [B]ut resigning is not the rational approach, no[r] does it solve anything. . . . Resigning will not be a solution . . . but there is a greater principle involved in this case. It is the trade union movement. . . ." WHS MSS867 Helstein Correspondence 1948, Box 2, folder 2. It is unknown whether this reasoning swayed Helstein. But suggesting that resigning was not a "rational approach" and that continuing as president was in the interest of the union movement was certainly in line with Helstein's thinking.

59. Halpern, n. 26, p. 224.

60. Johanningsmeier, n. 81, p. 326; Lichtenstein.

61. Stepan-Norris, and Zeitlin, p. 4.

62. Ibid., pp. 13–14, n. 28.

63. Johanningsmeier, p. 328.

64 Horton, Myles, with Judith Kohl and Herbert Kohl, *The Long Haul, An Autobiography* (New York: Doubleday, 1990), p. 97.

65 Stepan-Norris and Zeitlin, p. 22.

66 Walter Reuther, UAW president, stated at the CIO's 1949 convention that " 'the record is clear' that the CIO's Communists were 'not a trade union group' and has failed to carry out the kind of program geared to the needs of American workers . . . " Stepan-Norris and Zeitlin, p. 21.

67 Stepan-Norris and Zeitlin, p. 61. Most unionists were impervious to the red charges and to raids from right-wing unions, where these leaders consistently produced results like better wage and working conditions for them. Ibid, pp. 318–320.

68 Ibid., p. 115.

69 Ibid., p. 280. Even resigning from the Communist Party and signing the oath did not get unionists off the hook. In a number of cases, the government prosecuted these officials for perjury (supra, p. 282). A year after the law went into

effect, 81,000 union officers had signed the affidavits, including 30 of the CIO's 45 unions (Levenstein, p. 218).

70 Cochran, pp. 153–154.

71 MSS118, Box287, f1, House [of Representatives] Un-American Activities Committee (HUAC), Communist investigations, 1959. This information was contained in a letter to "Dear Sir and Brother," signed by "Russell R. Lasley, International Vice-President for the Committee, together with other union officials" The attachment was headed, "Questions l. Are you a member of the Communist Party; 2. Have you at any time since December, 1957 been a member of the Communist Party? 3. If your answers to either or both of the above questions is 'No,' do you now support or have you been at any time since December, 1957 a consistent supporter of, or have you actively participated in any activities of the Communist Party? If the answer is 'Yes,' to any part of this question, specify the occasion or occasions and the nature of the support or participation." Of course, by December 1957, almost all, if not all, union officials had left the Party.

72 Brody, p. 247. A particular provision that made it difficult to organize in the South was the provision giving individual states the power to outlaw the union shop (Lichtenstein, p. 239).

73 Ibid., Balanoff, p. 189.

74 Ibid., pp. 190–191. Helstein described the atmosphere while March spoke: "[I]t was a tense hall. You could just cut the tension in a large auditorium in this hotel. The Cosmopolitan Hotel in Denver was packed. They were sitting on the edge of their chairs. They knew this was a fight, knew that it was the result of the election that had taken place. When March came up to the podium and they recognized him you could have heard a pin drop. It was real tension and let me tell you it took an awful lot of courage to get up there and face those people at all. And he spoke . . . with feeling. You know he was a brilliant speaker, fantastically effective." Ibid., p. 194.

75 Ibid., p. 192.

Chapter 6

1. Information on Puerto Rico comes from http://www.welcome.topuertorico.org/history5.shtml.

2. WHS MSS Puerto Rican Correspondence January to August 1952, Box 538, folder 2.

3. Ibid.

4. Ibid.

5. Balanoff interview of Helstein, May 3, 1972, reduced to manuscript, in the possession of the Roosevelt University Library. n. 26, pp. 146–147.

6. Ibid., p. 154.

7. Ibid., p. 155.

8. Ibid., n. 26, p. 156.

9. Ibid., p. 153. Although Helstein did not specifically refer to the comparison, the parallel to his experience in becoming UPWA president is obvious, including the cultural and historical differences, no doubt one of the points of this recital.

10. Ibid., pp. 157–158.

11. Ibid., p. 148.

12. Ibid., p. 158.

13. Ibid., p. 161.

14. Ibid., pp. 163–164.

15. Ibid., p. 165.

16. Helstein had much earlier dropped adhering to Jewish dietary rules. Recall his daughter Nina's statement of eating bacon for breakfast.

17. Balanoff, p. 167. Helstein was obviously out of sync with the Latin culture. They drove too slow for him and seemed to be more interested in family relations and having a good time than in "getting down to business."

18. Ibid., pp. 167–168.

19. Ibid., pp. 168–169.

20. Ibid., p. 160.

21. Eva Sandberg, telephone interview by the author, October 7, 2006.

Chapter 7

1. Helstein, p. 170.

2. Ibid., p. 171.

3. Halpern, pp. 247–248.

4. Citing Troy, "Trade Union Membership, 1897–1962" (New York, 1962) in Lichtenstein, Nelson, *Labor's War at Home, the CIO in World War II* (New York: Leo Cambridge University Press, 1982), p. 80.

5. "Progress Report, Automation Committee, Formed under agreements of September 1, 1959 between Armour and Company and United Packinghouse Food and Allied Workers AFL-CIO and Amalgamated Meat cutters and Butcher Workmen of North America AFL-CIO," supra n., p. 544. This report details the job losses and the difficulties in obtaining further employment of laid-off workers, the hardest hit being the oldest, least skilled and educated, women and African Americans—in other words, exactly those groups that had heretofore most benefited from the UPWA's policies.

6. Interview with Eugene Cotton, September 21, 1995, by the author, transcribed by Deb Morrow. In the AFL-CIO's 1961 convention, delegate Charley Hayes, in a speech from the floor, pointed out that 10,000 jobs had disappeared in the previous six years and that those who were unemployed could find employment in lower paid jobs or on the relief rolls. He also said that there was double the unemployment among "Negroes" than whites and called on the Executive

Council to "implement the procedures" to help alleviate this problem. Foner, Lewis, and Cvornyek (eds.), pp. 67–68.

7. Eugene Cotton, September 21, 1995, interview by the author, transcribed by Deb Morrow. This statement by Cotton shows how the role of lawyer departs from the simple advocate to one who thoroughly understood how individual workers fit within the industry.

8. Helstein, Ralph, "Collective Bargaining in the Meat Packing Industry," in Arnold R. Weber (ed.), *Collective Bargaining, Problems and Perspectives*, Proceedings of a Seminar Sponsored by Graduate School of Business—University of Chicago and The McKinsey Foundation (Skokie, IL: The Free Press of Glencoe, IL, 1961), pp. 151–171.

9. Helstein, p. 152.

10. Ralph Helstein, Tape 1, November 23, 1982, interview by H. Targ and transcribed by the author.

11. "Progress Report," p. 1. The UPWA representatives were Jesse Prosten (contract administrator) and Howard McDermott (director of the Wage Rate Department).

12. "I think he contributed vision, and a mission, and I think that if Ralph not been in that position I don't think that the same degree of work or attention and focus on civil rights would have been there, and I don't think that the union would have developed the progressive kinds of collective bargaining program that they did" (Eugene Cotton, General Counsel of the union).

13. David F. Noble, *Forces of Production: A Social History of Industrial Automation* (New York, N.Y.: Oxford University Press, 1984), p. 252.

14. Ibid., pp. 252, 255.

15. Wilson J., Warren, *Tied to the Great Packing Machine, The Midwest and Meatpacking* (Iowa City: University of Iowa Press, 2007), pp. 23–24.

16. Horowitz, "Community," supra n., p. 118.

17. Deslippe, Dennis A., "Challenges to Gender Inequality in the United Packinghouse Workers of America, 1965–1974," in Stromquist, Shelson and Marvin Bergman (eds.), *Unionizing the Jungles, Labor and Community in the Twentieth Century Meatpacking Industry* (Iowa City: University of Iowa Press, 1997), pp. 195–196.

18. Deslippe, supra n. 121, p. 198.

19. Ibid., n. 121, pp. 198–202. The suit filed by Ottumwa women with the EEOC ended with a judgment of $450 for each complainant (p. 2020. Disputes between men and women became so heated that there was occasional violence and harassment against the female claimants.

20. Fink, Deborah, "Reorganizing inequity, gender and structural transformation in Iowa meatpacking," in Stromquist, Sheldon and Marvin Bergman (eds.), *Unionizing the Jungles, Labor and Community in the Twentieth Century Meatpacking Industry* (Iowa City: University of Iowa Press, 1997), p. 225. "I [the author] witnessed and experienced sexual harassment daily in the time I worked there,

and I saw no evidence that either management or the union was addressing it effectively" (p. 232).

21. Deslippe, supra n. 121, pp. 210–211.

22. Fink, supra n. 124, p. 257. There is "a significant difference between worker relations in the old Hygrade plant and the new plants: for the 'new breed' packer, the factor most easily manipulated to extract as much wealth as possible from every animal is the labor force, and they are perfectly willing to do so."

23. Fink, supra n. 126, pp. 228–230.

24. Horowitz, "Community," supra n., pp. 118–119.

25. Bruce R. Fehn, *Striking Women: Gender, Race, and Class in the United Packinghouse Workers of America (UPWA), 1938–1968*, Dissertation (Madison, WI: Graduate School, University of Wisconsin-Madison, 1991), pp. 155–106.

26. Horowitz, n. 30, p. 38; Barrett, n. 3, pp. 51–52, 54.

27. James Weinstein, *Ambiguous Legacy, The Left in American Politics* (New York: New Viewpoints, 1975), p. 164.

28. Halpern, n. 1, p. 428–434.

29. Cohen, n. 21, p. 348.

30. Cohen, n. 21, pp. 347, 358–359.

31. Orear, Leslie F. and Stephen H. Diamond, *Out of the Jungle, The Packinghouse Fight for Justice and Equality in Chicago* (Hyde Park, NY: Hyde Park Press, 1968).

32. MS118, Box 287, f2, HUAC Committee Investigation, 1960. Letter, dated July 27, 1960, from G.H. Hathaway, international secretary-treasurer of the UPWA-AFL-CIO to George Meany, president of the AFL and CIO. The letter in part stated: "For many years complaints have been registered by members in various areas of our operation—and particularly by those in canning, sugar, and stockyards locals—that the name of our organization inadequately reflected the actual scope of its membership and that on some occasions employers in these fields had made efforts to use the name as a device to promote disaffection or to obstruct organization."

33. Perry, Charles R. and Delwyn H. Kegley, *Disintegration and Change: Labor Relations in the Meat-Packing Industry* (Philadelphia, PA: Industrial Research Unit, University of Pennsylvania, 1989), p. 97.

34. Eugene Cotton September 21, 1995, interviewed by the author, transcribed by Deb Morrow.

35. Correspondence shows that Helstein was asked to be on the board of Saul Alinsky's Industrial Areas Foundation (January 8, 1948) and the University of Chicago's Citizens Board, WHS Helstein Correspondence 1948, Box 2, folders 2 and 5.

36. Jewish Vocational Service and Employment Center, December 29, 1947 (WHS Helstein Correspondence 1948, Box 2, folder 2).

37. The AFL-CIO Council warned any members of Congress in the mid-term 1966 election: "Those who would deny our military forces unstinting support are in effect aiding the Communist enemy of our country." Most rank-and-file members agreed with this sentiment. Tuchman, Barbara W., *The March of Folly, From Troy to Vietnam* (New York, Alfred A. Knopf, 1984), p. 327.

38. *The New York Times*, May 7, 1972, p. 21. Walter Reuther, his brother Victor and Emil Mazey UAW secretary-treasurer, came out against the war in 1969. Isserman, Michael, *The Other American, the Life of Michael Harrington* (New York: Public Affairs, 2000), p. 288.

39. Peter Kims, *The New York Times*, November 10, 1973, p. 1. Helstein was engaged in numerous other civic activities. For example in April 1960, it was reported that he was "named to the Midwest advisory board of the American Medical center, Denver, Colo. . . . The board is composed of business, professional, philanthropic, and labor leaders from the Chicago area." Included among the members was Earl B. Dickerson. "The American Medical center is a 56 year old hospital for the care of tuberculosis and cancer patients." *Chicago Daily Tribune*, April 14, 1960, p. S10.

40. Isserman, p. 319. The DSOC was an attempt by Harrington to create an organization "to take the place of the now defunct Socialist Party" with which he had been associated during most of his adult life. "The designation, 'organizing committee' conveyed a deliberately modest self-evaluation: It was meant to suggest a group that would be involved in an ongoing process of innovation and transition. . . . At the same time, for radicals . . . the name carried with it echoes of the heroic days of the Left in the 1930s, . . . like the CIO's Steel Workers Organizing Committee. . . ." Isserman, p. 311.

41. WHS, MSS 867, Helstein Correspondence 1956, Box 2, folder 7.

42. Ibid., Box 2, folder 6.

43. Ibid., Box 3, folder 2.

44. Isserman, supra n., pp. 304–305.

45. Ibid., supra n., p. 322.

46. WHS MSS 867, Helstein Correspondence 1955, Box 2, folder 6.

47. WHS MSS 867, Helstein Correspondence 1962, Box 3, folder 2. Helstein asked in the letter that deliveries of the paper be suspended during July, when he was presumably on vacation.

48. WHS MSS 867, Helstein Correspondence, 1954, Box, folder 1.

49. WHS MSS, Helstein Correspondence, 1947, Box 2, folder 1.

50. WHS, Helstein Correspondence, 1948, Box 2, folder 2.

51. WHS MSS 867, Helstein Correspondence, 1960, Box 3, folder 1.

52. WSH MSS 118 Contributions 1947–1948, Box 46, folder 1.

53. *The New York Times*, June 17, 1980, in which Helstein is listed as a "retired packing house union worker" and *The New York Times*, February 15, 1985, p. 1. WHS MS S867, Helstein Correspondence, 1951, Box 2, Folder 4.

54. WHS, MSS Helstein Correspondence 1947, Box 2, folder 1.

55. WHS MSS 118, UPWA General Correspondence and Subject file C-D (Colleges & Universities) & General.

56. WHS MSS 867, Helstein Correspondence, 1959, Box 2, folder 12.

57. WHS MSS 867, Helstein Correspondence, 1951, Box 2, folder 4.

58. WHS MSS 868, Helstein Correspondence, 1956, Box 2, folder 7.

59. WHS MSS 867, Helstein Correspondence, 1959, Box 2, folder 12.

60. WHS MSS 867, Helstein Correspondence ,1958, Box 2, folder 9.

Chapter 8

1. Brody, p. 263.

2. Helstein, p. 152.

3. Mergers were very common in union history. See Herberg, pp. 22–45.

4. Brody, p. 216.

5. Ibid., p. 237.

6. Ibid., p. 238.

7. Ibid., p. 239.

8. Perry and Kegley, p. 112.

9. Brody, pp. 242–244.

10. Ibid., p. 250.

11. Ibid., pp. 263–264. In that merger agreement, "Agreement for the Merger of the American Federation of Labor and the Congress of Industrial Organizations," signed February 9, 1955, under No. 2, "Principles of Merger," states: "The merged federation shall constitutionally recognize the right of all workers, without regard to race, creed, color or national origin to share in the full benefits of trade union organization in the merged federation. The merged federation shall establish appropriate internal machinery to bring about, at the earliest possible date, the effective implementation of this principle of non-discrimination...." Foner, Lewis, and Cvornyek.

12. Brody, p. 268.

13. Ibid., p. 269.

14. Balanoff, pp. 257–258.

15. Ibid., p. 258.

16. Ibid., p. 262.

17. Ibid., p. 273.

18. Brody, p. 265.

19. Ibid., pp. 265–266.

20. Balanoff, pp. 248–249.

21. Ibid., p. 250.

22. Brody, p. 267.

23. Ibid., p. 268.

24. Perry and Kegley, p. 115.

25. Helstein first learned about Highlander and met Myles through the union's civil rights work. "[W]e took our kids down to Monteagle and they fell in love with that area [in Tennessee].... We used to contribute some money and get more of our people going there; but we did that because Highlander and Myles represented the same things that we believed in. We knew he wasn't a communist. It was perfectly ridiculous [emphasis in original] to call someone who was as independent as Myles a communist . . . the end result was that we had this community of feeling that transcended ordinary relationships." Wiggerton, p. 69.

26. Zacharakis-Jutz, Jeffrey T., *Straight to the Heart of a Union, Straight to the Heart of a Movement: Worker's Education in the United Packinghouse Workers of America between 1951 and 1953* (DeKalb, IL: Northern Illinois University, 1991), pp. 167–177.

27. Glen, John M., *Highlander, No Ordinary School, 1932–1962* (Lexington, KY: University of Kentucky Press, 1988), pp. 6–7.

28. Ibid., pp. 11–12.

29. Zacharakis-Jutz, pp. 176–177.

30. Glen, pp. 19–20.

31. Ibid., p. 20

32. Ibid., p. 30.

33. Ibid., n. 152, p. 45.

34. Zacharakis-Jutz, n. 152, p. 179.

35. Dolnick, interview by the author, September 23, 1995.

36. Zacharakis-Jutz, pp. 186–187.

37. MSS 118, UPWA, General Correspondence and Subject file, April to December 1950, Box 70, Folder 5, Les Orear.

38. Zacharakis-Jutz, pp. 206–209.

39. Interview with Eugene Cotton, May 17, 1995.

40. Zacharakis-Jutz, pp. 260–267.

41. Ibid., pp. 267–268

42. Wiggerton, p. 93.

43. This narrative has been compiled from interviews with Les Orear, March 31, 1995, interviewed by the author, transcribed by Deb Morrow; interview, Ralph Helstein, January 14, 1981, interviewed by Les Orear; interview of Rachel Helstein by the author at her home; and interview of Catherine Brosman Carey, December 21, 1996, by the author by telephone.

44. During the Omaha convention (1944) at which Helstein, after discovering that the convention hotel discriminated against blacks, moved the convention elsewhere, Stephens, district director, took the floor to state that he accepted blame, apologized, and "confessed that Omaha's Jim Crow policy was 'something we never knew existed before.'" Halpern, p. 217. It is possible that Stephens'

receptivity to Durham's proactive black policies was his means of making up for his past delinquency in this area.

45. Balanoff, p. 269.

46. Horowitz, p. 120.

47. Balanoff, p. 183.

48. Stephens became romantically involved with Cathy Brosnan, his secretary, who at the same time, apparently unknown to Stephens, was also involved with Richard Durham.

49. According to a "Memorandum" dated January 7, 1952, from Russell Lasley, "The services of Richard Durham have been acquired to write a popular version of the Fisk studies.... He will also put into pamphlet form the Wilson and Swift arbitration awards. We have agreed to pay him a salary of $500.00 a month for a two month period, plus any necessary expenses." MSS 118, Box 246, F16, Dolnick and Durham, 1952.

50. "Dick [Durham] pointed out to [Stephens] that while the union had conventions and passed a whole lot of resolutions, there was never any particular action; they said we were going to defend the rights of women for equal pay for equal work. We're going to fight against discrimination or we're going try to get better relationships with the farmers who raise the cattle. Nothing really followed up on that so he said somebody needs to see these programs holistically, and act on them and coordinate activity of the international union and then of the districts, and then of the locals in working in their areas on these problems. So he got a job. A department was established in the union called the International Program Department, and it was then in its embryo stage and they decided they'd start with the coordinator in Chicago, and they were going to have one out in Kansas City, and I think one in Iowa and one perhaps in New York.... There were ten districts I believe at the time. But it was started with the Program Department in about four districts." Oscar Brown, Jr., September 23, 1995, interviewed and transcribed by the author.

51. Interview with Les Orear, March 31, 1995.

52. Ibid.

53. "Now I [Helstein] must introduce one other character in this drama and that was a man by the name of Russell Bull, a strong figure. A tough and stubborn guy, thin, lean, very black hair, an intense person. He was the fisherman that we all went fishing with but he was really a driving force and a wonderful guy. As a matter of fact one of the most dramatic stories I ever listened to was the story of how he and about four or five other people organized the Tobin Packing Company in Fort Dodge, Iowa under the worst of circumstances. This was back in the 30s.... He was strong and able, had a whole lot of guts. He'd get us into all kinds of problems." Balanoff, p. 184. In an interview conducted and transcribed by the author on March 24, 1995, Herb March stated that "Russell Bull was a good, militant unionist. He was the director of District 3. He took over from

Stephens, much better than Stephens; originally out of a packinghouse, and he didn't go for redbaiting. He was not a political person and he could be depended on to follow a course of honest, militant unionism, and organizing anything that had to be organized. When we were in the fight for a new International, he was a stalwart on anything where grievances arose, where militant action was required—especially in the Armour chain—that would involve a militant interpretation of the provisions of the contract. He was the best director they ever had. Helstein was not present when the Russell Bull incident with Durham took place so what he recounts is second-hand information he acquired."

54. Horton had been "beaten up, locked up, put upon and railed against by racists, toughs, demagogues, and governors. . . . [I]n 1932, in the mountains west of Chattanooga, in one of America's poorest counties, Myles Horton founded the Highlander Folk School. . . . At first he ran workshops to train organizers for the CIO. . . . In the early 1950s, Horton turned the emphasis of his workshops from union organizing to civil rights. Highlander was now the principal gathering place of the moving forces of the black revolution" Horton, p. ix.

55. Initially, Bull's reaction was to say, "'Look, this is my way of talking. I say, "Come on boys," and say it to anybody, and that doesn't mean that I think they're children.'" Finally, Charlie Hayes, who is black— . . . said to Bull, 'I'm a friend of yours, you like me. I know it. If I tell you that that term applied to me demeans me and insults me will you stop using it because you're a friend of mine?' . . . Bull said, 'Well, of course, I'm not going to insult you. Of course, I'll stop using it.'" Balanoff, p. 185.

56. Interview with Ralph Helstein January 14, 1981, by Les Orear, transcribed by the author. Civil Rights, Tape No. 5.

57. Interview with Rachel Helstein at her home.

58. I got to know Charlie Hayes quite well. While I was working for William Davies Packing, Hayes was the UPWA organizer who helped organize the plant and who helped us with the strike. Then when I thought of doing his biography, I interviewed several of his fellow workers. He took me down to Mounds, Illinois, where he grew up and where I interviewed several of his family members. Whenever I came to Chicago, we went to lunch together at a South Side restaurant where as you entered a life-size picture of Hayes appeared on the wall opposite one of former Chicago mayor, Harold Washington. As a former member of the House of Representatives from that district, he was greeted with great reverence. Relevant to this episode with Stephens, such an emotional outburst was uncharacteristic. I knew Charlie as extremely calm, always in good humor, warm, and normally never given to uncontrolled anger. He was emotional when he spoke to workers about their rights but otherwise was extremely amiable and even-tempered. Stephens and Hayes had a long-standing feuding relationship. In November 1955 during an organizing drive in the Chicago Swift plants, Stephens wanted Hayes to reassign a talented organizer, Leo Turner, currently engaged in

the Swift organizing drive, to the Kansas City Swift plant. In a three-page, single-spaced letter to Stephens, Hayes denominated the proposal as "ill-timed, ill-advised, illogical" and to be "profoundly shocked" by the purported suggestion "that the blame for our poor showing in organizing new members rests on the back of our Anti-discrimination Policy." In a letter of December 21, 1955, Stephens replied to "Brother Hayes," calling Hayes' letter a "dissertation . . . covering everything from 'Operation Dixie' to UPWA personnel practices to the Wilson shutdown to cynicism." Hayes was accused of "histrionics" and that he had been "carried away by your own sense of dramatics," concluding that "the enemy will be overcome by our unity and firmness of purpose. I ask you to join the fight. Your efforts are necessary to win." MS 118 Q16, Wisconsin Historical Society. Stephens was also critical of Herb March and Les Orear. In a letter from Stephens to Orear dated October 11, 1949, Stephens complained of an article published in the union paper that Orear edited, writing, "The facts are, Les, I told you to do this before, and you allowed it to happen the way it did happen. This campaign [Wilson boycott] . . . is a serious one . . . [and] demands precision on instructions. In the future, please take note." MSS 118, UPWA General Convention and Subject file, Les Orear, 1949, Box 59, folder 1. In a letter from Stephens to Herb March dated February 8, 1952, Stevens wrote, "I have noted your constant criticism of our efforts to organize. . . . Stephens asks March to offer his own plan, "You are obviously convinced that you possess a superior knowledge of these matters. . . . frankly, I am getting a little tired of your left-handed slaps at our efforts. . . ." MSS 118, UPWA general Convention and Subject file, Box 90, folder 3, Helstein Convention, General, January to March 1952, Wisconsin Historical Society.

59. Balanoff, pp. 259–260.

60. Ibid., p. 275.

61. Ibid., p. 276.

62. "The denouement came when Durham overreached himself, when Helstein got the impression that he was being surrounded by Stephens and Durham. . . . At the convention in New York, Stephens told poor Lasley that his head was in his lap and he could prepare to take a walk because he wasn't going to be reelected. Stephens had selected a black guy from Indiana to take over from poor Lasley. And Ralph was a party to that, uneasy about it. Then suddenly Charlie Hayes got word that there was going to be opposition to him and that was going to be Clayton Sales from Indiana—a guy who could be easily handled by Durham. Then Charlie and Ralph got their heads together and smelt what was brewing. When Ralph talked to Stephens about it, Stephens said he wasn't going to commit himself to support Hayes. Then Ralph saw all these pieces falling into place. There was going to be a new vice-president and a new district director in Chicago, not his people at all. Then he had a meeting with Lasley, put his head back on; he was going to be elected vice-president and Stephens wasn't. [Glen]

Chinander [director of District 2] afterward said we were not after you, only opposed because we thought Stephens was your fair-haired boy and we hate Stephens. So from then on it was clear sailing for Helstein for the rest of his career." Interview with Les Orear, March 31, 1995, interviewed by the author, transcribed by Deb Morrow. "Then the Sioux City convention came along and the black membership on the executive board was strengthened by addition of Don Smith from New York who took over from Meyer Stern, and George Thomas from Texas who took over from Pittman and Hayes who took over from Nielsen. All three occurred at that convention. Not going to say that Durham did it. Sure that Stevens was doing it. They were good changes . . . but those changes gave Durham a power platform for his own operation. Very interesting political situation because Helstein was also finding that his black face was excellent and he could use that black face to keep the 'right wing,' the anti-administration people boxed in. This was like Glen Chinander in St. Paul and Baker in Kansas City, and local union elements not in Helstein's camp. Helstein could beat them over the head that they were not good enough friends of the black people. This leadership could be neutralized—all lilly-white [sic] politics—did not follow the black-white line enough. Dumping Pittman was a good example, meaning that if you didn't tow the line, you could be replaced. Baker was getting this—not by blacks—by black forces. Helstein could do this because they loved him and he knew he was doing right." Interview with Les Orear, March 31, 1995.

63. Balanoff, p. 260.

64. "[Helstein] always believed that between, Durham, [Oscar] Brown [and] Kathy Brosnan . . . —this was the way to take over complete power in the union, . . . in the beginning not to take power directly, but to surround me so that I wouldn't be able to do anything without their approval; and then later, once they accomplished that it would be simple to take over the whole operation." Les Orear, undated, interview by Fehr, summarized by the author.

65. In this letter of May 9, 1958, from Stephens to Helstein, Stephens began, "This is a very difficult letter for me to write. . . . I now feel I clearly understand what you were trying to say. . . . (1) This is a power fight between you and me. (2) After 16 years my loyalty to you has ended and that I am attempting to control the Executive Board. . . . I have not in any way conspired against you. I am not in any way part of a power fight against you." Stephens offered to "give you my resignation as Vice President of this Union . . . and if you so desire. I will not be a candidate for Vice President of the International Union at the New York Convention." Obviously, by ignoring Stephens' offer to resign, Helstein preferred to maintain total control of this termination process.

66. Balanoff, pp. 278–279.

67. Letter from Tony Stephens.

68. MSS 118, Box 288, F2, HUAC—A. T. Stephens, Correspondence and Affidavits, 1959.

69. Ibid.

70. "The AFL-CIO Ethical Practices Codes were adopted as formal UPWA Policy at the May, 1958 Convention of the UPWA on the basis of the AFL-CIO Convention adoption of these Codes in December, 1957." MS 118, Box 287, F1, HUAC, Communist Investigation, 1959. This same document set forth "certain rules which will govern our decisions and procedure...."

71. MSS 118, Box 287, F1, HUAC, Communist Investigation, 1959. Given Helstein's career-long opposition to such "loyalty oaths," it is passing strange that the union adopted such a procedure. The only explanation I can think of is that, similar to the March firing, Helstein thought it necessary to save the union.

72. This letter came from the same source as the other material on this matter, but no source is indicated on the letter.

73. MSS 118, Box 287, F1, HUAC, Communist Investigation, 1959.

74. MSS 118, Box 162, F7, Communist Investigation, 1961 (Public Review Advisory Commission).

75. Interview with Nina Helstein, March 7, 1996, by the author, transcribed by Deb Morrow.

76. Eugene Cotton interview, September 21, 1995, interviewed and transcribed by the author.

77. Interview of Les Orear, April 11, 2007, at his office, Illinois Labor History Society, Chicago, Illinois.

78. Interview of *Catherine Brosman Carey,* December, 21 1996, by telephone by the author, transcribed by Deb Morrow. I have rearranged Brosnan's statements and added connectives to provide a coherent whole.

79. Oscar Brown, Jr., September 23, 1995, interviewed by the author at the home of Brad Lyttle, transcribed by Deb Morrow.

80. Warren, pp. 39–40.

81. Ibid., pp. 43–46.

82. Perry and Kegley, pp. 45–48.

83. Center for Economic and Policy Research, 1611 Connecticut Avenue NW, Suite 400, Washington, DC 20009, 202-293-5380, http://www.cepr.net/index.php/about-us. Economic and Policy Research, Washington, D.C., April 7, 2009.

Chapter 9

1. Copy of letter of November 30, 1972, with attached letter of the Illinois Labor History Society. The article in *The New York Times*, November 30, 1972, p. 16 stated: "Ralph Helstein, 64 years old, who was president of the United Packinghouse Workers of America from 1946 until the merger with the Amalgamated Meat Cutters and Butcher Workmen union in 1968, retired today with the title of president emeritus. He had served as vice president and special counsel of the merged union."

2. "The UPWA was renamed in 1964 the United Packinghouse, Food and Allied Workers of America to reflect the changing demography of the union as sugar workers affiliated, and vegetable packing workers and even Alaskan fishery workers affiliated too. That was the official name at the time of the merger. So it is often the practice to use the most recent name rather than the original one—it was still the same union before the merger" (e-mail from Les Orear, April 22, 2008).

3. The fund spent all its funds in producing the Memorial Day Massacre film and some other publications, e-mail from Les Orear, May 7, 2008.

4. Lichtenstein, p. 326.

5. Interview with Lester Orear, April 11, 2007 at this office, Illinois Labor History Society (ILHS), Chicago, Illinois.

6. This is exactly the reasoning he gave in a letter to his father when his father queried why he wanted to take the job as president of the union.

7. Interview of Les Orear, September 6, 2006, at ILHS office.

8. Ibid.

9. Obituary, headline, "Helstein, 76, activist, former union leader," *The New York Times*, February 15, 1985, p. C10.

10. Ibid., p. A24.

11. Isserman is Hamilton College Professor. Isserman is the author of a biography of Michael Harrington (author of *The Other America*, the book that inspired the War on Poverty in the 1960s), entitled *The Other American: The Life of Michael Harrington* was selected as a *New York Times* Notable Book of the Year in 2000, (p. 363).

12. This event recalls the incident when Helstein himself, as a law student, joined a protest against unjust wage practices and ended up in jail. His father merely admonished him to find a way to protest that would not land him in jail but encouraged him to continue to do what he thought was right.

13. According to the *Chicago Tribune* obituary, n. 8, "he became a member of Swift & Co, Local 28. He went into the cattle pens and slaughterhouses, studying operations, jobs and job classifications, of which there were hundreds. He wrote a 361-page brief on the economic, wage and working conditions of the industry for the War Labor Board."

14. Excerpts from his convention speeches are found in the Appendix.

15. Perry, Charles R. and Delwyn H. Kegley, *Disintegration and Change, Labor Relations in the Meat Packing Industry* (Philadelphia, PA: Industrial Research Unit, The Wharton School, University of Pennsylvania, 1989), pp. 1–2. See pp. 86–90 for a description of the reorganization of the packing industry.

16. Ibid., p. 20.

17. Ibid., p. 18.

18. Ibid., p. 70.

Bibliography

Book References

Anderson, Lewie, "Declining Union Power and Membership." Prepared by Lewie G. Anderson, UFCW Local 1142 Member President of Research-Education-Advocacy-People, July 22, 1994.

Andreas, Carol, *Meatpackers and Beef Barons, Company Town in a Global Economy* (Newot, CO: University Press of Colorado, 1994).

Auerbach, Jerold S., *Rabbis and Lawyers, The Journey from Torah to Constitution* (Bloomington, IN: Indiana University Press, 1990).

Barrett, James R., *Work and Community in the Jungle, Chicago's Packinghouse Workers, 1894–1922* (Urbana: University of Illinois Press, 1987).

Bays, Martha Dupree, *Drawing the Color Line: The Uses of Race in Manipulating Labor Markets* (Evanston, IL: Northwestern University, 1988).

Brody, David, *The Butcher Workmen, A Study of Unionization* (Cambridge, MA: Harvard University Press, 1964).

Cahan, Abraham, *The Rise of David Levinsky* (New York: Harper and Brothers, 1917).

Cohen, Lizabeth, *Making a New Deal, Industrial Workers in Chicago, 1919–1939* (Cambridge, UK: Cambridge University Press, 1990).

Davidowicz, Lucy S. A., "The Jewishness of the Jewish Labor Movement in the United States" in *A Bicentennial Festschrift for Jacob Rader Marcus*, ed. Bertram Wallace Korn (New York: American Jewish Historical Society/KTAV1976), reprinted in *The American Jewish Experience*, ed. Jonathan D. Sarna [New York: Holmes & Meier, 1986).

Deslippe, Dennis A., "Challenges to gender inequality in the United Packinghouse Workers of America, 1965–1974," in Stromquist, Shelson and Marvin Bergman (eds.), *Unionizing the Jungles, Labor and Community in the Twentieth Century Meatpacking Industry* (Iowa City: University of Iowa Press, 1997), pp. 195–196.

Diner, Hasia R. and Beryl Lieff Benderly, *Her Work Praises Her, A History of Jewish Women in America from Colonial Times to the Present* (New York: Basic Books, 2002).

Diner, Hasia R. and Beryl Lieff Benderly, *Profiles of Eleven, Profiles of Eleven Men Who Guided the Destiny of an Immigrant Society and Stimulated Social Consciousness Among the American People* (Detroit: Wayne State University Press, 1965).

Epstein, Melech, *Jewish Labor in the U.S.A., An Industrial, Political History of the Jewish Labor Movement* (New York: Trade Union Sponsoring Committee, 1882, 1914).

Fehn, Bruce, " 'The only hope we had,' United Packinghouse Workers Local 46 and the struggle for racial equality in Waterloo, Iowa, 1948–1960," in Stromquist, Shelson and Marvin Bergman (eds.), *Unionizing the Jungles, Labor and Community in the Twentieth Century Meatpacking Industry* (Iowa City: University of Iowa Press, 1997).

Fehn, Bruce R., *Striking Women: Gender, Race or Class in the United Packinghouse Workers of America (UPWA)* (Madison, WI: University of Wisconsin, 1991).

Fink, Deborah, "Reorganizing inequity, general and structural transformation in Iowa meatpacking," in Stromquist, Shelson and Marvin Bergman (eds.), *Unionizing the Jungles, Labor and Community in the Twentieth Century Meatpacking Industry* (Iowa City: University of Iowa Press, 1997).

Foner, Philip S., Ronald L. Lewis, and Ronald Cvornyek, "The Black worker since the AFL-CIO merger, 1955–1980," in *The Black Worker, A Documentary History from Colonial Times to the Present*, Vol. III (Philadelphia: Temple University Press, 1984).

Freud, Sigmund, *Leonardo da Vinci, A Study in Psychosexuality*, authorized translation by A. A. Brill, PhD, MD (New York: Vintage Books, Random House, 1916, renewed 1947).

Ginger, Ann Fagan, *Carol Weiss King, Human Rights Lawyer, 1895–1952* (Boulder, CO: University of Colorado Press, 1992).

Glen, John M., *Highlander, No Ordinary School, 1932–1962* (Lexington, KY: University of Kentucky Press, 1988).

Glenn, Susan A., *Daughters of the Shetl, Life and Labor in the Immigrant Generation* (Ithaca, NY: Cornell University Press, 1990), p. 1.

Gordon, Albert I., *Jews in Transition* (Minneapolis, MN: University of Minnesota Press, 1949), p. 18.

Greene, Melissa Fay, *The Temple Bombing* (Reading, MA: Addison-Wesley Publishing Co., 1970)

Halpern, Eric Brian, *"Black and White Unite and Fight": Race and Labor in Meatpacking, 1904–1948* (Philadelphia: University of Pennsylvania, 1989).

Harper, Steven J., *Straddling Worlds, The Jewish-American Journey of Professor W. Leopold* (Evanston, IL: Northwestern University Press, 2007).

Helstein, Ralph, *Oral History transcript*, Roosevelt University, January1986, Tape3867G.

Herberg, Will, Protestant, Catholic, Jew (New York: Doubleday & Co., 1960).

Herbst, Alma (AH), *The Negro in the Slaughtering and Meat-Packing Industry in Chicago* (New York: Arno & *The New York Times*, 1932, reprinted 1971).

Helstein, Ralph, "Collective bargaining in the meat packing industry," in Arnold W. Weber (ed.), *The Structure of Collective Bargaining, Problems and Perspectives*, a publication of Graduate School of Business, the University of Chicago, Third Series (New York: Free Press of Glencoe, 1961).

Horowitz, Roger, *The Path Not Taken: A Social History of Industrial Unionism in Meatpacking, 1930–1960*, Vols. I and II (Madison, WI: University of Wisconsin, 1990).

Horowitz, Roger, " 'This community of our union,' shopfloor power and social unionism in the postwar UPWA," in Stromquist, Shelson and Marvin Bergman (eds.), *Unionizing the Jungles, Labor and Community in the Twentieth Century Meatpacking Industry* (Iowa City: University of Iowa Press, 1997).

Horton, Aimee Isgrig (AIH), *The Highlander Folk School, A History of its Major Programs, 1932–1961* (Brooklyn, NY: Carlson Publishing Co., 1989).

Horton, Myles, with Judith Kohl and Herbert Kohl, *The Long Haul, An Autobiography* (New York: Doubleday. 1990).

Horwitt, Sanford D., *Let Them Call Me Rebel, Saul Alinsky—His Life and Legacy* (New York: Alfred A. Knopf, 1989).

Hyman, Paula E. and Deborah Dash Moore (eds.), Je*wish Women in America, An Historical Encyclopedia*, Vol. I, A-L (New York: Routledge, 1997).

Kushner, Tony, Foreword, in Sholem Aleichem, *Wandering Stars* (New York: Viking Press, 2009).

Levenstein, Harvey A., *Revolution at the Table, The Transformation of the American Diet* (New York: Oxford University Press, 1988).

Lichtenstein, Nelson, *Walter Reuther, The Most Dangerous Man in Detroit* (Urbana: University of Illinois Press, 1995).

McKillen, Elizabeth, "American labor, the Irish Revolution, and the campaign for a boycott of British goods, 1916–1924." *Radical Labor History*, Winter 1995, 61: 35–61.

Newman, Bonnie (ed.), *Helstein Family Reunion, 1894–1994*, August 19–21, 1994.

Noble, David F., *Forces of Production, A Social History of Industrial Automation* (New York: Alfred A. Knopf, 1984).

Orear, Leslie F. and Stephen H. Diamond, *Out of the Jungle, The Packinghouse Fight for Justice and Equality* (Chicago: Hyde Park Press, 1968).

Palmer, Bryan D., *James P. Cannon and the Origins of the American Left, 1890–1928* (Urbana: University of Illinois Press, 2007).

Perry, Charles R. and Delwyn H. Kegley, *Disintegration and Change: Labor Relations in the Meat-Packing Industry* (Philadelphia: Industrial Research Unit, University of Pennsylvania, 1989).

The Worker Speaks His Mind, On Company and Union (Cambridge, MA: Harvard University Press, 1953).

Blue Collar Man, Patterns of Dual Allegiance in Industry (Cambridge, MA: Harvard University Press, 1960).

Rabbi Marc, Shared *Dreams, Martin Luther King, Jr. and the Jewish Community* (Woodstock, VT: Jewish Lights Publishing, 1999).

Rabinowitz, Victor, *Unrepentent Leftist, A Lawyer's Memoir* (Urbana: University of Illinois Press, 1996).

Rachleff, Peter, *Hard-Pressed in the Heartland, The Hormel Strike and the Future of the Labor Movement* (Boston: South End Press, 1993).

Research-Education-Advocacy-People (REAP), *The Meat Packing Industry, The Workers Plight and UFCW.* Second Regular REAP National Convention, July 23, 1994, Canton, Ohio.

Richter, Irving, *Labor's Struggles, 1945–1950, A Participant's View* (New York: Cambridge University Press, 1994).

Satmar, Ger. Bobov, and Belz, religiousmovements.lib.virginia.edu.

Schloff, Linda Mack, *And the Prairie Dogs Weren't Kosher. Jewish Women in the Upper Midwest since 1855* (St. Paul, MN: Minnesota Historical Society Press, 1996), pp. 29–31.

Schoenbaum, Eleanor W. (ed.), *Political Profiles, The Truman Years* (New York: Facts on File, 1978).

Schrecker, Ellen, *Many Are the Crimes: McCarthyism in America* (Boston, MA: Little Brown & Co., 1998).

Singer, I. J., *The Family Carnovsky* (New York: The Vanguard Press, 1969).

Slayton, Robert A., *Back of the Yards, The Making of a Local Democracy* (Chicago: University of Chicago Press, 1986).

Sorin, Gerard, *Irving Howe, A Life of Passionate Dissent* (New York: New York University Press, 2002).

Stach, Reiner, *Kafka, The Decisive Years*, translated from the German by Shelley Frisch (Orlando, FL: Harcourt, 2005), p. 10.

Stepan-Norris, Judith and Maurice Zeitlin, *Left Out: Reds and America's Industrial Unions* (Cambridge, UK: Cambridge University Press, 2003).

Storch, Randi, *Red Chicago, American Communism at its Grassroots, 1928–35* (Urbana: University of Illinois Press, 2007).

Stromquist, Sheldon, "Promise and perils of the postwar era," in *Solidarity & Survival* (Iowa University Press, 1993).

Tuchman, Barbara W., *The March of Folly, From Troy to Vietnam* (New York: Alfred A. Knopf, 1984).

Wade, Louise Carroll, *Chicago's Pride, The Stockyards, Packingtown, and Environs in the Nineteenth Century* (Urbana: University of Illinois Press, 1987).

Warren, Wilson J., "The limits of social democratic unionism in Midwestern meatpacking communities, patterns of internal strife, 1948–1965," in Stromquist, Shelson and Marvin Bergman (eds.), *Unionizing the Jungles, Labor and Community in the Twentieth Century Meatpacking Industry* (Iowa City: University of Iowa Press, 1997).

Wenger, Beth S., *New York Jews and the Great Depression* (New Haven, CT: Yale University Press, 1996).

Wilensky, Harold L., *Intellectuals in Labor Unions: Organizational Pressures on Professional Roles* (Glencoe, IL: The Free Press Publishers, 1956).

Wyman, David S., *Abandonment of the Jews, America and the Holocaust, 1941–1945* (New York: Pantheon Books, 1984).

Zacharakis-Jutz, Jeffrey T., *Straight to the Heart of a Union, Straight to the Heart of a Movement: Worker's Education in the United Packinghouse Workers of America Between 1951 and 1953* (DeKalb, IL: Northern Illinois University, 1991).

Transcribed Interviews

United Packinghouse Workers Union Interviews

	Page
Annotated Bibliography	i–xvi
Anderson, Lewie (4/27/95) (two tapes)	1–47
Barton, Charles (5/24/94)	48–68
Brown, Jr., Oscar (9/23/95)	69–99
Brown, Jr., Oscar (9/24/95)	100–173
Cantor, David (5/13/95)	174–197

(Continued)

	Page
Carey, Catherine Brosnan (12/21/96) (by telephone)	198–231
Cotton, Eugene (3/9/93)	232–236
Cotton, Eugene (3/9/93a)	237–241
Cotton, Eugene (3/14/95)	242–256
Cotton, Eugene (3/14/95a)	257–289
Cotton, Eugene (3/17/95)	290–300
Cotton, Eugene (9/21/95)	301–303
Cotton, Eugene (9/21/95a)	304–318
Cotton, Eugene (9/21/95b)	319–333
Covey, Jill (5/6/95)	334–346
Dolnick, Norman (9/23/95)	347–398
Dolnick, Norman (9/23/95a)	399–408
Hayes, Charlie (1986)	409–412
Hayes, Charlie (1986a)	413–415
Hayes, Charlie (5/27/86)	416–418
Hayes, Charlie (11/24/92)	419–422
Hayes, Charlie (12/7/92)	423–424
Hayes, Charlie (12/14/92a)	425–427
Hayes, Charlie (3/10/93)	428–432
Hayes, Charlie (1/10/94)	433–466
Hayes, Charlie (1/14/94)	467–514
Hayes, Charlie (2/10/94)	515–530
Hayes, Charlie (3/4/94)	531–564
Hayes, Charlie (3/5/94)	565–581
Hayes, Charlie (3/7/94-3/8/94)	582–584
Hayes, Charlie (3/9/94)	585–604
Hayes, Charlie (2/21/94)	605–627
Hayes, Charlie (11/23/94)	628–653
Hayes, Charlie (3/18/95)	654–674
Hayes, Charlie (3/23/95)	675–693
Hayes, Charlie (9/21/95)	694–703

	Page
Hayes, Charlie (9/28/95)	704–714
Hayes, Charlie (9/16/96)	715–734
Hayes family (11/20/92)	735–739
Hayes family (1/20/93)	740–762
Helstein, Nina (3/7/96)	763–795
Helstein, Rachel (11/23/94)	796–811
Helstein, Rachel (12/14/94)	812–821
Helstein, Ralph (9/18/80)	822–830
Helstein, Ralph (9/17/80)	831–834
Helstein, Ralph (10/22/80)	835–838
Helstein, Ralph (11/20/80)	839–850
Helstein, Ralph (11/14/81)	851–866
Helstein, Ralph (5/3/72); Balanoff, Elizabeth interview, in the possession of the Roosevelt University Library.	
Helstein, Rosen (11/23/82)	867–883
Johnson, Henry (n.d.)	884–885
King, Irving (9/25/95)	886–912
Lasley Russell (n.d.)	913–913
Long, Felix (6/14/94)	914–945
March, Herb (7/77)	946–946
March, Herb (12/19/79)	947–957
March, Herb (7/15/85)	958–976
March, Herb (10/21/86, Tapes 293, 295)	977–1027
March, Herb (10/21/86a, Tapes 296, 297)	1028–1045
March, Herb (3/19/95)	1046–1051
March, Herb (3/20/95)	1052–1063
March, Herb (3/21/95)	1064–1076
March, Herb (3/21/95a)	1077–1080
March, Herb (3/24/85)	1081–1082
March, Herb (6/21/95)	1083–1093
March, Herb (10/4/95)	1094–1126

(Continued)

	Page
March, Jane (3/24/95)	1127–1177
March, Richard (3/20/95)	1178–1216
Nielsen, Harold (8/21/83)	1217–1289
Nielsen, Harold (9/4/85)	1290–1304
Orear, Les (n.d.)	1305–1309
Orear, Les (3/29/83)	1310–1312
Orear, Les (3/31/95)	1313–1366
Orear, Linn (11/3/96)	1367–1387
Parks, Sam (1/28/80)	1388–1391
Parks, Sam (12/19/80)	1391–1392
Pierce, Eunetta (5/23/94)	1393–1452
Prosten, Ann (4/28/95)	1453–1480
Prosten, Ann (4/28/95a)	1481–1501
Prosten, Ann (4/28/95b)	1501–1548
Prosten, Jesse (12/18/85)	1549–1552
Saunders, Richard (5/24/94)	1553–1592
Starr, Vickie (5/15/95)	1593–1599
Turner, Ruth (5/21/94)	1600–1664
Vaughn, Jesse (5/24/94)	1665–1681
Weightman, Philip (10/7/86)	1682–1700
Weightman, Philip (10/8/86)	1701–1717
Weightman, Philip (10/8/86a)	1718–1734
Wyatt, Addie (6/94)	1735–1763
Wyatt, Addie (9/28/95)	1764–1780
ZPackhist (6/95)	1781–1897

Transcripts are located at the University of Wisconsin, Madison.

Annotated Bibliography of Interviews

Anderson, Lewie

1) 4/27/95 (Two tapes, interviewed by the author, transcribed by Deb Morrow)
   Interview regarding information on Jesse Prosten, including his work experience with Armour and Company in 1963 in Sioux City, and Iowa Beef Processors

in 1966. He first joined the UPWA in 1967 and became a steward in 1969 after the merger of UPWA and Amalgamated. Had previous union experience in machinists union. Was full-time union staff person from 1972 to 1975 and then became a full-time staff person in the international union in 1976 working for Jesse Prosten. Tape talks about definition of "militant" and impressions of Jesse Prosten. (Original tape includes an interview on 4/28/95 with Ann Prosten.)

Barton, Charles

1) 5/24/94 (Interviewed by the author, transcribed by Deb Morrow)
    Information regarding his knowledge of Charlie Hayes after meeting him in 1953 and his continuing friendship with Hayes (negotiations). Includes racism and civil rights issues.

Brown, Jr., Oscar

1) 9/23/95 (interviewed by the author, transcribed by Deb Morrow)
    Charlie Hayes works as organizer of Swift; black advancement movement within union; Dick Durham's role; romantic relationships within union; Charlie Hayes and the Black Caucus; role of the Communist Party; Neilsen's role; union politics and Tony Stephens; Durham's firing.

2) 9/24/95 (Interviewed by the author, transcribed by Deb Morrow)
    A continuation of an interview with Oscar Brown, Jr. Includes information regarding Black Caucus beginnings, black leadership, and the roles played by Dick Durham and Charlie Hayes.

Bull, Russell

There are no known interviews of Russell Bull, who was a director of District 3. Herb March comments on him.

Cantor, David

1) 5/13/95 (Interviewed by the author, transcribed by Deb Morrow)
    Talks about his experiences with the packinghouse workers union; forming their newspaper; and discussions with Herb March, R. R. Martinez, Jesse Prosten, Sigmund Wlodarczyk, Pete Brown, and Vickie Starr (Cramer), as well as several others from the early 1940s.

Carey, Catherine Brosnan

1) 12/21/96 (Two tapes, interviewed by the author, by telephone, transcribed by Deb Morrow; tape 2 appears to be lost)

Talks about her time as an employee of the international office between 1951 and 1958 Worked directly with Helstein and with Tony Stephens. Talks about her relationship with him; talks about Stephens' relationship with Dick Durham, black–white issues as developed by Durham; mention of Jesse Prosten and Russ Lasley.

Cotton, Eugene

1) 3/9/93 (Interviewed by Dan Collins, transcribed and summarized by the author)
   Cotton's legal education, his career as UPWA general counsel, and his reflections and experiences on the early years of the union and the people he encountered. Also discusses his functions, the civil rights policies of the union, Un-American Committee hearings, his views of Helstein, and other's views of him.

2) 3/9/93a (Interviewed by the author, transcribed by Deb Morrow)
   Cotton's evaluation and experiences with Charlie Hayes, Hayes' importance in union affairs and Hayes' relationships with others inside and outside the union.

3) 3/14/95 (Interviewed and summarized by the author, transcribed by Deb Morrow)
   Cotton describes his upbringing, how he became a labor lawyer, and the New Deal outlook of many of his colleagues. Discussion regarding his law school career and professor influencing him before joining the UPWA, including work with the U.S. Court of Appeals, private law firm, the FCC, and Labor Board.

4) 3/14/95a (Interviewed by the author, transcribed by Deb Morrow)
   Political influences in law school, his teachers, and fellow law students; work experiences; his marriage; early experience and practice with federal agencies in Washington, D.C.; and his entry into labor law practice.

5) 3/17/95 (Interviewed by the author, transcribed by Deb Morrow)
   Cotton comments on a history of the UPWA prepared by the author (see last file, zPackhist, and in the process comments on that history.)

6) 9/21/95 (Interviewed by the author, transcribed by Deb Morrow)
   Includes discussions regarding plant closures, a discussion regarding Helstein's concepts of how the UPWA should react to several technological changes that were occurring within the industry, and some discussion to Helstein's ability to keep contacts with so many groups and individuals throughout the nation on so many issues.

7) 9/21/95a (Interviewed by the author, transcribed by Deb Morrow)
   Cotton's comments on the union's reaction to the threat of plant closings and technological changes.

8) 9/21/95b (Interviewed by the author, transcribed by Deb Morrow)

Cotton's comments on the 1948 convention, attempts by the Congress of Industrial Organizations (CIO) to decertify the union, Reuther's participation, reactions of major labor leaders to the Taft-Hartley Act, and the firing of Herb March. Includes his recollections of Charlie Hayes, Jesse Prosten, and Lew Clark.

Covey, Jill Richmond (daughter of Les Orear)

1) 5/6/95 (Interviewed by the author, transcribed by Deb Morrow)

Talks about her father's work and character and her impressions of the people with whom he worked.

Dolnick, Norman

1) 9/23/95 (Interviewed by the author, transcribed by Deb Morrow)

Dolnick's comments on the origin of the black–white handclasp, black–white problems in the union, Dick Durham and the black power movement. Also includes information about Leo Turner, the union newspaper operation, and Dolnick's contacts with Ralph Helstein. Also discusses Ralph Helstein's management and negotiating style.

2) 9/23/95a (interviewed by the author, transcribed by Deb Morrow)

Dolnick's evaluation of Russ Lasley, Herb March, Jesse Prosten, and other union officers.

Ellis, Franknd

1) There is no known interview of Frank Ellis. This file is a compilation from various sources compiled by the author.

Hayes, Charlie

1) 1986 (Halpern and Horowitz, 1106A, 152 side 1, transcribed and summarized by the author)

Importance of Communist Party in the organization of the UPWA, union's antidiscrimination efforts, organizing blacks, 1946 election of Helstein, 1948 strike.

2) 1986a (Charlie Hayes, Halpern and Horowitz, Tape 153-1, transcribed and summarized by the author)

His election as district director of District 1 of the UPWA, including the resolution passed by the district.

3) 5/27/86 (Halpern and Horowitz, No. 1106A, side I, Wisconsin Historical Society, transcribed by the author)

Early work experiences; early organizing; effect of charges of Communism; 1946 election and 1948 strike; civil rights; left and right elements in union;

Hayes' nomination and election to as District 1 director; "boys" issue about black–white relations.

4) 12/14/92 (Tape no. 3, side 2, interviewed by Les Orear)
Hayes discusses the merger negotiations with the Amalgamated and his dispute with Tony Stephens.

5) 12/14/92a (Tape No. 3, interviewed by Les Orear, summarized by the author)
Hispanics in union; merger with Amalgamated, and dispute between Hayes and Tony Stephens.

6) 12/7/92 (Interviewed by Les Orear, summarized by the author)
Union political activities; election as director; problems of black organizers in the South.

7) 11/24/92 (Interviewed by Les Orear, transcribed by the author)
Early working years of the UPWA, early organizing in Wilson & Co., people who helped in the organization of Wilson local, election of Helstein, political orientation of locals, Chicago administration's reaction to plant closings.

8) 3/10/93 (Interviewed by the author, transcribed by Deb Morrow)
His earliest experience in representing union, starting work in packinghouse in Chicago, early work experiences, early experiences as African American.

9) 1/10/94 (Interviewed by the author, transcribed by Deb Morrow)
Early years and education; his family; discrimination and life in Southern Illinois.

10) 3/4/94 (Interviewed by the author, transcribed by Deb Morrow)
His first and second marriages; how he gave up smoking; his divorce; how he was nominated for Congress; union activities around 1969; drinking at union activities. Goes into more detail regarding his third wife and his run for Congress; his failure to win his congressional seat; and information on Ralph Metcalf, Sam Parks, and Harold Washington.

11) 1/14/94 (No. 3, interviewed by the author, transcribed by Deb Morrow)
His early life and schooling and the problems of growing up black in Southern Illinois, meeting his first wife, marriage, early organizing efforts.

12) 2/10/94 (Interviewed by the author, transcribed by Deb Morrow)
Organizing and the difficulties of organizing in the South and the conditions under which black organizers had to live in the South, his living in Altgeld Gardens in Chicago, automation and the results on workers, his work history, Congressman Dawson's influence.

13) 11/23/94 (Interviewed by the author, transcribed by Deb Morrow)
His becoming director of District 1, replacement of Harold Nielson; merger with Amalgamated Meatcutters; Mayor Daly's relation with the union; his relations with Eugene Cotton; the change to Sikora Hall; the union's meeting hall.

14) 2/21/94 (Interviewed by the author, transcribed by Deb Morrow)

Hayes' early childhood in Southern Illinois; first marriage; his move to Chicago and living in Altgeld Gardens; second marriage and death of his second wife; his trip to Israel; his third marriage.

15) 3/5/94 (Interviewed by the author, transcribed by Deb Morrow)

Organizing his campaign for Congress, persons who helped with the campaign; Adam Clayton Powell as an aid; his philosophy on the Gulf War and other matters; election in 1983; his first months in Congress; redistricting his district; the check cashing "scandal"; the factors incurring the loss of his congressional seat; his economic situation.

16) 3/7/94–3/8/94 (Interviewed by the author, transcribed by Deb Morrow)

Problems for blacks in Congress; problems for blacks growing up in Southern Illinois; problems in first job; first attempts at forming a union; segregation in unions; organizing in the South; Martin Luther King, Jr., in Chicago; criticism of Jesse Jackson; questions about contributions, political action committee monies; civil rights activities

17) 9/21/95 (Interviewed by the author, transcribed by Deb Morrow)

Dick Durham, his characteristics, and his importance at the Highlander Folk School about 1952. Includes information on Les Orear and Norm Dolnick, Pete Brown, Oscar Brown, Jr; influence of the Communist Party on the union; Hayes' firing of Oscar Brown, Jr.; testimony before the House Un-American Activities Committee.

18) 9/28/95 (Interviewed by the author, transcribed by Deb Morrow)

How Dick Durham was hired; "boy" incident in which Russell Bull used the word "boy" and it became a big issue for Dick Durham; the various political moves within the union that ended up in Hayes' becoming director of District 1; dispute between Hayes and Stephens concerning the merger with the Amalgamated; the firing of Oscar Brown, Jr.

19) 3/18/95 (Interviewed by the author, transcribed by Deb Morrow)

Recollections of Herb March and Jesse Prosten, Hayes membership in the Communist Party, the Party's influence on union affairs and others who may have been members, 1948 strike, how Jesse Prosten and Helstein worked together.

20) 9/16/96 (Interviewed by the author, transcribed by Deb Morrow)

Communist influences in the union and his own personal experiences, Party meetings, local leadership of the Party, Black Labor Council, assertion of black rights in union.

21) 11/20/92 (Interviewed by the author, transcribed by Deb Morrow)

Interview with childhood friends and relatives of Charlie Hayes, recollections of his childhood and conditions for blacks in Southern Illinois and in Chicago.

22) 1/20/93 (Interviewed by the author, transcribed by Deb Morrow)
Interview with Deirdre Smith, Charlie Hayes' granddaughter. Includes information regarding her impressions of Charlie as a young child and during his
run for Congress. Interview with childhood friends in Cairo, IL, and his siblings.

Helstein, Nina (daughter of Helstein)

1) 3/7/96 (Interviewed by the author, transcribed by Deb Morrow)
Recollection of her memories of her father; early years as well as negotiation
skills; character traits; and impressions of Jesse Prosten, Gene Cotton, Saul
Alinsky, and Myles Horton.

Helstein, Rachel (wife of Ralph Helstein)

1) 11/23/94 (Interviewed by the author, transcribed by Deb Morrow)
Talks about her childhood; Ralph Helstein' childhood and education; hiring by
union; his Jewish influence, philosophy; relations with management; election as
president of the union; relations with Charlie Hayes and Herb March; his firing.

2) 12/14/94 (Interviewed by the author, transcribed by Deb Morrow)
Talks about Norman Dolnick, Jesse Prosten, and changes in his attitudes
over automation, Eugene Cotton, salary issues, negotiating skills.

Helstein, Ralph

1) 10/22/80 (Interviewed by Les Orear, transcribed by the author)
Healing the strains caused by the 1948 strike at the 1948 Convention;
factions on the left and right seeking control of the union; factions in election
of officers; position of Canadian locals; problems caused by automation and
contract provisions negotiated to protect workers.

2) 11/20/80 (Tape IV Interviewed by Les Orear and transcribed by the author)
Helstein compares the bargaining styles of the major packing companies
and the approaches of their attorneys.

3) 9/15/80 (Interviewed by Les Orear, transcribed by the author)
Considerations for his decision to run for president; different groups within
union for and against him; left and right; position of Canadians; development
of his philosophy of governing; his speaking before convention; competition
with Amalgamated.

4) 9/17/80 (Interviewed by Les Orear, transcribed by the author)
Canadian Fred Dowling, administrator during course of strike; Frank Ellis;
hiring of Eugene Cotton as counsel; how strike was financed; Taft-Hartley Act;
negotiations and his understanding of the effects of the Act; union politics.

5) 1/14/81 (No.5, interviewed by Les Orear, transcribed by the author)
  Side 1: Jewish identity as a child; early childhood experiences made him sensitive to discrimination; union's antidiscrimination policy; Local 100 discrimination against whites; antidiscrimination policy of union removed one cause of left–right splits; his union philosophy; union was supportive of civil rights movement; different approaches to civil rights of the UPWA and UAW. Side 2: election of district officers; "boy" incident and all the internal politics flowing from it; education of Tony Stephens by Durham; issue of Durham editing UPWA newspaper; merger and civil rights; break between Tony and Charlie Hayes over Tony's merger actions; opposition by Charlie Hayes re-election; end of Tony Stephens and Durham's union employment.

6) Interview by Eliot Wigginton, 5/4/81, at Highlander Folk School, 93 pages.

7) 11/23/82 (Interviewed by H. Targ, transcribed by the author)
  Attempts of UPWA to deal with automation.

8) n.d. (Interviewed by Stan Rosen, transcribed by the author)
  Helstein's Jewish upbringing and how his religious beliefs affected his job as union president.

Johnson, Hank

1) n.d. (No interviews, compilation of others statements of him)
  Organizer and assistant national director for Packing Workers Organizing Committee (PWOC); left PWOC in 1940 over Willkie nomination; worked as organizer for United Mine Worker's District 50; killed in 1944 by fellow organizer who accused him of selling out workers.

King, Irving

1) 9/25/95 (Interviewed by the author, transcribed by Deb Morrow)
  Discusses the place of lawyers within union negotiations, styles used by different unions. Talks about Eugene Cotton, Charlie Hayes, Ralph Helstein, and Russ Lasley.

Lasley, Russell (Russ)

No interviews available. Comments by others.

Long, Felix

1) 6/14/94 (Interviewed by the author, transcribed by Deb Morrow)
  His work history, organizing Agar, work floor actions, relations with management, organization of plant according to gender and race, his dealings with and impressions of Charlie Hayes, Hayes re-election problems.

March, Herb

1) 7/77 (Interviewed by Bob Slayton, transcribed by the author; only about a paragraph of this interview could be transcribed because of problems with the tape)

Effect of Nazi-Soviet pact on PWOC leadership.

2) 12/19/79 (Interviewed by Les Orear)

Early organization packinghouse workers; influence of Democratic machine, union's work in the back-of-the yards neighborhood; influence of the Catholic Church, various ethnic worker groups; black–white relations and the Dies Committee. Separate collection of quotes from various sources prepared by the author about Herb March.

3) 7/15/85 (Interviewed by Roger Horowitz for the State Historical Society of Wisconsin United Packinghouse Workers of America Oral History Project, San Pedro CA Project Tape #2, Sides 1 & 2, M3297; transcribed by Deb Morrow) Discusses organizing before and during World War II, the no-strike pledge, job actions, how workers viewed the Communist Party, the cause of his leaving in 1954, the Dies Committee, his testimony, union elections.

4) 10/21/86 (Tape 293, M3818, Tape series 1106A; the interview was conducted on October 21, 1986 by Rick Halpern and Roger Horowitz for the State Historical Society of Wisconsin UPWA Oral History Project. Tape 293, transcribed by Deb Morrow)

March's growing up in Brooklyn, how he was employed by the Young Communist League (YCL), his organizing activities for the YCL in Kansas and Oklahoma, activities in the South, the Scottsboro case.

5) 10/21/86a (Tape 296, Tape Series 1106A. Interview with Herbert March, continued. Tape 296, Side 1, M3821.The interview was conducted on October 21, 1986, by Rick Halpern and Roger Horowitz for the State Historical Society of Wisconsin UPWA Oral History Project, transcribed by the author)

Work stoppages during the war years; activities of the Communist Party in various plants; March's firing and reinstatement; Hank Johnson and District 50; his killing; Saul Alinsky's activities and Back of the Yards Council.

6) 10/4/95 (Interviewed by the author, transcribed by Deb Morrow)

March's impressions of Dick Durham, Oscar Brown, Jr., and Tony Stephens; his career in the Young Communist League and the Communist Party; Smith Act indictments; leaving the Party, his going to California and joining the Sheetmetal Workers.

7) 3/19/95 (Interviewed and transcribed by the author)

March's childhood, becoming a political radical and member of the Communist Party; early organizing activities; becoming involved with the Packinghouse Workers Union; organizing efforts in the South.

8) 3/20/95 (Two interviews; interviewed and transcribed by the author)

Depression-area activities; unemployed councils; activities as young Communist Party member; unemployment councils; starting to work at Armour early packing organizations; activities as union speaker; early organization of union; relationships to other unions; battles with police; reaction of city; company union; organizing in plant; no strike policy in World War II; Wilkie-Roosevelt union dispute.

9) 3/21/95 (Tape 3, interviewed and transcribed by the author)

Career in Communist Party; Dies Committee hearings; attempt on his life; drafting of union constitution; organization during World War II; evaluation of Weightman; working with community organizations; Back of the Yards Council; work as a Communist Party member; contacts with churches; second attempt on his life; elected director of District One; left and right wing; proposal of Ralph Helstein as president; going to Communist Party school.

10) 3/21/95a (Tape 5, interviewed and transcribed by the author)

Work as labor attorney in California, interplay between Communist Party and union, how issue played out in union.

11) 3/21/95b (Tape 5, interviewed and transcribed by the author)

Work as labor attorney in California; clients he represented; interplay between Communist Party and union; his heart attack; going to Yugoslavia; his law practice; work as a labor lawyer; relationship of Communist Party to union; activities as a Communist Party member; his views of Helstein for firing him.

12) 6/21/95 (Tape 4, Side 1, interviewed and transcribed by the author)

Coming out as Communist Party member, Communist Party representative, intra-party disputes, resignation from party and trip to California, work in California, FBI visits, union activities, expelled from union, law school and fight to be admitted to Bar, career as lawyer; Side 2, 1946 and 1948 strikes, organizing after loss of 1948 strike, antidiscrimination policy, anti-Communist oath, non-Communist affidavit, March's firing by Helstein and its affect on Helstein.

March, Jane (wife of Herb March)

1) 3/24/95 (Interviewed by the author, transcribed by Deb Morrow)

Her childhood; political influences; her marriage to Herb; the difficulties of being married to an active union organizer; the machinations of the Communist Party; their going to California; Herb's firing and Joan's reaction to it and how she believes others in the union should have reacted to it; women's place in the union; Joan's aspirations.

March, Richard

1) 3/20/95 (Interviewed by the author, transcribed by Deb Morrow)
   Describes the Croatian background of mother and its influence on her and on Herb; the marriage and their personality conflicts; Herb's Jewish background; how he got his name, March; what Herb was like as a father; how he was influenced by Herb's political activities; Herb's character; influence of his mother and father on him.

Nielsen, Harold

1) 8/21/83 (The UPWA Oral History Project, an interview with Harold Nielson, conducted by Rick Halpern on August 21, 1985. Original tape, 1106A, Number 3, Side 1, transcribed by Deb Morrow)
   His union beginnings, 1940, from his conversion of total anti-union to being a member of the PWOC in Cudahy; arrests of strikers; corruption in the court system; struggle with Cudahy management; early union organization; relations with black workers and women; working conditions in plants, discrimination, antidiscrimination policies, and racism; move to new hall and security problems; problems with the CIO; his view of the UPWA in relation to other unions.

2) 9/4/85 (Interviewed by Roger Horowitz and Rick Halpern for the state Historical Society of Wisconsin's Packinghouse Workers Oral History Project. Tape 5, Side 1, transcribed by Deb Morrow)
   Government takeover of the Cudahy plant; information regarding *The Milwaukee Journal*; relations with Milwaukee government; local businessmen of Milwaukee and Paul Robeson, both supporters and nonsupporters.

Orear, Les

1) 3/29/83 (Interviewed by Sue Davenport, transcribed by the author)
   Comments by Herb March; why Orear started Illinois Labor History Society; early years; entry into union; organizing; relations with Herb March, Dies Committee, early organizers; start of *Packinghouse News*.

2) 3/31/95 (Interviewed by author, transcribed by Deb Morrow)
   Orear's early background, parents, and schooling; introduction to Herbert March in 1933 or 1934; Orear's joining the YCL and the influence of the Communist Party on union decisions; black power problems within union; Durham and Cathy Brosnan; problems in editing UPWA newspaper; early union activities.

3) n.d. (Interviewed by Fehr, transcribed by the author)
   Organizing Swift plant in Kansas City; work during 1948 strike; after-strike efforts; move of Chicago office to black areas; taking over packinghouse

newspaper; black–white dispute at Highlander staff retreat and its aftermath, plant shutdowns.

Orear, Lynn (daughter of Les)

1) 11/3/96 (Interviewed by the author, transcribed by Deb Morrow)
   Her recollections of her father and the influence he had on her in terms of unions and in general, forming her values; events she went to with her father; her exposure to union activists such as Martinez, Herb and Jane March, and memories of going to union events; Orear's taking care of his sick wife; Orear's philosophy.

Parks, Sam

1) 12/8/80 (Interviewed by Les Orear, summarized by the author)
   His early years, early organization at Wilson, Weightman, and 1946; election of Helstein; his views on Helstein and the speed with which Helstein pushed black advancement; valuation of union on race relations compared with other unions; criticism of organized labor in terms of salaries paid to officers; and the effect of check-off and other union protections.

2) 12/19/80 (Interviewed by Les Orear, Tape UC 1117A UPWA ILHS Tape 21, side 1, part 1; summarized by the author)
   Theory and philosophical questions; Trade Union Educational League. Left-wing objective; education in industrial unionism; the left; Communist Party; syndicalist; 1920s to 1930s.

Pierce, Eunetta

1) 5/23/94 (Two tapes, interviewed by the author, transcribed by Deb Morrow)
   Her early work experiences, including working in packing; her work with Charlie Hayes, his wives, and his personality; mention of many of the union leaders.

Prosten, Ann

1) 4/28/95 (Interviewed by the author, transcribed by Deb Morrow)
   Events in Russia that motivated her parents to emigrate to the United States; early moves of her parents; how she came to her left-wing and pro-union view; her college years and getting her first job.

2) 4/28/95a and b (Continuation of interview No.1, interviewed by the author, transcribed by Deb Morrow)
   WPA job where she met Jesse; demonstration where arrested; her romance with Jesse; Jesse's move as organizer in Boston; Italian workers there; her work

as journalist for *The Chicago Worker*; civil rights work; knowing Helstein and Herb March.

Prosten, Jesse

1) 12/18/85 (Interview of Jesse Prosten by Halpern and Horowitz c.f. M3431; 25:05, Tape 48, side 1, UPWA OHP summary and transcription by the author)

Lewie Anderson's importance discussed; closing plants; Austin plant; 1946 election of Helstein; Herb March and Taft-Hartley Act; 1948 strike; civil rights; enforcement of racial equality policy; job actions; John Hope racial survey; attitudes toward blacks and Jews.

Saunders, Richard

1) 5/24/94 (Interviewed by the author, transcribed by Deb Morrow)

Recollections of his family; coming to Chicago; union organizing before UPWA; discrimination; antidiscrimination actions; his recollections of Charlie Hayes beginning in the early 1940s.

Starr, Vickie

1) 5/15/95 (Interview and transcribed by the author)

How she came to Chicago and moved in with the Marches; job in stockyards; Marxist education; working in the packinghouse; discrimination against and harassment of women; recruiting for the Communist Party; youth activities; school training.

Turner, Ruth

1) 5/21/94 (Interviewed by the author, transcribed by Deb Morrow)

She worked as Charlie Hayes' secretary beginning in 1960 until he became a congressman.

Vaughn, Jesse

1) 10/23/86 (JV No. 300, interviewed by the author, transcribed by Deb Morrow)

He is discussing becoming active in the 21st Ward during the latter part of the 1950s, with information regarding the elections. Also information regarding Hank Johnson, Herb March, and others.

2) 5/26/95 (Interviewed by the author, transcribed by Deb Morrow)

His early union activities; impressions of Charlie Hayes and Herb March and their union activities.

Weightman, Philip

1) 10/7/86 (PW No. 286, interviewed by Halpern and Horowitz, transcribed by Deb Morrow)

He was offered, by Amalgamated Meatcutters to be placed on their payroll at a full staff pay and stay in the plant; work and get my salary; efforts of Communist Party to recruit him; influence of Communist Party on union; Hank Johnson and his activities for union; Johnson's killing by Shelton; how Weightman was approached to become a member of the Communist Party and the part played by Herb March.

2) 10/8/86 (PW No. 290, interviewed by Halpern and Horowitz, transcribed by Deb Morrow)

Information regarding the 1946 Montreal convention at which Helstein replaces Clark as international president.

3) 10/8/86a (PW No. 291, interviewed by Halpern and Horowitz, transcribed by Deb Morrow)

Continuation of difficulties in union after 1946 convention; information regarding his being hired by CIO in 1948; various jobs he for the union; his activities as political consultant in various campaigns; his activities in the civil rights movement with Dr. King and others.

Wyatt, Addie

1) 6/94 (Interviewed and transcribed by the author)

2) 9/28/95 (Interviewed by the author, transcribed by Deb Morrow)
Discusses her activities and the activities of the union as a leader in antidiscrimination.

Zpackhist

1) 6/95

A compilation of the history of the unionization of the packinghouse workers from various sources.

Index

About the Author

CYRIL ROBINSON is a lawyer and emeritus professor of criminal justice at Southern Illinois University, Carbondale, Illinois, and has written numerous articles in legal and historical journals on matters of criminal justice, criminal law and procedure, police history, and police-community relations. His published works include Greenwood's *Police in Contradiction: The Evolution of the Police Function in Society and Legal Rights, Duties, and Liabilities of Criminal Justice Personnel: History and Analysis.*